DODDIE

DODDIE

MY AUTOBIOGRAPHY

ALEX MACDONALD

WITH BRIAN SCOTT

BLACK & WHITE PUBLISHING

First published 2012
This edition first published 2013
by Black & White Publishing Ltd
29 Ocean Drive, Edinburgh EH6 6JL

1 3 5 7 9 10 8 6 4 2   13 14 15 16

ISBN: 978 1 84502 697 4

Typeset by RefineCatch Limited, Bungay, Suffolk
Printed and bound by Grafica Veneta, S. p. A. Italy

For my wife Christine's sister, Isabel, who died suddenly on 14 March 2007, as well as Christine herself, our daughter Lisa and sons Nick and Kris.

I dedicate this book also to my mum and dad; my younger sister Ann; my Granny Watson (with whom I lived for a few years before getting married); and Christine's parents, Roy and Isa Jones.

I shouldn't forget in this context, either, my pal from boyhood Jimmy Lumsden and his family – not least Jimmy's father, Michael, who was a great source of encouragement to me as a youngster with dreams of being a footballer.

Oh, and the Tradeston 'old lads' as well. They looked out for me when I was a kid in that part of Glasgow and know who they are.

CONTENTS

ACKNOWLEDGEMENTS

I am indebted to Black & White Publishing for giving me this opportunity to publish my memoirs; also to the host of other people who helped me do so. They include a good friend and Ibrox historian, David Mason, for keeping me right about matters relating to my twelve years with Rangers, and freelance journalist Ray Hepburn, for doing likewise in regard to my spell – almost as long – with Hearts.

Thanks, too, to Jim Masson of the *Evening Telegraph* in Dundee; Paul Smith, St Johnstone's commercial manager; and Jim Slater, a Saints' historian, for re-kindling memories of my formative years at the Perth club.

But my career as both player and manager may not have been worth talking about without the support of someone like Sandy Jardine. He helped me immensely in both capacities and my thoughts have been with him lately during his fight against cancer, which was diagnosed late in 2012. You can imagine my shock when he told me about it. Sandy was one of the fittest guys I know. He never smoked and rarely drank. It just goes to show none of us can be sure of what lies ahead.

I remain grateful also to every manager who ever signed me, in particular Davie White, who invited me to fulfil my boyhood dream by joining Rangers in 1968. I was saddened by his recent death at the age of eighty. That is not to forget Willie Waddell, who changed my style of play for the better at Ibrox, and Jock Wallace, who raised my fitness levels and helped imbue me with the team spirit which made us winners. Lifting the European Cup Winners' Cup in Barcelona in 1972 was the absolute highlight for me, and I thank all my old team-mates, the Barca Bears, for making that possible.

Let me express my gratitude, too, to all the players, staff, and sprint coaches at Hearts who allowed me (and Sandy) to turn things around at Tynecastle and go as close as we did to winning honours there.

I should make particular mention here of one of the Hearts coaching staff, John Binnie – not just for his input to our efforts, but also for his friendship, both of which I continued to rely on once he joined me at Airdrie.

Yet nothing could have been achieved at Airdrie without the help of the honest bunch of players we had there. Between us, we did things many people thought we couldn't – things like qualifying for Europe.

A word, finally, about my daughter-in-law, Donna, who encouraged me to go into print, and Tommy Stark, who gave me employment once football had had enough of me – many thanks to them also.

Alex MacDonald

FOREWORD
BY SANDY JARDINE

Alex, like myself, will remember 2012 for the collision of emotions that occurred during the first few months of it. While both of us, along with our old Ibrox team-mates, were looking forward to celebrating the fortieth anniversary in May of Rangers winning the European Cup Winners' Cup, the club was plunged into administration in February. This came as a huge blow to all concerned. With Rangers' very existence at stake, maybe it was as well the likes of Doddie and I had our memories to sustain us.

Doddie is my closest pal in football, and I'm delighted he asked me to provide this foreword to his memoirs. He came to Rangers from St Johnstone in 1968 and we spent the next twelve years not just as team-mates, but roommates before big games and on tour as well. I used to put him to bed at night! We probably saw more of one another during all that time than we did our own families. Then, after he'd moved to Hearts in 1980 and became their manager soon enough, we renewed our association when I joined him at Tynecastle for what was another memorable spell of working together.

We got on really well and always enjoyed a very comfortable relationship. We were two lads from a working-class background who had the good fortune to make our way in football. Doddie was always quite shy and didn't really like the hassle of talking to the press and TV. He only ever wanted to get on with the job, whether it was playing or managing. He was (and remains) very honest and down to earth. But the biggest factor with him was his desire to succeed. He was a winner, and not just at football. If even we were playing table tennis or tiddlywinks, he wanted to win. Same with snooker – and I'll tell you a story about that shortly.

Doddie the player had good ability, of course, but he had a fantastic engine also. He could get up and down the park like few others. He was one of the fittest boys I ever played with. The pair of us were always out in front at training, with the rest tucked in somewhere behind us. But I can't over-emphasise the importance of his will to win, and needless to say, he was hugely important to Rangers when we won the Cup Winners' Cup in Barcelona in 1972. Doddie was a player's player, if I can use that old expression. Everybody appreciated what he did for the team. He played for the team and was rewarded with a dozen medals.

A lot of supporters might not have appreciated the work he put in, but we – his colleagues – always did. If as players we had been picking the team, his name would have been among the first on the list. I mentioned earlier his ability to get from box to box, but allied to that was his capacity to ghost in behind opposing defenders and score goals. It was amazing, the number he scored in big games. His talent for getting himself into the penalty box at exactly the right time was terrific. So many of his goals were important ones as well. It wasn't easy to get a cap back then, and in Alex's midfield position Scotland had the likes of Asa Hartford, Archie Gemmill and Bruce Rioch. I'm quite sure if he were playing now, he'd have about fifty caps.

I remember him asking me – this would have been in 1981–82 season – if I would join him at Tynecastle. My Rangers career was coming to an end, the old team were breaking up, so I asked John Greig, who was manager by then, if I could be released. John put my request to the directors, who because of my length of service said they would let me go. So things were kind of put in place for me to join Hearts, both as player and assistant to Doddie, about six months before I actually made the move.

Doddie had never had much ambition to be a manager. I recall him phoning me when he was offered the job and asking what he should do. I told him, 'Take it. With all your experience, it won't be a problem for you.'

'Hearts have got good potential,' I went on to say. 'They're just a bit down on their luck at the moment.' Doddie had told me also that things at Tynecastle were a joke compared to what he'd experienced at Rangers. By the time I went there, I discovered they were worse than he'd said.

The job confronting us was all about trying to build things up, getting players up to a certain standard. If they couldn't achieve that, we had to look for others. Yet we were fortunate in having a clutch of good, young players – John Robertson, Davie Bowman and Gary Mackay – whom we worked on and brought through to first-team level.

A lot of players think they know the game. Believe me, they dinnae. But Doddie had this great ability to make it simple enough for them to take in and understand. I would say that was one of his greatest assets as a manager. Working at Hearts was a great adventure for both of us. We took them from the First Division to the Premier, qualifying for Europe on several occasions. That was great. But what happened to us in 1986 when we missed out on winning the league title and lost the Scottish Cup Final on consecutive Saturdays left us devastated.

It was just a few months later that I was sounded out about going to Aberdeen as a replacement for Alex Ferguson. In the event, after speaking to Wallace Mercer I was made co-manager alongside Doddie. In fact, I got him a rise in wages at that point, with Wallace giving us new contracts. But this didn't change the way Doddie and I operated together. Titles didn't mean anything to us. When you work in management, there's always club politics to be considered – speaking to the chairman, etc. Doddie couldn't be bothered with that. He just wanted to work on the playing side of the business. To be honest, I'd become a bit bored with that, so I took over all the other things.

I mentioned earlier I would get around to telling a story about Doddie playing snooker. It involves Wallace Mercer, who at the start of every season would invite us to his house in the Barnton area of Edinburgh for dinner. After we'd eaten, he would take us into his snooker room, which had a lovely big table. What Wallace didn't know was that he had to watch Doddie like a hawk. Wallace would play a shot, then it would be Doddie's turn to pot an easy ball.

'Oh,' Wallace would say. 'I never noticed that.'

The reason he never noticed was because while he was hanging over the table, Doddie had placed a ball on the edge of the pocket. The same thing happened every year, and Wallace never twigged. It was funny.

Doddie and I always knew our time at Hearts wasn't going to last forever, and so it proved when I got sacked in 1988. It was Alex's turn about eighteen months later, and after a short time out of the game, he was appointed manager of Airdrie. What he'd done at Tynecastle was fantastic, but in many respects his achievements at Airdrie were even greater. They were a wee club, with wee gates. Yet he took them to two Scottish Cup finals and into Europe for the first and only time in their history. It was quite amazing, really. That was their most successful period, certainly of the modern era. For them to treat Doddie the way they did, by not renewing his contract in 1999, was crazy. In saying that, the even bigger surprise for me was that no other club came in for him.

Maybe the reason for that was that he never toadied to people. He never promoted himself. He just drifted away and got forgotten about, and was a great loss to the game. Perhaps if he had done all the coaching badges it might have helped. But, like me, he never got around to that. When we were players together at Rangers, there never seemed to be time for us to attend the courses at Largs. I recall later, when Doddie and I were at Hearts, Andy Roxburgh coming through to Tynecastle and telling us he wanted all the Premier Division managers to have a coaching badge. I agreed with that, and Andy was desperate for us to go down to one of the courses at Largs. But when he went out of the room, I can recall Doddie saying, 'That'll be right.' His point was that we were telling the likes of Jimmy Bone to play on a Saturday. How could we then go to Largs and have Jimmy, who was part of the set-up there, tell us how the game should be played?

Sandy Jardine

ALEX MACDONALD . . . OF CELTIC?

What is it people say – don't believe everything you read in the press? Tell me about it. I remember once after a midweek match with Rangers going back to my local near Kirkintilloch for a quiet pint. I had a lot to mull over to be honest, having fallen out with our then manager Jock Wallace at half time, in circumstances I'll reveal later on in this book.

The owner of the pub, knowing I was on the premises, duly appeared at the bar, brandishing a newspaper. 'How about this then?' he asked, showing me the back page, which carried the blaring headline: 'MacDonald Joins Celtic'. No kidding, I just about fell off my stool. But it was his idea of a joke. The paper was a spoof copy he'd had made up at a stall in, I think, the Kelvin Hall in Glasgow.

MacDonald Joins Celtic, indeed. Those who know me for the Rangers man I am and always have been would have thought the very possibility nothing short of preposterous. Yet there was a time going on nine years earlier when the unthinkable could have been true. I was still with my first senior club, St Johnstone. Here's what happened.

After a night game at Perth in 1968, I'd made my way back to Glasgow by train and was waiting just along from George Square for a bus when a big Mercedes pulled up about fifteen yards past the stop. A lady hung her head out of the front passenger window and shouted, 'Alex!'

I looked at the only person, a guy, waiting with me and asked if his name was Alex. He shook his head, so I stepped nearer the car and said to the lady, 'Can I help you?'

She said, 'No, but you can help this man,' and pointed inside towards the driver, who I couldn't see at that point. It turned out to be the manager of Celtic, Jock Stein. 'Where are you going?' he asked.

'Govanhill, to my granny's,' I told him, because I was staying with her at the time.

'I'll give you a lift then,' he said. 'Jump in.'

I should tell you this wasn't the first time I'd met him. Once after a midweek game between St Johnstone and Celtic at Muirton Park, when the trains were off for some reason, I'd asked him if I could get a run back to Glasgow on their bus and he said, 'Aye, no problem, so long as you sit at the front, not at the back with the players.'

Anyway, there he was giving me a lift again and asking all sorts of things, like where I saw my career going, what money I was earning, and the sixty-four thousand dollar question: how would I feel about joining Celtic? To be honest, I can't remember exactly how I answered that one. What I do recall is that when we reached Govanhill, I was shaking with excitement.

But looking back then, yes, I probably would have jumped at the chance to sign for Celtic. Why? At that particular time, 1968, I just wanted to be with the best, and Celtic were the best. They'd won the European Cup the previous year and were in the throes of creating a monopoly on winning the Scottish League title. Then there was Jock Stein himself, one of the best managers in the business.

Of course, I was Rangers mad. When I was that bit younger, I had photographs of their players plastered all over the house. Even after getting into senior football, I had a picture of Jim Baxter on the front of my first cuttings album. Still, if it had come to the bit, with Jock Stein following up his interest in me, I think I would have had to say to him, 'I'm your man.'

He is supposed to have gone on record once as saying that if he had the chance to sign two players of equal merit, one a Protestant, the other a Catholic, he would choose the Protestant. Why? Because Rangers then, but not now, wouldn't sign the Catholic. Maybe, in my own case, that was where he was coming from. Who knows?

As things transpired, it wasn't very long before I actually signed for Rangers and began to revel in playing against Celtic. I appeared in more than forty Old Firm games during my twelve years at Ibrox and loved every one. If we'd had to face Celtic every week, it would have suited me to a tee. Some of my team-mates used to be quite nervous – sick even – before kick-off, but I'm happy to say I wasn't affected like that. The sooner I got out there onto the pitch – be it at Ibrox, Celtic Park or Hampden – the happier I was. I'd grown up knowing what it meant to Rangers if they beat Celtic, so I felt as if I was carrying all the hopes of the supporters on my shoulders.

If you got beat in an Old Firm game, you just knew half of Glasgow would be laughing at you, while the other half would be giving you stick. Every ball was there to be won, and you didn't hold back from trying to win it. You didn't dare, because that would have meant more stick. My view was that if you got hurt then it was only for a wee while. The doctor was there to take away the pain. I actually took that maxim into management with me and was forever telling players not to worry about the physical contact. All too often, of course, when Rangers and Celtic faced one another, the physical exchanges tended to be highlighted with the skill factor being overlooked to a degree. Yet who could say the teams I played in didn't have skill?

Celtic themselves had some unbelievable players, and I don't just mean the likes of Jimmy Johnstone and Bobby Murdoch. I thought the wee boy John Clark was brilliant as well. He was a right hardy man in defence, one who did his job for the team. He sorted you out when he had to. Needless to say, I had great respect for Billy McNeill also. Yet as we lined up before a game, I never had any communication with any of them. Well, that's not strictly true. The one guy I would shake hands with was George Connelly. Don't ask me why that was, other than that I thought of him as a magnificent footballer and one who wouldn't look to do you any harm in fifty–fifty situations.

Don't get me wrong. I got on well with the Celtic lads, but at the time I had this attitude that Rangers were MY team and nothing and nobody would distract me from doing my very best to stop any team – especially their greatest rivals – from beating them. I was totally focused on winning and took the same attitude with me to Hearts, although as far as playing Celtic was concerned, something involving Danny McGrain made me mellow a bit.

My daughter Lisa was diagnosed as having diabetes when she was in her teens in the mid-1980s, and unbeknown to me, Danny, who is diabetic as well, went to visit her in hospital. He gave her an autograph and a Scotland shirt, which I thought was an absolutely fantastic gesture. I'd always thought of him as being a great player but that confirmed he was a good man as well. I respected him all the more as a result.

But before I go on here, let me track back to the thought that I could have ended up playing for Celtic. Would I, in that event, have competed as hard as I did for them as I did for Rangers, especially in Old Firm matches? It goes without saying that of course I would. I remember once asking my old Rangers team-mate, Alfie Conn, why he had chosen to join Celtic after his time down south with Spurs and he answered, 'Jock Stein. The power of Jock Stein.'

I knew where he was coming from. I would have felt like that, too. In my own experience, the great majority of times you went out with the aim of trying to please the manager. He, after all, called the shots. He needed to know he could hang his hat on you. If so, he only had to concern himself with the next guy, and so on. Then you tried to please the supporters. Only after that, and when you were a bit older and more established, did you attempt to fulfil your own ideals as a footballer, to express whatever was in your head.

Fortunately for me, I was never intimidated by the atmosphere of big games and they didn't come much bigger than Old Firm ones. People used to ask me, 'How come you play so well against Celtic and in Europe?' If that was true, then it may have been for the reason that nobody wanted to make mistakes in those games; therefore, they were less inclined to linger on the ball. So I would see more of it. Do you see what I'm driving at? In lesser games, I would make a run and shout, 'Here I am!' But the ball wouldn't come. Whoever was on it wanted to do a little more before parting with it, leaving me to come back out of the position I'd got myself into before making another run. In short, I liked the bigger games more because I tended to be involved a lot more. The noise of the crowd was never a factor that bothered me. Only if the ball went out of the park for, say, a throw-in and I went to retrieve it, was I ever aware of actual comments.

. . . Which reminds me of a time we were playing at Celtic Park. I went to get the ball for a throw-in and who did I see amid this sea of faces in front of the main stand, but a boy called Bobby McClung who used to live up the stair from me and who I knew to be a Rangers fan. I shouted, 'Bobby, what are you doin' there?' Next thing I'm getting total abuse. But it turned out he got the same. He was where he shouldn't have been, in a Celtic section of the crowd, and told me some time later, 'You nearly got me done in for speaking to me.' At least by then he could laugh about it, although I'm sure he wasn't laughing at the time.

My first Old Firm game was on 3 January 1970 at Celtic Park, and it finished 0–0. What do I remember from the occasion? Not a lot, in fact. But less than a couple of months later, we found ourselves back there in a Scottish Cup quarter-final tie that still sticks in my mind for a reason which has haunted me for long enough: I got sent off. One minute I was clearing a shot off my own line and feeling quite proud of myself, the next I was lunging in to challenge Celtic's goalkeeper, Evan Williams, for the ball. I felt it was there to be won, so why not? Jim Brogan breenged in all of a sudden and pushed me off my feet. He could have gone off along with me.

We ended up losing 3–1 and I had to live with the thought of having let my team-mates down in that one moment of rashness. The referee, by the way, was Big Tiny Wharton, the most respected match official of his day. Sometimes if you fell foul of him, he would call you over and at the same time reach for his pocket. More than once in these circumstances I can recall being aghast and saying, 'You're no' going tae book me?' Then he would pull out a hanky and give you a ticking off. But on that occasion there was no such jokey gesture on his part, and I still have his report of the incident, which he filed to the SFA, by way of testimony. It reads that on 21 February 1970, he had cause 'to order off Alex MacDonald (No. 10) Ranger FC for deliberately kicking an opponent'. Then it goes on to explain the circumstances, saying: 'Following a corner kick, Celtic goalkeeper Williams threw himself on the ball as Stein (Rangers) tried to make contact. A. MacDonald, a few paces to the side, ran in and deliberately kicked Williams on the neck as he lay covering the ball.' Shame on me, although I have to say Mr Wharton's version of events sounded much graver than the way I saw them at the time.

How many times have we seen the same thing happen: a goalkeeper makes to grab the ball and a player running in jabs out a foot in the hope of knocking it away from him? When the adrenalin is boiling up, it's difficult to hold back. Mr Wharton said I 'deliberately kicked Williams'. How could he be sure? It was no accident that Jim Brogan sent me flying but he stayed on the field. It was all heat-of-the-moment stuff yet, on reflection, highly regrettable from my point of view as well as Rangers'.

If there was a lesson to be learned, then I'm sorry to say it must have been lost on me.

Some five years later, 30 August 1975 to be precise, I was sent off again in an Old Firm game. My only consolation was that, this time at Ibrox, Rangers won 2–1. It was a real, rowdy affair off the park as well as on it, with eighty-four arrests made among fans. Ian Foote was in charge and he gave me my marching orders for something that happened at a bounce-up involving Danny McGrain. The referee's report actually stated: 'McGrain had cleared the ball when MacDonald deliberately kicked him.' So far as I was concerned, I didn't even make contact with Danny, but maybe the intent was there . . .

These games generate so much passion they're akin to powder kegs which can blow up at any moment. Few if any, in my experience, had the potential to be more explosive than the League decider between ourselves and Celtic at Parkhead in May 1979. Celtic needed to win to lift the title, and win they did. But unlike those occasions I've just covered, I found myself the innocent party in an incident involving Johnny Doyle. Mike Conroy had just brought me to the ground with a crunching tackle. Johnny then had a boot at me and was sent packing. Much good it did, us being left to face only ten men, right enough.

I'd actually given Rangers an early lead that night. But with Doylie off, Celtic managed to equalise through Roy Aitken. George McCluskey proceeded to put them 2–1 in front, only for Bobby Russell to equalise. Colin Jackson then scored an own-goal, and Murdo MacLeod struck virtually on the whistle to give Celtic a 4–2 win. Dramatic stuff, but pity about the ending. No matter how upset Johnny Doyle was at being sent off, I don't suppose it took him too long to get into the swing of Celtic's after-match celebration.

I liked Wee Doylie as a guy and a player. It was a terrible that he died in an accident at home. Like myself, he was nothing if not competitive. I remember after one Old Firm game us coming off the park and him saying to me, 'I'm no' goin' to shake your hand but well done anyway.' We must have had a right few tussles that time. Then again, who didn't I have a right few tussles with? In quite a few of the Rangers Supporters Clubs I've visited, there's a photograph of me inviting Roy Aitken to box. Hopefully he would have taken pity on me since I'm a lot smaller. In various publications, there's another of me saying to Lou Macari, 'Gie's a kiss.' No wonder he's laughing. I should have offered to box Lou instead. After all, he's even wee-er than me.

Who said Old Firm games didn't have their lighter moments? But what was I thinking about, having a go once at Billy McNeill, who is so much taller? One report from the time, in September 1974, said I 'swung a boot at him then dived theatrically'. Don't ask me, 'Now what that was all about?' It sounds as if I'd rather not be reminded, although diving wasn't exactly my style. Big Billy must have forgiven me because a few years later, when he was in charge of Aberdeen, he sounded me out about joining him at Pittodrie.

Anyway, it wasn't as if I was always the aggressor. Paddy McCluskey, never the quickest, resorted on one occasion to bringing me down with a rugby tackle – in the New Year fixture of 1973 at Ibrox, it was. In so doing, he gave away a penalty with which Derek Parlane sent us on the way to a 2–1 win. What a start to our centenary year. Come the start of the following season, in a League Cup tie at Celtic Park, it was Jimmy Johnstone's turn to get embroiled with me.

Celtic had been all over us in the first half and gone 1–0 up. Then, soon after the break, I equalised. That racked up the tension in the game, and it wasn't long before Derek Parlane put us in front. But, with the Celtic lads protesting the goal was offside, I got involved in an argument with Wee Jimmy which resulted in him being sent off. I got away with a booking. Alfie Conn, by the way, ended up scoring to give us 3–1 win that saw us through to the later stages of the tournament.

I don't know this for a fact, but I think sometimes the Celtic players looked to draw me into trouble, hoping I would react and pay the same penalty Jimmy Johnstone did that time. What makes me say so? Well, I was told once that Jock Stein said in effect before an Old Firm game, 'Just needle him and he'll lose the head.' To think that when I was with St Johnstone he seemed to be interested in signing me. If only my memory were better, I could highlight a hundred mad moments in our games with Celtic – and not all of them involving yours truly.

But seriously, how can I forget it was against Celtic, in the Old Firm League Cup Final of 1970, that I won the first of my medals with Rangers? It's not an occasion Derek Johnstone could have forgotten either – still ten days short of his seventeenth birthday, he got the only goal. I've seen umpteen re-runs of the magical moment in which Big DJ rose superbly between Billy McNeill and Jim Craig to head in a cross by Willie Johnston. What that film clip doesn't show is me helping to set up the attack by passing the ball wide to Bud on the right flank.

Willie Waddell, to whom I ended up owing so much in my career, hadn't long taken over as manager, with Jock Wallace his coach. The result signalled great times ahead for Rangers as we began to emerge from the shadow of Celtic and, of course, the man whose influence over them registered as quite extraordinary. I'm talking, obviously, of Jock Stein. Yet it remains an intriguing thought that I could have been playing for his team, not against them.

2

ME, A HOOLIGAN?

Everyone who was around at the time knows exactly where they were when they heard President Kennedy had been assassinated. Me? I was caught up in a gang fight inside the Barrowland Ballroom in Glasgow, a favourite haunt of a few pals and mine at weekends. It would be wrong to say we went there looking for trouble. We were more interested in the dancing and always dressed for the part, but if we saw anybody we knew in a bit of bother then we were only too willing to help them out.

So it was that fateful Friday night of 22 November 1963. The fists were flying when all of a sudden we heard somebody shout, 'President Kennedy's been shot.' That was the end of the scrap. Everybody just sloped away into the darkness.

I was a spotty-faced fifteen-year-old back then, charged up with hormones and probably a few scrumpy ciders as well. It's probably stating the obvious to say I wasn't an angel, although I was a bit put out a couple of years later by something supposedly said about me by the then manager of Partick Thistle, Willie Thornton. Gordon Whitelaw, a team-mate of mine at St Johnstone, apparently had recommended me to Willie, only to be told I was 'a hooligan'. Quite where Willie was coming from, I don't know. Maybe he'd heard about me getting into the odd scrape on the field as a juvenile player. As fate would have it, when I signed for Rangers in 1968, he'd actually become assistant to the then Ibrox manager, Davie White. But he never said anything to suggest he thought of me as a delinquent. Quite the opposite, really. He was never anything other than helpful.

Fighting was just a natural part of growing up, so far as I was concerned, although I didn't think of myself as any latter-day Benny Lynch. My ma spotted me once from the window of our tenement trading blows with some guy out in the street and was all upset. But my da just said to her, 'Leave him be. He'll sort it out.' I would fight with anybody – even my best pal, Jimmy Lumsden. We went at it for fully two hours on one occasion – about what, I can't remember. Given that our friendship endures to this day, the issue between us couldn't have been very serious.

Football was my real passion though. When we were in our early teens, me and Jimmy cleared this big bit of spare ground to create our very own pitch. We even painted goals on the derelict buildings at either end, and a crowd of us would play there for as long as our legs held us up. In my case, that was longer than most. I could run all day and, in the summer nights, till well after the sun went down. The energy I seemed to be blessed with was to prove a great asset to me as a professional footballer. In training at St Johnstone and Rangers even, older guys were forever saying, 'Are you no' gonnae slow doon?'

Being born with an aggressive streak helped also. When the midwife slapped my backside to make me cry, I threw her a look which said 'Keep yer hauns tae yersel, hen.' I jest, of course, and my tongue is slightly in my cheek when I say it took me long enough to figure out why my birthday in 1948 was celebrated so widely year upon year. Then somebody told me the date in question, 17 March, is St Patrick's Day.

Home was a room and kitchen in Kinning Park, and after moving about a mile within that same district, we flitted to Tradeston, which is next to the Gorbals. My ma was a machinist, my da a semi-skilled labourer. Great party people, they were. Both could play the piano, and my ma knew a thousand songs. So you can imagine ours wasn't exactly a quiet abode. But that didn't stop me complaining about us all living in the one room. So, when we got the chance of going to Easterhouse, I was all for it. Talk about the lure of luxury. This new accommodation actually had a bathroom, and separate bedrooms for me for me and my younger sister, Ann. I would have been about thirteen at the time and felt like I was living the life of a toff. Then something happened which made me yearn for a return to my roots on Clydeside.

We were playing football in these new surroundings of mine and when I nutmegged this lad, he thumped me. I nutmegged him again, and he thumped me a second time. All of a sudden, his whole team were ganging up on me. Fair enough if that had been the end of the matter but it wasn't. The reprisals got worse, with somebody trying to throw a midgie bin through one of our windows. Then they found their mark with a brick. What were these guys trying to tell me? That I wasn't welcome in their sprawling scheme?

I hadn't changed schools when we went there. I was still travelling back and forth by bus every day to the city. So I decided, with my parents' consent, I would move in with my Granny Watson in Govanhill, which is on the way to Hampden but not too far removed from my old stomping ground of Tradeston. It was while living there I finished my education, such as it was. In fact, I continued staying with my granny until I got married. Whoever it was who came up with the slogan 'Glasgow Smiles Better' could have had my very own upbringing in mind. Life in the city was much more to my liking.

Granny MacDonald and I were close as well. She came to Glasgow from Uist and spoke the Gaelic. Hers was the Catholic side of the family. But my da wasn't much into religion, so didn't press it on me. He took the view that all the church's teachings were just a form of brainwashing. So far as schools were concerned, my ma insisted I go to non-denominational ones, Crookston Primary and Secondary. What religious education I did receive was mainly from attending a Bible class at what they called Paddy Black's Mission in Tradeston. It also provided various recreational facilities for youngsters in the area.

It was at Crookston, by the way, that I began playing football with Jimmy Lumsden, who was to join Leeds United, then Morton and Clydebank. I also played for the Lifeboys, then the Boys Brigade. Happy days, indeed. I was on the go all the time, even if it was just running errands for my Granny MacDonald. I remember her rewarding me once with three half crowns (37.5p), which set me running again – straight to the post office to buy savings stamps. I never walked anywhere in those days. Sometimes, just for the fun of it, I would run round and round the block to see how long I could last.

The more serious running came when I was at secondary school and won the cross-country championship at Bellahouston Park three years in a row. Oh, yes, I had trophies to prove it. I just wish now I'd hung onto them. A cousin of mine, Alfie Lilley, was at Bellahouston Academy. I would go to see him play rugby and he would reciprocate the gesture by coming to watch me play football. A team I trained with but never played for were Plantation Hearts. Was that an omen, signalling the fact I would end my playing days with another team called Hearts?

Some pals and I were into birds in a big way in those days too – pigeons, to be exact. We would climb up to the top-storey level of a tenement, where I would hang out of the window and grab the birds from the edge of the roof. What to feed them was another matter, but thank goodness for our ingenuity. Nearby was a flour-mill, with a hoist moving up and down non-stop at the side of it. If we were careful and the night watchie didn't catch us, we could jump on this contraption, stick out an arm when it reached an open hatch and grab a handful of grain each. If we'd got our timing even slightly out, we could have beheaded ourselves.

Then came the question of where to keep the pigeons, which we'd stowed in a basket. Jimmy Lumsden said he would take them home with him, which he did. But he hid the basket under his ma's bed, which was a dead give-away. She heard them cooing and made us return them to nature. It was better that we stuck to playing football, although I did talk my granny into getting a budgie. We named it Billy and I can remember the fun we had trying to get him to speak. All this while, my interest in Rangers was being nourished. Don't ask me who they were facing the first time I saw them. I can say only it was a night match because the one thing I remember is seeing this big red moon above the Celtic end at Ibrox.

I recall much more about the first time I actually played there. I must have been all of thirteen and scaled the wall on the railway side (that's the one where the Govan Stand is situated now), before pulling a few of my pals up after me. Then we jumped down onto the back of the terracing and onto the park for a kick-about. I can see myself yet, scoring at the Celtic end. In fact, I can hear myself, too, shouting, 'How about tha-a-at?' How long did we play? Half an hour, maybe. Well, we didn't want to abuse the privilege, or damage the turf. Seriously though, something must have alerted Bobby Moffat, the doorman who was in charge of security, for out he came and chased us back the way we'd come. So we crossed over the street to the Albion training ground and continued our game there.

It must have been around that same time I used to take the odd day off school and go into Ibrox, as anyone could at the time walk through the open gate at the side of the Main Stand and watch some of the players, Willie Henderson among them, playing heidie tennis in the tunnel. Talk about being starry-eyed. Even then, I itched to play for Rangers. It wouldn't matter if they freed me after a few weeks, I remember thinking, just so long as I could say I'd pulled that blue jersey over my head. The reality was, of course, I'd to keep working at my game, but that didn't seem like hard graft to me. By then I was playing every night on the spare ground, right below where the southern end of the Kingston Bridge is now, and both morning and afternoon for teams on a Saturday.

Jimmy Lumsden, with whom I'd more or less grown up, moved eventually to Castlemilk, but we stayed as close as ever. Sometimes I stayed overnight at his place. I even went on holiday with him and his family once. He duly got into the Glasgow schoolboy team, while I only made the trials. That wasn't the fault of Jimmy's da, a great man, who really pushed me to make it as a footballer.

I just wish I could have thanked him when finally I went professional, but am sorry to say he had died by then.

My own da stood back. I remember once him saying to me, 'Aye, you didn't do too well on Saturday, did you?'

I replied, 'How would you know? You weren't at my game.'

'I was there, all right,' he came back. 'You just didn't see me.' He'd been a player himself, by the way – up to junior level. His brother was due to play trials for Celtic just when the Second World War broke out and so that put a stop to a lot of things.

My daft period came that bit later when, as well as getting involved in the odd skirmish at places like the Barrowland Ballroom, a pal and I got a hold of a mo-ped on which we careered around town. When I say got a hold of, I mean my pal pinched it from somewhere. He had a beard so looked old enough to drive the thing. I settled for hanging on to his back. The scooter's starter was broken so whenever we were ready to push off, I had to pull this wire to get the motor spluttering into life.

It was the time of the Mods and Rockers craze which swept through Britain, with the Rockers favouring actual motorbikes. We considered ourselves Mods. My ma, at her work, was making these plastic coats with a wee bit suede on the collar. I got a hold of one of these to make me look the part. Fitba was fitba, but fun was fun, and I had plenty of it in those days.

What else did I get up to during this crazy phase after I'd left the school? Well, I joined the Orange Order in the Gorbals, but when I was nominated to do something or other, I left.

My first job was as a van boy with the Co-operative, delivering all around the area. My Granny Watson never went short of a half-pound of butter. On Saturdays, I had the task of washing the bosses' cars, sleek big Rovers and the like. It gave me a taste for fancy motors, and after joining Rangers, I managed to afford one. Before signing for St Johnstone, I became an apprentice cooper and thereby hangs a tale of which I'm not especially proud.

When the old barrels came into our place, we had to strip off the lead which was strapped around them. It was worth a fair bit of money. One day, this guy I was working with nodded upwards and said to me, 'There's a lot of lead up on that roof there.'

I said, 'Well, what do you want to do about it?' I imagine you can guess the rest. Suffice to say, that was the end of my time, and his, in the cooperage. Maybe it's better I stick to talking about my real fixation, the fitba.

I'd been used to playing on the spare ground, often with lads who were much older than myself. Some of them were married even, but that fact didn't drive them home early. My granny was never sure when I'd be home. It could be after midnight. These guys looked after me, the young kid on the block, you might say. If somebody was giving me a problem, they would sort it out. I learned a bit about growing up just by being in their company, and on a serious level of football, I was making progress.

Jimmy Lumsden and I got invited to train with Kilmarnock Amateurs, which meant meeting up after school, hopping along to his auntie's in the Gorbals for pie and chips, then jumping on the red bus which took us down to Ayrshire. Training under the floodlights at Rugby Park, with the nets shimmering in the glow of them, was absolutely brilliant. Jimmy got picked to play for the Under-16s who were a right good team. They wanted me then to play for the Under-18s, but I didn't fancy that idea.

On the day I left school, there was a knock on my granny's door. I went to answer and could hear her shouting, 'Who is it?' It was Don Revie, the manager of Leeds United, along with his chairman who, from memory, was a Mr Reynolds. They wanted me to go to Elland Road for trials, so the next day I found myself on a train down to Leeds, where I stayed – initially at least in a hotel along with a guy called Mick McGowan, I think it was. Then it was into digs, which were ok, apart from the fact I wasn't getting fed enough. It came to the point I had to go out for fish suppers.

Enough of this, I thought. I decided to go and speak to Don Revie, but when I got to his office, it was his brother who was there. I said to him, 'I'll need to go back to Glasgow because I'm homesick and hungry.'

He replied, 'No, no. I'll move you.'

So he did, into a new set of digs alongside Jimmy Greenhoff and Norman Hunter, who were to become big names with the club. That was great, and I stayed there for the rest of the fortnight or so I was down there. But that got me thinking, did I really want to go to England?

It must have been a while after that – in fact, I was working at the cooperage – when Wolves wanted to take me down the road. I remember saying to their representative, 'I can't take my apprenticeship with me, and anyway, I'm a Glasgow boy. I don't really want to move from here.' I was playing for Glasgow United by then. They had a good set-up and were run by men called Sam Beck and Archie Lawrie, and then St Johnstone soon came in for me. That was in 1965, when I'd just turned seventeen.

Archie actually took me along to my first trial game for their reserves, against Third Lanark at Cathkin. Just about the only thing I can remember was nutmegging an ex-Celtic player – Jim Conway, maybe. I got a fair bit of pleasure out of that, I can tell you. I must have done well enough in the game, for I was invited then to play a second trial game, this time against Dundee at Muirton Park. The guy I found myself up against on that occasion was big George Ryden.

I can see him yet. He was the first player I'd encountered who smeared his brow with Vaseline. He was brown as a berry, as well, and positively gleamed under the floodlights. Again, I can't recall much if anything about the game itself, apart from the fact I played as a frontrunner with the number 9 on my back. But, given the events of a couple of weeks later, I guess I must have done all right. I was actually playing on the spare ground this night when a car drew up and out stepped the St Johnstone manager, Bobby Brown, and the scout who had recommended me to him.

If I'd known they were coming, I might have smartened myself up a bit because I was wearing a t-shirt, an old pair of corduroy trousers and sannies. Happily, they accepted me as they found me, and the three of us went to this wee café across from the Kingston Halls where I had a glass of milk as I negotiated my own deal. My signing-on fee was £250, which I split between my ma and Granny Watson, who was still looking after me most of the time. Well, maybe I kept a wee bit back for myself.

I think I remember the wages too: £12 a week during the season, dropping to £8 in the close-season. It seemed like a fortune. I was on my way as a footballer and wouldn't be back at the Barrowland Ballroom for a while, if ever.

3

JIMMY JOHNSTONE AND A CASE OF MISTAKEN IDENTITY

The Alex MacDonald who emerged soon enough in St Johnstone's first team seemed to remind one journalist of a player whose reputation was established internationally by that point. Here, I quote from the article which that reporter felt moved to write after seeing me in a night match against Dundee United at Tannadice: 'With his fitba' legs and his hair made to look reddish in the glare of the lights, I got to thinking how like Alan Ball he is.' Well, it's all in the eye of the beholder, I suppose, but there was at least an obvious resemblance between me and a player who arrived at Muirton Park some time after I did, Kenny Aird. We were pretty much the same height, build and age, and as another newspaperman observed, 'They even have the same, carrot-coloured hair.'

Kenny and I, both attackers, decided we would try to fox opponents by playing on these similarities in our appearances. One ploy we worked was a scissors movement, both of us going for the same ball then breaking away in different directions. Our hope was that the guys supposed to be marking us couldn't tell Kenny from me, and vice versa. The first time we did it in an actual match, the opposing full-back and wing-half started arguing with one another about who they were meant to be picking up.

Even our own team-mates sometimes had problems telling Kenny and me apart. For example, I can recall one of them pushing upfield in a game with the ball at his feet, then shouting, 'Right,

Kenny' as he prepared to make a pass. But he wasn't looking at Kenny. He was looking at me. Confusing or what? All the more so when, as often was the case, we switched positions in the forward line. We certainly fooled Jimmy Johnstone on one notable occasion in a 1–1 draw at Celtic Park in September 1967 in which I scored our goal.

I gave Jinky a wee smack near the touchline and he got up again no bother. Then I gave him another wee smack and he wanted to argue. Kenny and I duly swopped over, with him going wide and me moving inside. So Kenny, a good wee tackler, was close to Jinky by then, and when he gave him a smack, it was one too many for the Celtic man. Jinky took a swing at Kenny in retaliation, knocking out one of his teeth. Then he looked over at me and said to Kenny, 'Sorry, I thought you were that other guy.' You won't be surprised to learn Jinky got sent off for that. In fact, he began walking the instant the incident happened and ended up being suspended for twenty-one days by the SFA and missing that season's League Cup Final as a result. All told, it was an unfortunate episode for him but certainly not one Kenny or I set out to script, so to speak.

Sometime later, by the way, when Kenny and I were coming out of Queen Street Station in Glasgow after training at Perth, we saw Jimmy standing there, speaking to somebody. I remember joking with Kenny, 'C'mon, we'll get him now.' Kenny, needless to say, let the opportunity pass him by. He wasn't carrying a grievance by then, regardless of being short of a tooth. How long Jimmy bore a grudge, if at all, I don't know. He had a sense of humour and maybe saw the funny side of the situation. Well, eventually at least.

But I've got ahead of myself here. Let's track back to my actual joining St Johnstone, straight from juvenile football with Glasgow United. I had to go through the formality of signing for Luncarty Juniors, just up the road from Perth. This was because if I didn't make the grade as a senior I could be re-instated to the next highest level: junior football. If I hadn't at least been registered as a junior, the rule at the time would have prevented me from taking that one step down. Complicated, did you say? It was hard for me, a daft seventeen-year-old, to get my head round that one.

Luncarty wasn't somewhere I knew. Even yet, it's a place I've never been, although I've seen it signposted off the main road going from Perth to Pitlochry. People who know these things tell me a largely forgotten battle was fought there a very long time ago. The battle I girded myself for back in 1965 was getting into St Johnstone's first team just as quickly as I could, and I counted myself fortunate to be in with good set of guys who gave me all the encouragement I needed.

Among those I travelled by train from Glasgow with were Benny Rooney and Gordon Whitelaw, as well as Ian McPhee, who I'd known of old, as he came from my part of the city. The banter between us was good and became better still when we were joined by another real Glasgow character, John Connolly.

My ma actually bought me a suit so I could look semi-smart for the journeys. Using her expertise as a machinist, she sewed a crease into the trousers to make sure they didn't become crumpled through sitting in the carriage for a couple of hours a day. Mothers think of everything, don't they?

Many was the laugh we had, not only on our daily commute but also in training, with guys like Willie Coburn and Bill McCarry, who was known throughout the Scottish game as Buck. They were St Johnstone stalwarts, as was Ron McKinven, who'd had the honour as an amateur of playing for the British team at the 1960 Olympics in Rome, along with Davie Holt and Hunter Devine of Queen's Park and Billy Neil of Airdrie. One of their matches, by the way, was against Italy, who had Giovanni Trapattoni and Gianni Rivera, virtually unknown to the rest of the world at the time, in their side. I mention all of this for topical reasons, what with the waves of controversy there have been about a 'British' team being fielded – for the first time since Rome – when the Games came to London in 2012.

McPhee, Coburn, McCarry, McKinven, as well as Willie Renton and Neil Duffy, were all in the St Johnstone team in which I made my debut against Clyde at Shawfield midway through my first season with the club. If I were solely reliant on memory, I couldn't have told you a single detail about the match in question in January 1966, so it's as well my family had begun to compile a cuttings book, which I still have. Let me blow some of the dust off it and extract from a report of the time what, from my personal stance, were the most pertinent snippets.

One relates: 'Saints' young centre-forward, Alex MacDonald, proved that he will be hard to displace as the leader of the Perth side. He gave Clyde a fright in the fourteenth minute. The home keeper could only parry one of his power drives then, and Neil Duffy was right on the spot to tap the ball home.' Another testifies: 'The Shawfield side always looked as if they could pull the goal back. But when MacDonald caught their defence on the wrong foot in the minute before half time and raced on to score, they were in deep trouble.'

I must have been feeling quite pleased with myself when we went in at the interval – as you can well imagine – only to become rather disillusioned once we re-emerged from it for the second half. Clyde knocked in three goals during that period – two of them by Joe Gilroy – to spoil my afternoon and of course St Johnstone's by beating us 3–2. In fairness, Clyde weren't a bad team back in the mid- to late-1960s, one of their best players being Davie White, who was to become manager of Rangers before long and sign me for £50,000.

Now and again, I would drop back into the reserves, and it was while playing for them in a match against Rangers I came up against one of my boyhood heroes, Jimmy Millar. As every Ibrox fan knows, Jimmy had made his name as a centre-forward, with Ralphie Brand playing alongside him. Between them, in what was an excellent team, they scored the proverbial barrow-load of goals. But on this occasion, Jimmy was playing at wing-half, and I must have been at inside-forward, directly in opposition. I was in about him throughout the game, to the point that any time I saw Jimmy afterwards, he would laugh and say, 'Aye, here's the wee whippersnapper who tried to kick me.' My answer to him was always the same: 'Jimmy, I wouldn't kick anybody in a blue jersey.'

It wasn't strictly true, though. The first time I came up against Rangers at top-team level, in the Scottish Cup of 1965–66 at Ibrox, I didn't hold back any. Playing as we did that day, in front of a crowd of 32,000, really fired me up. They had a good side at the time, with Willie Henderson, Alex Willoughby, Jim Forrest, Jorn Sorensen and Willie Johnston in attack, but managed to beat us only 1–0, with a goal by Willoughby. Also for the record, Rangers went on to win the competition that season, beating Celtic in a replayed final, with Kai Johansen the scorer.

My early role with St Johnstone was as a frontrunner and I found myself up against some of the toughest customers around, among them Roy Barry of Dunfermline. But I did my best to make sure that nobody got the better of me. It wasn't in my nature to back down, regardless of how much bigger than me they might have been. I can still hear opposing defenders discussing who was to be marking me. 'Have you got him?' one would ask, and the other would say, 'Aye, I've got him.' I'd be saying to myself: 'You just think you've got him.' Then I'd drop off and appear somewhere else. It was, to use the modern phrase, a good learning curve for me. Later, when I moved into a midfield slot, Big Ian McPhee taught me how to take an opponent for a walk so he could push through from his deeper position.

Learning simple wee things like that helped my development as a player and ensured that by the end of my first season at Muirton I could reflect on having gone a fair way to establishing myself. Bobby Brown was the complete gentleman, brilliant to play for. Frank Christie, his trainer, could be a hard taskmaster, though. I can recall being joined at the club by Billy Clark and saying to him, 'Don't let Frank get you down. You've got to stand up for yourself.' In fact, Frank was only trying to help the pair of us improve. Billy was a good player, by the way, and became a great pal of mine. He remains so to this day. But, as the brother of Arnold, Scotland's biggest car dealer, he was wanted by him in the business. That meant working Saturdays, which effectively put paid to his time as a professional footballer.

I must have been one of the fittest guys in the country back then, despite having a problem with one of my feet. Thereby hangs an unlikely tale. When I was a kid on Clydeside, I used to help a coalman on his rounds. One day, his horse tramped on my toes. It was sore at the time but, after a while, everything seemed to be ok. Only after joining St Johnstone did the injury start flaring up. X-rays suggested a fragment of bone had been floating about in my foot for all those years, so I had to undergo an operation to remove it.

Horses obviously didn't fancy me because later in my time at St Johnstone we were up north somewhere for a game and staying in a hotel set beside an open field. A few of us went out for a walk and were approached by this horse on the other side of the wire fence. Somebody thought it would be a good idea if I climbed over and got on its back. I was daft enough to agree, but no sooner had my mates helped me up than the startled beast threw me. I had a sore back at the time and that experience didn't help it any.

St Johnstone had been promoted from the Second Division a couple of seasons before I signed for them, and in my first term on their books, they finished fourteenth out of the eighteen teams making up the First Division. Celtic won the title, thereby beginning their historic run which saw them installed as champions nine times on the trot. Little could I have imagined I would be in the Rangers side who, in 1975, stopped them making it ten in a row. My thoughts at the time were focused solely on making further progress at Muirton. I wasn't earning a fortune but had enough to fund a lifestyle which was by no means extravagant.

Then something happened which made me wonder if I was being – how to put this – short-changed just a bit. I can remember yet standing in the clubhouse this day as we were handed our pay packets. Felix McGrogan and Harry Fallon opened theirs, each of them pulling out five fivers. I was still on a basic £12. Now then I didn't consider myself to be motivated by money. If I had been, I might still be in football. But in this instance there was a principle at stake. So it wasn't long before I found myself knocking on the manager's door to ask for a rise. Give Bobby Brown his due, he saw to it I got one.

That have may been an admission on his part that I had begun to pay my way in the team and I'd like to think I continued giving St Johnstone their money's worth all the way through to my time of leaving them late in 1968. For what it's worth, in that first season at Muirton after my debut against Clyde in January 1966, I ended up playing a total of eleven games. Eight were in the league, three in the Scottish Cup, and I netted three goals. Not bad for starters, I would say. The following term, 1966–67, saw me play sixteen games in all and again score three times. But then in 1967–68 came quite a rapid upturn in my fortunes, with fourteen goals in thirty-nine games.

I could consider myself pretty well established by that point, despite Bobby Brown having left to take over as national manager. His first game in charge was against England at Wembley in April 1967. It's one that remains embedded in the memory of every Scotland fan, ending in a 3–2 win over the world champions to which my boyhood hero, Jim Baxter, made a spectacular contribution. What do you mean you can't remember, or never heard of him, taking the mickey out of the opposition at one point that day by playing keepy-uppy? I won't forget it.

Like a lot of our guys at St Johnstone, I was sorry to see Bobby leave. He'd given me my start in the senior game, and I am ever grateful to him for that. Still, I was to become no less indebted to his successor at Muirton, Willie Ormond, whose arrival at the club pretty well coincided with my development into a fully fledged member of the side. Willie had what, in hindsight, I would describe as an old-fashioned approach to the game. He could spot a player blindfolded and knew how to put a balanced team together. Nothing scientific about that. He was also very funny – great with the one-liners.

Everybody knew he liked a drink, or to use his terminology, 'a wee wet'. After I'd left for Ibrox, Ian McPhee told me of the time the lads on the bench one particular day were a bit put off because they could smell alcohol off Willie's breath. Ian was deputed to go speak to him about it, so he went to his room and asked for a quiet word.

'Aye, sure, big fella, what's on your mind?' Willie asked.

'Well . . . ' Ian said, before starting to stutter. 'It's, er, like this, boss. The boys aren't happy, that, er, you know, they could – how can I put this? – smell drink off you, er, on Saturday and they're, well, not happy about it.'

Willie, sharp as ever, came back at him in a flash, saying, 'Christ, if you had to watch what I have to watch every match, you'd need an effing drink, as well.'

Willie's first season in charge was memorable for two reasons, the first of them being that we reached the semi-final of the League Cup in which we faced Dundee at Tannadice. Naturally, the encounter caused a big stir on Tayside and attracted a crowd of 18,000. We took the lead in the first half through one of my fellow travellers from Glasgow, Gordon Whitelaw, but Dundee came back at us after the break to win 3–1 with a penalty by one Jim McLean, and what the records stated were two own-goals by our wing-half, George Miller. Dundee went on to meet Celtic in a rousing final, which produced no fewer than eight goals, five for Jock Stein's team who were beginning pretty well to monopolise the honours in Scottish football at the time.

After the turn of the year came the second highlight for us as we progressed to the last four of the Scottish Cup and found ourselves drawn against Dunfermline. The 1960s were good for them. First under Stein, then Willie Cunningham and George Farm in turn. Their record of qualifying for Europe was terrific. Still, we managed to hold them to a 1–1 draw at neutral Tynecastle, with Tam Wilson our scorer. Might we be that bit luckier second time around and win the replay, again at Tynecastle? We certainly didn't want for confidence but lost 2–1 after extra time. Yours truly scored our goal, though, and, if I can say so myself, it was a cracker, struck from wide on the right flank.

Within a week or so I went to the pictures in Glasgow with Christine, who was to become my wife later that same year, 1968. On came the Pathe News and I can still hear the voice saying, 'And now we go to Scotland for the Scottish Cup semi-final replay between St Johnstone and Dunfermline.' Next thing I'm looking at ME scoring this goal and feeling like I should stand up and shout, 'Hey, everybody, here I am!' Tickled pink I was, even if a bit disappointed still that we didn't get through the tie. Dunfermline, for the record, went on to beat Hearts 3–1 in the final at Hampden, Hearts having beaten Morton in the other semi.

I don't suppose I attached much significance at the time to the fact Davie White, not long installed as Rangers' manager, was in the stand for that replay. Subsequent events were to suggest I must have made a sound impression on him but, then, it may not have been the first. He had just taken over from Scot Symon at Ibrox in November 1967, when Rangers played St Johnstone at Muirton. It was a tight game, with Rangers winning 3–2, but I scored one of our goals with a flick from close in, which sailed between two men who were to become team-mates within a year, Erik Sorensen and Willie Mathieson.

I was nineteen by then, and according to the press, beginning to attract the attention of far bigger clubs than St Johnstone. One newspaper snippet in my cuttings book says: 'Sunderland have been asking about St Johnstone's talented utility forward, Alex MacDonald, the former Glasgow University player.' Glasgow UNIVERSITY? With my academic record? It was a slip of the reporter's pen, of course. What he meant to write was 'the former Glasgow UNITED player'. I suppose I would have had a wee chuckle to myself at the time. Liverpool were said to be interested also, with their scout, Geoff Twentyman, having seen me play at Aberdeen. The word was he went to Pittodrie specifically to watch Aberdeen's Jimmy Smith who, by the way, ended up a few seasons later at Newcastle. But, while Jimmy didn't play too well on that occasion, I was meant to have caught the Anfield man's eye. One thing in particular might have appealed to him, that being the way I managed to set up a goal for Gordon Whitelaw. Having beaten a couple of opponents, I slipped and went to ground. Up I got, still with the ball at my feet, beat another couple of red shirts, then stuck a pass through for Gordon to finish the move.

Fulham and Ipswich were two others whose scouts were reported to be keeping tabs on me around that time, albeit with Willie Ormond going on record as saying there had been 'no bids for MacDonald – or any other of my players'. He went on to point out he wasn't interested in selling anybody, that he was in the business of strengthening his side, not weakening it. That sounded fair enough to me. I was happy enough to be where I was. England didn't hold any greater attraction for me then than it had done a few years beforehand when, still a juvenile player, I knocked back the chance to go on trial with Wolves. I wasn't bothered what, if anything, might be waiting for me beyond the horizon. Getting more games under my belt in the then Scottish First Division continued to be my most realistic ambition.

One thing I haven't mentioned so far is my disciplinary record. That's for the reason that, in my first couple of seasons with St Johnstone, it was flawless. Not a single booking did I pick up, although more and more players were being pulled up for kicking me. But in that third season, I collected three cautions. Willie Ormond was quick in coming to my defence, saying opponents were paying more attention to me than they might have done previously and I was showing signs of frustration as a result. He may have been right, but young though I still was, I might have known better than to get involved the way I did with big Davie Provan of Rangers in the summer of 1968.

The occasion was a five-a-side competition at Musselburgh – hardly prestigious although keenly contested by us players. No sooner had I beaten Davie a first time than he punched me in the ribs. I beat him a second time, and he had another dig at me. So what did I do by way of retaliation? I booted him, that's what, and he got carted off. What I didn't realise at the time was that Davie was just getting over a bad injury and my reaction had set him back a bit. But I ended up suffering as well. The SFA banned me for the opening two games of the new season as a result of that moment of rashness.

Willie Ormond spoke up for me again, saying, 'We have told Alex to lay off his man a bit more and try to get the ball in open space. But we cannot really expect the boy to give up the close dribbling skills at which he excels.' Willie duly likened me to a player with whom he had appeared in Hibs' Famous Five forward line of the 1950s, Bobby Johnstone. 'He has the same, easy style of beating his man and runs all day,' he said. Given that Bobby Johnstone played a few times for Scotland and starred for Manchester City in an FA Cup final, I took those remarks as a compliment, indeed.

Once the new season got underway and I returned from suspension, the conjecture about which clubs were in for me intensified. Spurs were said to be looking, Middlesbrough also. In fact, Middlesbrough's manager, Stan Anderson, had come to a match between ourselves and Airdrie towards the end of the previous season, supposedly to watch big Sam Goodwin in opposition to us. Whether or not Sam impressed him, I don't know. But Anderson told reporters he had 'formed a favourable impression of MacDonald'.

As the summer of 1968 gave way to autumn, my name was linked with Newcastle and Derby County, Newcastle supposedly posting a bid of £40,000 which the St Johnstone board knocked back. 'We don't want to lose MacDonald, who is one of the best young players in the country,' Willie Ormond was quoted as saying. 'But if, and when, he does go, it will be for a big fee.'

I could sense the club's attitude was changing slightly. No longer was it quite the case of 'hands off MacDonald'. Perhaps Jock Stein had picked up the same vibes, because it would have been around that time which I highlighted earlier that he offered me a lift home and sounded me out about signing for Celtic. What I don't recall is who, if anybody, I told about that chance meeting while I was waiting near George Square for a bus to my granny's. Then again, since I was travelling to Perth and back every day with Celtic-minded people like Benny Rooney, whose dad was the physio at Parkhead, maybe I let slip what was meant to be my big secret. It could be, too, that Rangers got to hear about Celtic's interest because very shortly I had an approach on the QT from them. Such approaches were against SFA rules. That said, they happened all the time, more often than not with a journalist acting as the middleman. The deal was that he did the tapping, then claimed the story as an exclusive when the transfer was about to go through.

I won't say who was the intermediary in the case of Rangers and me. No kidding, my recollection is a bit fuzzed, although the reporter, Jim Rodger, who got involved in a lot of these machinations, could have had a part to play. But I do remember being told to go and see one of the Rangers' directors, Matt Taylor, at his business premises in Glasgow. His instruction to me was, 'Don't do anything. We'll get you.' I was beside myself with excitement at the prospect of going to Ibrox but had to bide my time and wait for their move to become official. I needed something to distract me from all the speculation but could have done without what happened one night in early November.

Picture, if you will, Ian McPhee and me walking back from Hampden after watching Scotland play Austria. Christine and I weren't long married at the time and had got a flat in Govanhill, near where I'd lived with my granny for so long. We were just about to turn into my street when we saw this lassie being dragged into a car. Something not right, Ian and I thought. So, in an instant, we collared this policeman who had been on Hampden duty and reported the incident. He promptly stopped the car and got the girl out. Ian and I were feeling quite proud of ourselves, having done our civic duty and – who knows – very possibly saved some helpless soul from a fate we wouldn't have cared to think about.

Anyway, just then, Ian spotted a fire engine up the street and said something daft to me like, 'Hey, wouldn't it be funny if your house was up in flames?' No, I didn't think it would be at all funny. But as fate would have it, it WAS my place that had been set ablaze. This I discovered after racing up the stairs to find Christine and her pal, with rollers in their hair, in a great flap. They'd been giving one another a perm or something and quite forgot they had the chip pan on at the time. See women! Our kitchen was charred and we'd to move out and accept temporary board and lodgings with Christine's uncle, Dougie Skimming, who just happened to live in the school jannie's house across the road from Ibrox. Coincidence or what? There was me waiting for Rangers to make their move – and living on their doorstep.

Still young as I was, twenty and a bit, I had the nous to realise that nothing in football remained a secret for long. But you can imagine how I felt when I bought a paper one day and read a banner headline that had falsely quoted me as saying, 'I want to join Rangers.' I wasn't so much surprised as shocked, for I hadn't been aware even of speaking to the reporter whose name was on the story, never mind saying any such thing. I phoned him up and complained bitterly. All he could say, a bit apologetically, was, 'That's one I owe you, Alex.' I could only deduce that the headline writer had taken a bit of a liberty and put words into my mouth.

My concern was this: if Rangers didn't follow up their interest in me, Jock Stein could withdraw his once he'd read what I was purported to have said in this particular paper. So the waiting went on, with me getting more nervous by the day. Eventually, I slapped in a written transfer request, hoping it might draw the whole issue to a head. Still, I had to wait until the board at Muirton Park got around to discussing it. Here's the irony. For weeks on end, I'd been travelling back and forth to Perth for training all dolled up with collar and tie. Come the day I might sign for Rangers, I had to be smartly dressed, didn't I? The lads on the train, Benny Rooney, Ian McPhee, Kenny Aird and the rest, were forever ribbing me, saying, 'Got the good gear on again, eh? What are you up to?'

Guess what, the very day I reverted to going casual was the one that changed my life forever.

4

IBROX, HERE WE COME

More fool me for not anticipating the call from Ibrox when it came that day in late November 1968. The speculation about my going there had been mounting for a week or so, since the St Johnstone directors agreed to the transfer request I'd handed in. Rangers were in the Republic of Ireland at the time, preparing for a Fair Cities Cup tie against Dundalk, and chairman John Lawrence was reported as having told manager Davie White to put a bid in for me right away. How much? Mr Lawrence was coy on that question, saying only it would be 'substantial'.

According to the papers, the manager made the offer verbally by telephone, promising to confirm it in writing just as soon and he and the team got back from what turned out to be their 3–0 victory, 9–1 on aggregate. But St Johnstone weren't of a mind to do business immediately. While insisting they didn't want to set up an auction for my services, they seemed intent on waiting over the weekend, at least, to see if any other clubs, Spurs, in particular, might follow up their earlier interest.

Needless to say, there was only one place I wanted to go. Perhaps other clubs knew that and backed off. So I was delighted when the deal went through within days of what proved to be my last, and not exactly memorable, game for St Johnstone: a defeat by Airdrie at Broomfield. Willie Ormond drove me from Perth to a hotel in Falkirk to complete the move in the presence of Davie White and director Matt Taylor. There I was, dressed in a casual shirt, putting pen to paper. From then on, it would be blazer, collar and tie. Such was the Rangers way.

Little did I sense at the time that, having been signed for St Johnstone by one future Scotland manager, Bobby Brown, I had been sold by another in Willie Ormond. I was grateful to both for the help they gave me in advancing my career, thankful also to my Muirton team-mates who had given me all the backing I could have wanted as I made the transition from novice to established player. A good bunch of lads, they were, with a few real characters among them. How can I forget goalkeeper Jimmy Donaldson? He spoke with a stutter and, once at Celtic Park, I think it was, as a cross came into his area, he shouted, 'It's mmmm-ma . . . ' Before he could complete what he wanted to say – 'It's ma ba'' – the ba' was in the back of his net.

Jim Kerray, who had played with Huddersfield and Newcastle, among others, was another who made a lasting impression on me, not least for his snappy dress sense. Then there was John Kilgannon, who came to us from Dunfermline. I liked him a lot, as well. Tragically, he died in a car crash near Cumbernauld in 1967 when he couldn't have been any older than thirty.

Maybe we didn't have the best of teams. In my three and a bit years with St Johnstone, we were rarely out of the bottom half of the league although, with Kenny Aird and Fred Aitken having come in, and Henry Hall arriving around the time I left, the future was promising. What we didn't lack at any time was camaraderie. There was always a bond between us, but in saying that, it didn't stop the likes of Buck McCarry kicking me any time thereafter I played for Rangers against him. Benny Rooney wasn't one to hold back either. I remember once, when I was lying flat out on the deck, him running all over me. I had his stud marks to prove it. That's friends for you!

By the way, those papers which had speculated that Rangers would be prepared to pay £50,000 for me were spot on. I think I got £4,000 in the form of a personal sweetener. It was a small fortune at the time. Mr Lawrence, who was one of the country's biggest and most successful house builders, asked me what I would do with the money. I seem to remember saying I would use the greater part of it to put down a deposit on a new house. That appeared to please him, but in the end I bought one from a rival company, Wimpey, in Kirkintilloch.

Davie White hadn't gone into the transfer market for a whole year after becoming Rangers manager. Then, as if to flag up the first anniversary of his appointment, he'd paid out £100,000 to Hibs for Colin Stein. I arrived just a couple of weeks later for half that amount, but not wanting for ambition. Still, it was hard for me to take in that I'd actually signed for the club I'd grown up supporting. For several weeks, since we'd moved in with Christine's uncle across the road from Ibrox, I'd walked past the stadium on my way to the underground thinking but hardly believing it could soon be my place of work. When I duly reported for my first day's training, I found myself standing nervously on the front steps of Ibrox and thinking, 'Do I go in here? Have I really signed for Rangers?'

It was a totally mad feeling. I hoped some member of the public – a Rangers fan preferably – would come along and say something like, 'Good luck, Alex.' Then I would know I wasn't dreaming. But nobody did. Maybe the daftest thought that crossed my mind was that when I walked inside, the doorman, Bobby Moffat, would recognise me as one of those he had chased from playing on the field a few years earlier. Surreal or what? Yet, in a first-person article in that morning's *Scottish Daily Express*, I'd come across as being a whole lot more coherent than I actually was. Full marks to the ghostwriter for unscrambling my jumbled thoughts. Here, in essence, is what he wrote in my name. It goes some way to encapsulating my story until then – and of course, how I felt about this huge upturn in my career:

For a Glasgow boy born on St Patrick's Day, I suppose it's a bit of a joke joining Rangers. But there never has been any other place for me but Ibrox. From the moment St Johnstone decided to accept offers for my transfer, I dreamed Rangers would put in a bid . . . but was frightened to hope too much. I figured, after spending £100,000 on Colin Stein, they could hardly go into the transfer market for an unknown like myself. Now all the anxious waiting is over and I'm with the club I used to nip down the road from my boyhood home to see. My pals and I used to get lifted over the turnstiles to watch Rangers and now I'll be out there myself in a light blue jersey.

And if my first game is against Clyde at Shawfield on Saturday, I can truly say this is exactly where I came into senior football. My new boss, Davie White, will look on it as a kind of coincidence too, for he was at left-half in the Clyde side that beat St Johnstone when I made my senior debut almost three years ago. I had the number 9 on my back that day and though we were beaten 3–2, I managed to score a goal and went home feeling very pleased with myself. I also remember Davie White taking the ball off me several times and asking myself if he, Clyde's number 6, never stopped running. This isn't a plug to get into the first team right away. Obviously that's for the manager to decide, but I'll be happy to play anywhere he wants me to. I've played in every forward position at Perth.

The first thing I want to do at Ibrox is make it up with big Davie Provan, for we had a private feud the last time we met – in the five-a-sides at Musselburgh during the summer. After several clashes, Davie was carried off and I was ordered off and finished up with a two-match suspension at the start of this season. It has worried me that Davie was injured, but I'm happy to see he is again challenging for a place through the reserve side. I just hope there is no illfeeling. Another thing I'll be trying to sort out is a way of steering clear of trouble on the field. I was suspended for three cautions last season and have two against my name at the moment.

Yet, in my first two seasons at Muirton, I wasn't cautioned once. The only reason I can find is that, back then, no defender took particular notice of me and I was allowed to play my normal game. But, after that, I started getting marked closer and closer, with some of the attention I got not being exactly of the gentle sort, and I began landing in trouble by retaliating. It's stupid, I know, but when you're with a less fashionable side like St Johnstone, you've got to fight for every point, and it's hard keeping a cool head all the time.

I still can't believe I've landed at Ibrox, especially when I think of my boyhood heroes like Ian McMillan and Jim Baxter. When Baxter was transferred to Sunderland, I remember being angry with Rangers, for I thought he was the tops as a player. When St Johnstone first showed interest in me, I'd to ask where they played. I should have known, of course. But, to Glasgow boys like myself, the football world was bound by Ibrox and Parkhead, with all the other teams 'foreigners'. Thankfully, I'm a bit wiser since those days and look back gratefully to the Perth club for giving me a start, then seeing their way to let me join Rangers.

I'll be a full-timer at Ibrox, something I never dreamt possible when I was working away as an apprentice cooper before making football my career. My wife, Christine, is happy I've got my wish and now we can settle down after a few topsy-turvy weeks. The night of the Scotland–Austria game, I returned home to our Govanhill flat from Hampden to find our newly decorated kitchenette ablaze after a chip pan caught fire. We're still clearing up and have been staying with relatives at a school house . . . the one facing the main stand at Ibrox!

The thought of that fire haunts me to this day, by the way. I can see Christine and her pal yet, bits of silver paper sticking out of their heads after they'd been giving each other a hair-do, while close to tears because they'd forgotten about the boiling fat on the stove. In fact, I remember that incident at least as clearly as I do my actual Rangers debut against Clyde, in front of an all-ticket crowd of 25,000 at Shawfield on 23 November. I played at inside-right, in place of Andy Penman, in what was billed by the press as the most expensive forward line ever fielded by a Scottish club. It read: Alex Willoughby, myself, Colin Stein, Willie Johnston and Orjan Persson. Estimated value in the transfer market? In excess of £300,000, I suppose.

Yet you wouldn't have guessed as much from the fact the match ended in a 1–1 draw, Steinie scoring for us early in the second half, with Clyde equalising towards the end with a headed goal by Harry Glasgow following a free kick. I was quoted afterwards as saying, 'It was a bit of a strain out there. I felt very nervous, afraid to try things in case they didn't come off for me. I feel more tired now than I've ever felt after a game.' It was to be a familiar refrain from me, in that I took so long to settle with Rangers and always seemed to be knackered. But more on that later.

Rangers' form in the months before I joined them had been a bit erratic. They'd won 4–2 against Celtic at Parkhead in September but lost away to St Johnstone – who else? – in October. Then came a 3–2 defeat by Aberdeen at Ibrox.

This inconsistency may have strengthened Davie White's resolve to bring in Colin Stein, whose impact was both spectacular and immediate. Steinie scored a hat-trick in his debut, a 5–1 win at Arbroath, and followed it up with another in his second game, a 6–1 victory over his old Hibs mates at Ibrox. But then came a 1–0 defeat by St Mirren at Love Street, the 1–1 draw with Clyde at Shawfield and another with Airdrie at home. So it was on to Starks Park in early December when, with me scoring my first goal for the club, we beat Raith Rovers 3–0. Thereafter, we went thirteen league games without defeat, but a few more stumbles towards the end of the season saw us finish five points behind the title winners, Celtic.

Among the young players emerging with Rangers back then was Willie Mathieson, who had taken over at left-back from the man I'd had my infamous bust-up with at the Musselburgh Fives the previous close-season, Davie Provan. I must hand it to Davie for making me feel welcome on my arrival at Ibrox. The press wanted photographs of the pair of us together, as if making up for what had gone before, and Davie was happy to oblige them by posing alongside me. 'It would be senseless to talk of any trouble between Alex and myself,' he was quoted as saying. 'He's a Rangers player now and will get all the help I can give him.' I reciprocated the goodwill by admitting, 'Davie is a great fellow. He was among the first to greet me and helped me tremendously in my first training stint.'

Colin Jackson and Alfie Conn were breaking through then also, but we didn't want for experience either. John Greig was already a Rangers stalwart; likewise Norrie Martin and Ronnie McKinnon. If Bud Johnston was pretty much ages with myself, he had been several times round the block by that point and played quite a few times for Scotland. This is not to forget Willie Henderson, who had burst into the team in the early 1960s and been hailed as the finest winger of his generation. Willie, like Alex Willoughby, was always on hand to offer advice, although he was as dumbfounded as me when Davie White sent both of us out to practise taking corner kicks from the right side of the field. I remember confessing to Willie, 'Er, I cannae kick the ball wi' my right foot.'

The manager, of course, had seen me play on the right flank for St Johnstone in the Scottish Cup semi-final replay with Dunfermline at the back end of the previous season – and score a good goal from there. But I was naturally left-footed and, given my pick of positions, would have been far happier playing at inside-left (as the left midfield role still was known at the time). Maybe Davie White didn't recognise this and had made a mistake in buying me, I found myself thinking.

Many other negative thoughts weighed down on me during my first few months with the club. Making the transition from Rangers fan to player was not easy. I would look around at the

Ibrox crowd and think, 'I must know almost every one of you.' That in itself was a pressure of sorts. It may have made me try too hard just to please the support.

The upshot was that, while I did switch to the left side for a couple of games, I found myself in and out of the first team during the remainder of my first season at Ibrox. Training wasn't a problem to me. Far from it. Sandy Jardine and I were always out front when it came to running. But when it came to a match day, I just felt so tired because of the nervous energy I must have been burning up. That really concerned me, even though I retained a belief in my ability. Whether or not Davie White had doubts about me, I really don't know. I certainly never knocked on his door to let him know what was going on in my head, or how heavy my legs felt.

Still, with Rangers competing in the Fairs Cup that same term, I had the consolation of playing in Europe for the first time, against DWS Amsterdam at Ibrox in what was the return leg of our third-round tie with the Dutch club. The team had got off to a good start in the tournament, winning 2–0 at home against Vojvodina with a penalty by John Greig and a follow-up goal by the man who would become my soul-mate, Sandy Jardine. Greigie won't wish to be reminded that he was sent off for retaliation in the away game which Rangers lost only 1–0 to go through on aggregate. Easier by far was the Dundalk tie which, coming immediately before my move from St Johnstone, I mentioned at the start of this chapter.

Both Willie Henderson and Alex Ferguson got doubles against the Irish in Glasgow, Rangers winning 6–1, while Colin Stein got a brace in the 3–0 win in Ireland. Next up then were DWS, with us winning 2–0 away, thanks to goals by Willie Henderson and Willie Johnston. Davie White entrusted me to play in place of Orjan Persson in the return, with Orjan's accustomed number 11 on my shirt, and I don't think I let him down as we won 2–1, with Davie Smith and Stein the scorers. For better or worse, I wasn't involved in the quarter-final with Bilbao but can recall we won the home leg by the emphatic margin of 4–1.

Ferguson, Andy Penman, Persson and Stein got our goals that night, in front of a 62,000 crowd. In so doing, they gave us the cushion we needed for the return game in Spain, which we lost 2–0, to progress once more on aggregate. Again, I wasn't involved – until Willie Johnston got sent off and I had to go and unlock the dressing room door to let him in. Well, it was a role of sorts. If nothing else, I helped keep Bud away from the guy who had been dismissed along with him after an incident in which the pair of them ended up trading punches.

The fact we were drawn against Newcastle United in the semi-final caused quite a stir, as you could well imagine. The papers went to town for days on end in the build-up to this so-called Battle of Britain, albeit the tie became a battle of unimagined sorts in the return game which followed a goal-less draw at Ibrox. Hordes of our fans invaded the pitch at one point, causing a hold-up of close to twenty minutes as police tried to restore order. If I remember correctly, the chairman, John Lawrence, even went down onto the field to appeal for an end to the trouble, only to be ushered away by police. Nasty stuff, it was, and the result isn't best remembered, either. Newcastle won 2–0, with goals by two of their Scottish contingent, Jim Scott and Jackie Sinclair, and went on to beat Újpest Dozsa by 6–2 over two legs in the final.

If my involvement in Europe that season was only fleeting, I contributed even less in the Scottish Cup that got underway shortly after the turn of the year. In fact, apart from coming on as a substitute in our 1–0 quarter-final win over Airdrie, I found myself relegated to the role of spectator. We set out in that competition by beating Hibs 1–0 with a goal by Steinie. How they must have rued selling him those few months earlier. Then we beat Hearts 2–0, and with Airdrie taken care of thereafter, we thumped Aberdeen 6–1 in the semi-final, with Bud Johnston scoring a hat-trick. So it was on to an eagerly anticipated final against Celtic at Hampden. Dare I recall the score – a 4–0 win for Rangers' greatest rivals?

That was the match in which Alex Ferguson, supposedly detailed to mark Billy McNeill at corner kicks, was made to shoulder the blame for allowing the Celtic captain to open the scoring with a header from one such set piece. What a setback it proved to be for Alex, one which I'm quite sure niggles him to this day, despite everything he has achieved in management. He never played for Rangers' first team again and left the following season for Falkirk. Alex has alleged since that certain people within Ibrox had been out to get him; this, because he was married to a Catholic. All I could sense at the time was that, despite the goal-threat he carried, and his acutely competitive spirit, his place in the side had been under threat since the arrival of Colin Stein. In fact, just before I signed for Rangers, there was much speculation about Alex going south to join Charlton.

So it was that, with Rangers having failed to qualify for the quarter-finals of the League Cup that season, they ended it without a trophy. As for my contribution to their efforts, well, it amounted to a total of eleven appearances, two of them as a sub. That disappointed me. I'd hoped to repay their faith in me by offering them rather more. In short, I hadn't done myself justice, but if Davie White was disappointed in me, he never said as much. Maybe he understood, as I myself came to recognise in later years, that it can take time for a player to meet the demands of a big club like Rangers. In my case, it took at least a year.

Not the least of my concerns was that, in the games I did play, Rangers seemed to look on me as something of a utility man by fielding me in turn at (I use the old expressions here) inside-right, inside-left, left-half and outside-left. This prompted me to go on record at one point as saying, 'I've never felt more frustrated than I am right now. Sure, I'm overwhelmed at having realised my life's ambition by signing for Rangers. But I've had the feeling they just can't make their mind up about me and what my position might be. When all of a sudden you find yourself playing alongside your boyhood heroes, it's almost too much to take in all at once. In my very first week at Ibrox, someone came up to me and said, "Kinning Park boy, are you, Alex? Well, there shouldn't be much you can't do with a ball." I realised right then what was expected of me and that the £50,000 transfer fee weighed a ton on my head.'

Fair to say, things could only get better for me at Ibrox – and they did, eventually.

5

DRINKS ARE ON JIM BAXTER

What was it going to take for Rangers to get the better of Celtic who under Jock Stein had won four successive titles by the end of season 1968–69? Scot Symon, a much-respected manager at Ibrox, had lost his job towards the end of 1967 because of their ever-increasing dominance of the Scottish game, with Davie White taking over from him. Davie, if he wasn't to become another victim of Celtic's success, had to pull some kind of master-stroke, and there was hope he might have done just that when he re-signed Jim Baxter, albeit on a free transfer from Nottingham Forest, before season 1969–70 got underway.

Nobody knew better than I did what Jim meant to the fans. I'd watched him from the terraces in his first time around with the club and marvelled at the way he could orchestrate games with that magical left foot of his. It was with great sadness that the support – myself included – saw him leave for Sunderland in the spring of 1965 for a fee of £72,000. Would we ever see his likes again? Well, here he was, four years later, back in a blue jersey which, it would have to be said, didn't hang quite as loosely on him as his old one had done. To put it another way, Slim Jim wasn't slim anymore.

He hadn't led a monastic life in England. He hadn't led one before going there, for that matter. Jim's reputation for enjoying himself off the field was hardly his or the country's best-kept secret. Yet against world champions, England, at Wembley in 1967, he had given a virtuoso performance in a famous 3–2 win for

Scotland. Even now, I can picture him on that memorable occasion taking the mickey out of opponents like Alan Ball and playing keepy-uppy in front of the Royal Box. Rangers could use some of that same brilliance, if Jim still had any left to offer.

It was a big 'if', of course, yet he began the season in good style. One of his first games was against Celtic in the League Cup at Ibrox and he positively revelled in what was a 2–1 win for us. I didn't feature in the match, although I was delighted to be in the same side as Jim, as we beat Raith Rovers 3–2 at the outset of the competition. I even scored in that game at Starks Park. I saw myself as a grafter and was happy trying to put in enough work for the two of us, leaving him to do the fancy stuff.

The likes of John Greig, Ronnie McKinnon and Willie Henderson knew Jim of old, having played with him prior to his Sunderland move. They'd also been team-mates of his at international level. All of us could recognise the problems he'd brought upon himself by his excesses, but still, he was a great character to have in the dressing room. I'll say this for him, too: he was nothing if not a good host. Picture a few of us gathered in his hotel room after we'd lost 3–1 to Gornik Zabrze away in the second-round first leg of the European Cup Winners' Cup. The talk was all about where we'd gone wrong on the night.

Jim was dispensing some cheap champagne he'd ordered and, as he passed the glasses around, I told him, 'I don't drink the stuff. It doesn't agree with me.' At that, he said, 'Ok, son, stick your hand under my bed and pull out my bag.' Jim duly delved into it, producing half a dozen cans of Tennent's lager which he'd brought with him for the trip. 'Get tucked into these, then, son,' he said. Brilliant, I thought. Another thing which sticks with me from then was that, big star though he may have been, he always let youngsters like myself have their say on whatever issue was being discussed.

In the event, my actual experience of playing in such exalted company as Jim's didn't endure beyond mid-September of that season. Following a 2–1 league defeat by Ayr United at Somerset

Park, I found myself out of the side. As a result, I missed out on what I hoped would be my Old Firm debut at Ibrox the following week. Rangers lost 1–0 but, if I'm being honest, I couldn't really complain. I still didn't feel I had been doing myself anything like a full measure of justice. A bundle of energy I may have been in training throughout the week, but on match days, because of the pressure I felt under, I was tired before kicking a ball.

Our European campaign got underway against Steaua Bucharest at Ibrox, with me looking on from the sidelines and admiring what was a convincing enough win, 2–0, with Bud Johnston the scorer of both goals. That result stood us in good stead for the return in Romania, which ended goal-less. Among my memories of that trip was being among a group of players strolling down this street in Bucharest the day before the game. A man we thought was a wee Romanian guy, minding his own business, overtook us and accidentally cut in front of Jim Baxter. Jim gave him a clip on the back of the head, whereupon the wee guy turned round, fists raised, wanting to fight – Bud Johnston!

Rangers had strung a few decent results together in the league by the time of the next round in which we were paired with Gornik, but having lost to them in Poland, we were up against it for the return leg. I was selected as a substitute for that game, coming on in place of Orjan Persson, I think, in the second half. But for all the difference I made, I would have been as well staying on the bench. We lost by the same score as in the first leg, 3–1, Jim Baxter scoring our goal.

And as a funny aside, he and Willie Henderson had found themselves enveloped in controversy in the lead-up to the game, the pair of them missing a day's training at Largs because, er, they'd slept in.

The critics felt they should have been dropped by way of punishment, but Davie White, not one to hold a grudge, evidently felt the team would be much weakened without them. Who could argue with him, particularly when Baxter opened the scoring to give Rangers a fighting chance of overturning the advantage which

Gornik had established on their own patch? Unfortunately midway through the second half, the Poles equalised. Then, with fifteen or so minutes remaining, their top player (and what a player!), Vladimir Lubanski, struck a sensational goal to put them in front. Any chance we had of taking the tie to extra time was gone in that instant, with Gornik promptly scoring a third goal to confirm their superiority.

Our fans ended up giving them a standing ovation, but at the same time, a few of them rounded on Davie White by calling for his head. The following day, I think it was, he was summoned to a board meeting and given his books. Harsh or what? We'd lost to a very good side in Gornik, but the board obviously weren't prepared to countenance that as an excuse to offer the manager a reprieve. Maybe the directors felt he should have been stronger on the pre-match disciplinary issue involving Jim Baxter and Willie Henderson. Maybe they were further miffed by the fact that, while we were getting a going-over from Gornik, Celtic were progressing in the European Cup on the toss of a coin after losing to Benfica in Lisbon.

What seemed to be beyond argument was that Celtic's continuing success, both at home and in Europe, had rendered Davie White as vulnerable as Scot Symon before him. From a personal point of view, I was sorry to see him go. He'd signed me, after all, and I thought of him as being sound in the tactical sense. But how vulnerable was I, after slightly less than a year on Rangers' books and still far from being established at top-team level? I couldn't help thinking my jaicket might be on the proverbial, shaky peg.

As things transpired, I needn't have worried. Willie Waddell's appointment as manager in succession to Davie turned out to be the best thing that could have happened to me, even if it took a while for that realisation to dawn.

Willie had been a great player in his time with Rangers and Scotland, then a successful manager with Kilmarnock who he led in 1965 to the only championship title in their history. To everybody's surprise, not least Killie's, he quit the game on the back of that triumph to work as a football columnist with the *Scottish Daily Express*. So when Rangers appointed him, they were buying into not only his vast experience as a football man but also his knowledge of how the press worked. Jock Stein, of course, was strong in both areas, but the hope within Ibrox appeared to be Willie could emerge as his match.

So far as I was concerned, he soon set about changing me fundamentally as a player. While I'd always been a grafter and a runner, from my schooldays through my time at St Johnstone I'd liked to linger on the ball as well. Jim Baxter, my absolute boyhood hero, wasn't the only one who could nutmeg opponents, you know. But the message Willie Waddell preached to me was 'push and run, push and run'. I think he may have seen the likes of Spurs follow this code and believed it to be the way forward. Day after day, week after week, he went on at me about it – to the point I went home one day, close to tears, and complained to Christine about this guy never being off my back.

Yet as I adapted to his demands of me, I got back in the side for a couple of games pre-Christmas, and after another spell out, I had a further and longer run which spanned my Old Firm debut in a goal-less draw at Celtic Park and our participation in that season's Scottish Cup. We actually set out in the competition with a 3–1 win over Hibs at Ibrox, in which I scored a couple of our goals. Then we thrashed Forfar 7–0 at Station Park, and once more I managed to get myself on the score sheet. That result propelled us into the quarter-finals and a match with Celtic which I don't look back on with any sense of fondness. Why? Well, as I recalled in a previous chapter, it was the one in which I was sent off, supposedly for having a boot at Evan Williams.

The SFA hit me with a twenty-one-day ban and Willie Waddell took them to task for doing so. 'Alex MacDonald has suffered rather badly,' he was quoted as saying after the sentence had been meted out at a gathering of the disciplinary committee at Park Gardens. 'His only previous sentences before he joined us from St Johnstone were for throwing away a ball and being sent off in a five-a-side tournament. He has been a player of good behaviour with Rangers. Players with far worse records have missed fewer matches than he stands to miss. I am not pleased with this decision.' Who knows, maybe I would have got off with a lighter punishment had the committee chairman, George Fox, been there to preside over my case. It turned out that, because of a hitch with the train between Dundee and Glasgow, his arrival had been delayed.

I ended up missing five games, which given the progress I felt I had been making under the new manager, was a huge disappointment to me. By the time I was free to play again, we had only two league games left and had fallen so far behind Celtic in the title race that they won it by twelve points from us. But while I couldn't have sensed as much as we broke up for the close-season, happier days were not too distant. The arrival of Jock Wallace as coach to Willie Waddell served as a signal of the success which was to be delivered just a few months later in the shape of the League Cup, the club's first trophy in four years.

Jim Baxter had played only a handful of games since Davie White's departure, so his way-going that same summer wasn't exactly a surprise. He just didn't have the fitness required of him by Willie Waddell, which, I suppose, was a sad indictment of the way he'd led his life. His first spell at Ibrox, which lasted five distinguished years for him and the team, yielded three League titles, three Scottish Cups and four League Cups. His second, lasting only one year, delivered nothing. If Jim had any regrets, he never voiced them publicly. He just walked away with all his memories, never to play football again.

Prominent members of the backroom staff, among them Davie Kinnear and Harold Davis, went with him. Willie Waddell wasn't going to allow sentiment to get in the way of all the restructuring he had planned. In came physio Tommy Craig, coach Stan Anderson and, of course, Big Jock, who had earned the respect of Hearts' players during his time of coaching them. Needless to say, this man who been Berwick Rangers' player–manager when they knocked Rangers out of the Scottish Cup three and bit years earlier, wasn't long in gaining ours. His prime aim was to make us fit, probably fitter than any of us had ever been. That he did, although his methods weren't entirely conventional.

I'd never been to Gullane before Jock came to Ibrox, but in keeping with my team-mates, I was to become very familiar with the place in the years that followed. Even in my sleep I can see those huge sand dunes he had us running up until, in some cases, guys were physically sick. This was a regular routine for us prior to a new season starting and sometimes once the season had got underway. There were no complaints from me. The tougher the training, the more I liked it. All that cross-country running I'd done as a schoolboy must have stood me in good stead. Colin Stein lapped up the hard work as well. He had great lungs.

Big Jock's time in the British Army, serving as he did with the King's Own Scottish Borderers during the Malayan Crisis in the mid-1950s, obviously hadn't been wasted on him. If his aim was to mould us into a fighting unit – albeit one to fight on the park rather than in the jungle – he succeeded. The bond he created between the players was strong, and allied to the confidence he set about instilling with his boundless enthusiasm, he made even me, at 5 feet 6 inches, feel akin to a colossus. Jock's mission, in short, was to imbue us with what he called 'character', and in time, it would go a long way to arresting the success being enjoyed by Celtic under his namesake, Jock Stein.

By way of putting the finishing touches to our preparations for season 1970–71, we played a couple of games in West Germany, losing the first 3–1 to Hamburg and drawing the second 1–1 against Kaiserslautern. These were followed by a 2–0 defeat at home by Spurs. But not too much store was put in these results and they were forgotten quickly enough as we kicked off in the League Cup with a 4–1 win over Dunfermline at Ibrox. Morton and Motherwell were the other teams in our section against whom we proceeded to win with some ease.

Once the championship got underway and we'd stabilised after a couple of early upsets, including a 2–0 defeat by Celtic away, we could feel a sense of optimism growing in the dressing room. It couldn't have been much more evident than in the quarter-final of the League Cup in which we beat Hibs, both home and away, by 3–1. Graham Fyfe, who was just emerging, did especially well in those games, with two goals at Easter Road and another at Ibrox. I managed to get one myself, in the second of them. So we went on to meet Cowdenbeath in the semi-final at Hampden and beat them by the rather unconvincing margin of 2–0.

We'd already turned them over, by 5–0, in the championship at Ibrox, with a certain Derek Johnstone making his debut on that occasion and scoring twice. Little did we know that come the League Cup Final against Celtic on 24 October, this sixteen-year-old novice was to claim a special place in the history of Rangers. But lest I get ahead of myself here, I should point out that our participation in Europe that season hadn't gone so well. Indeed, it ended after just one round. Bayern Munich, Franz Beckenbauer and the rest, were our opponents in what was still called the Fair Cities Cup, and after they beat us 1–0 at home, we could only draw 1–1 with them at Ibrox. So much for Rangers getting even a hint of revenge for the painful defeat inflicted by the Germans after extra time in the Cup Winners' Cup Final in Nuremberg a little more than three years earlier.

I can't remember now whether it was prior to us playing Bayern at Ibrox that time in 1970 or before the home leg of one of our subsequent meetings with them that Willie Waddell was issuing instructions on how we should deal with some of their players. He mentioned one particular name – don't ask me whose – and said to me, 'You mark him.' Then he went on to say, 'And when Beckenbauer comes over the halfway line, you pick him up.' Was he still talking to me? I looked over my shoulder, thinking he had someone else in mind, but Willie fixed his gaze in my direction, saying, 'Aye, bloody you.' There I was, believing I had my work cut out already without having to worry about doing a job on probably the finest player in Europe as well.

But back to the League Cup Final on 24 October, with John Greig being counted out because of flu. Well, that's how some reports explained his absence. In fact, he had a whole lot more to worry about, a gash on his shin from the previous week's defeat by Aberdeen at Ibrox having turned septic and giving him and the doctors cause to fear his career could be over if he wasn't careful. Happily, he was back playing soon enough, although in the meantime we had to face Celtic at Hampden in the unsettling knowledge that he could be a big loss to us. The fact that our Old Firm rivals had won the competition five times in a row by that point was further good reason why they were listed as strong favourites to lift the trophy.

Alfie Conn was picked in place of John, and despite his relative lack of experience, he had obvious qualities to offer us. What, though, could the sixteen-year-old Derek Johnstone provide, youthful enthusiasm apart? Fair to say that while his selection as a nominal replacement for Graham Fyfe surprised everyone, the manager must have had a clear sense that Derek's power in the air, particularly, could upset the Celtic defence. So it proved when shortly before the interval, he connected with a cross by Willie Johnston to head the only goal of the game. What a turn-up for Big Ba', as we came to call him. What a turn-up for Rangers, who hadn't won a trophy in four years. A celebration was in order, surely?

Hundreds of our fans later made their way into the city, hoping to catch a glimpse of us with the cup at the St Enoch's Hotel where we still tended to end up after big matches. In fact, we made straight to Ibrox for a champagne party – which was over almost before it began. Chairman John Lawrence explained to the press the following day, 'The change in policy, away from the traditional hotel with players being joined by wives and girlfriends for a longer celebration, is part of Willie Waddell's economy drive.' Trust the manager to be thinking of the pounds and pence – when some of us players were in the mood to get plastered!

6

TRAGEDY FOLLOWED BY TRIUMPH

When Willie Waddell bellowed an order, we players were bound to obey it. But, on this occasion, I found myself questioning him as he shouted, 'You lot, out' to the five or six of us left in our dressing room after a 1–1 draw with Celtic at Ibrox. I'd come on late as a substitute, and between taking gulps of air, I told the manager I was still trying to get my second wind. 'OUT,' he repeated, this time more forcibly. It was the first hint any of us had that something was seriously amiss. I'm referring, of course, to the Ibrox Disaster, on 2 January 1971, when sixty-six Rangers fans died in a crush on the infamous Stairway 13 at the stadium. Let me recount the circumstances leading up to the tragic events of that day, indelibly marked as they are in the memory of everyone affected by them.

Jimmy Johnstone had given Celtic the lead with only a couple of minutes remaining, prompting hundreds of our supporters to make their way to the exit in the belief the contest was over. Then, in the brief time remaining, Colin Stein scored for us. We can but speculate on what happened next. Did those already making their way down Stairway 13, on hearing the roars that greeted our equaliser, decide to turn back and find themselves caught up in a hellish clamour? Such was the initial theory, albeit the official enquiry cast doubt upon it. Subsequent testimony from witnesses suggested the calamity occurred five minutes after the game ended, so had nothing to do with what happened towards the finish.

All that could be established for sure was that the steel barriers on the stairway had given way under stress, thus causing people to pile on top of one another with appalling consequences for many of them. Yet, like tens of thousands of other fans, players of both sides knew nothing at the time of this horrific occurrence. Most of my team-mates, certainly, had dispersed before the word began to filter through that a catastrophe had taken place. With Willie Waddell roaring at those of us who remained in the changing room to get out, we then saw ambulance men bringing people in on stretchers. Some were going into the treatment room, others to the wee gymnasium close by.

All we could think, at that point, was that a few people had been hurt. The enormity of what had actually happened continued to elude us. In my own case, it was only when I stopped off at a pub quite close by and saw a news report on the television that the scale of the things began to sink in. Then I went to my mother-in-law's and saw a bit more on the TV. Still, the fact that sixty-six people had been killed was almost too much to contemplate. In the great scheme of things, and against such a grievous backdrop as this, football suddenly didn't matter one whit. Ibrox, like the homes of the bereaved, became a place of mourning.

Willie Waddell, not for the last time in his career with Rangers, responded in a statesmanlike manner, splitting us players into groups and delegating each to visit the families of the dead to express sympathy on behalf of the club. I remember my group arriving at one particular house in Kirkintilloch and the guy who opened the door being very upset at seeing us. I wondered if this might have been a 'mixed' family, with Rangers players unlikely to be welcomed at the best of times by some of its members. We backed off at first but ended up being ushered inside and offering our condolences. Believe it or not, I can't even remember who was with me on that occasion but I do recall going with Gerry Neef and Willie Henderson on a similar mission to a house in Airdrie.

Those visits were harrowing enough for us. But how much worse was the experience of those who had lost loved ones – for the sake of a football match, as well? Then the funerals started. Again we split into groups and attended as many as we could. How many did I go to? Too many for me to recall now. I doubt if even I counted at the time. It was constant for days on end, and the grieving, the feeling of absolute despondency, stayed with us for a long time afterwards. Throughout the country, no corner of the football community was immune to the distress arising from such a shocking event.

A fund was duly set up for the benefit of those families directly affected, and within weeks football rallied round the cause by staging a match at Hampden involving a Scotland XI and an Old Firm Select, which included stars from the south like Bobby Charlton and George Best of Manchester United and Peter Bonetti of Chelsea. The fact that 80,000 fans attended showed how widespread the public's sympathy for the victims of the Ibrox Disaster and their dependents was. Among the many other donations made was a sizeable one, said to have been of five figures, from Rangers. So, some good at least emerged from the grimmest episode in the club's history, with more emerging in time. Never again, Willie Waddell said, would anybody's safety be endangered at Ibrox. And having made that pledge, he initiated a bold plan to convert the stadium into an all-seated arena along the lines we see and admire today.

A pall of depression still hung over the place when, a fortnight later, we resumed in the championship with a 1–1 draw there against Dundee United. We were left then with thirteen league games to play and managed to win only six of them. As a result, we finished in fourth-top position, fifteen points behind Celtic, with Aberdeen and my old club St Johnstone between us and them. This was an unacceptable situation for Rangers to find themselves in, although I had to doff my hat to St Johnstone for finishing third.

Willie Ormond had built a good squad in the time I'd been away from Muirton Park. Quite obviously, he hadn't missed having me about the place. His side beat us 2–0 at Ibrox, with goals by

Henry Hall and John Connolly, in the second-last league match of the campaign, and assured themselves of European football the following season for the first time. Didn't they do well too, overturning a 2–1 deficit against Hamburg in the opening round of the UEFA by winning 3–0 at home? My old pal Gordon Whitelaw was among the scorers on that notable occasion. They proceeded to knock out the Hungarian team, Vasas Budapest, on a 2–1 aggregate before their luck ran out against Zeljeznicar of Yugoslavia, to whom they lost 5–2 overall.

As for Rangers, the only path we could follow into Europe was via the Scottish Cup. We'd set out in that competition with convincing enough victories, 3–0 and 3–1 respectively, over Falkirk and St Mirren, then beaten Aberdeen 1–0. Hibs were our semi-final opponents, and after a 0–0 draw at Hampden, we beat them 2–1 in a replay at the same venue. Who awaited us in the final? None other than Celtic, league champions for the sixth successive season under Jock Stein. Our chances of winning seemed not to be helped by the fact that my mate Sandy Jardine, emerging by then as a candidate for Scottish caps, had to be counted out because of injury. Missing for the same reason also were Alfie Conn, who had become a regular in our side by then, and Mr Cool himself, Davie Smith.

Yet underdogs though we may have been, we could have beaten our Old Firm rivals had Willie Johnston not missed one glorious chance to score. In the event, we drew 1–1, Derek Johnstone picking up where he left off in the League Cup Final by cancelling out a goal by Bobby Lennox with a late equaliser. So it was back to Hampden a few days later, when our personnel problems were compounded by the loss of Alex Miller. In came Jim Denny for his first-team debut. What an occasion it was for him, playing in front of a crowd of 103,000. Then again, it was a big deal for the rest of us also. Could we win at the second attempt? Sadly, no. Celtic beat us 2–1, through Lou Macari and Harry Hood, the latter converting a penalty, while our goal was credited to the opposition's Tommy Callaghan.

Our consolation was that, with Celtic having qualified for the European Cup, we went into the Cup Winners' Cup as beaten finalists. Little could we have foreseen how well we would do in that tournament, but for the moment, manager Willie Waddell and coach Jock Wallace were intent on taking stock. We'd shown a good level of consistency in the domestic cups, winning one of them and finishing as runners-up in the other. Where we'd let ourselves down was in the league, losing seven times away and twice at home. We appeared to be missing something, and if it wasn't an actual goalscorer, maybe it was someone to provide more chances. Hence the gaffer's move in the summer for a player he knew and rated highly from his time of managing Kilmarnock, Tommy McLean.

Rangers paid £65,000 for Wee Tam and, given his sterling service over the years that followed, they surely got more than their money's worth out of him. He certainly helped me immensely with his crosses from the right flank, as he did Derek Johnstone. Yet there was nothing about our domestic form in the early part of season 1971–72 to suggest it would end momentously for us in Barcelona. Celtic beat us twice in our League Cup section, both times at Ibrox. What should have been their home tie had to be switched to our place because Parkhead was undergoing renovation. Then they beat us in the league, again at Ibrox.

The championship continued to unfold disappointingly for us, to the degree we could do no better than finish third – sixteen points behind Celtic, as they won yet another title, and six adrift of second-placed Aberdeen. Having failed to qualify for the latter stages of the League Cup, we managed to reach the semi-final of the Scottish Cup but lost 2–0 to Hibs in a replay. It was a totally different story in Europe, though, starting from when we knocked . out Stade Rennes on a 2–1 aggregate. Willie Johnston scored for us in a 1–1 over there, and I particularly remember how the French fans reacted to his pace. Cries of 'O-o-oh' were heard from them every time Bud ran at the opposition's defence.

Come the return leg, in front of a crowd of 42,000, I managed to score with a shot from close-in after thirty-eight minutes to give us a 1–0 win. The Rennes coach, a guy by the name of Jean Prouff, had got up our noses by saying beforehand his side would beat us, no bother. Didn't we enjoy shutting him up? So that was us into the second round, and an epic tie with Sporting Lisbon. The teams really went at one another in the first leg at Ibrox, Colin Stein scoring twice and Willie Henderson once in what resulted in our 3–2 win. We actually led 3–0 at one point, only to give ourselves unnecessary problems by conceding two goals. The return match proved to be at least as exciting, but first we had to get to the Portuguese capital, and that was a trial in itself. Rangers at the time weren't in the way of travelling by chartered aircraft. Maybe it was to do with Willie Waddell's cost-cutting measures. So the idea was we should set out early on the Monday morning, on a scheduled flight to Heathrow, and pick up a connection there. Talk about the best-laid plans.

Our departure from Glasgow was delayed because of an air traffic controllers' dispute, and once we got to London, it was to discover we'd missed our flight to Lisbon. From memory, the baggage handlers at Heathrow were on a go-slow, which only complicated the situation. We hung about endlessly in one of the lounges, not knowing when we might be able to complete our journey. But it proved impossible to do so that same day. The manager finally had us all bussed to Stansted where we stayed overnight in a hotel. Then what? A flight was chartered the following day from a Dutch airline and some thirty-six hours after congregating at Glasgow Airport, we finally landed in Lisbon. By the time we got to our hotel in Estoril, it was too late for us to fit in a training session. Bed beckoned instead.

Bear in mind this was now the Tuesday night. We were due to face Sporting the following evening. Fair to say our build-up had been far from ideal. Nonetheless, we proved to be up for the challenge that lay ahead, taking the tie into extra time by holding Sporting to the same score as we'd beaten them by at Ibrox, 3–2. Colin Stein got both of our goals, by the way. Then, during the additional thirty minutes, Willie Henderon scored for us, and while Sporting struck still later to make it 6–6 on aggregate, we were through on away goals. Or so we thought. The referee decided differently, ordering a penalty shoot-out, which we lost miserably and trudged back to our dressing room to grieve over our misfortune.

Just then, one of the journalists on the trip, John Fairgrieve of the *Daily Mail*, burst in with a rulebook in his hand and showed it to Willie Waddell. Contrary to what the referee had thought, John pointed out our goal in extra time should have counted double. We were into the next round after all, with the match official acknowledging as much once his error was pointed out to him. Yet something tempered the delight we all felt at that moment. Ronnie McKinnon, having been carried off, was discovered to be suffering from a double fracture of his leg. A row of seats had to be left clear on the flight home for the big fella to stretch out with his stookie.

While Europe was beginning to take notice of us, so too were people in England. We caught their attention when, within a couple of weeks of coming back from Lisbon, we were invited to provide the opposition for Chelsea in Ron Harris's testimonial match at Stamford Bridge. The London club weren't short of star players at the time, Peter Osgood and Charlie Cooke among them. Yet we won 1–0 with a late goal by Sandy Jardine and earned a fair amount of praise for our '£700,00 attack'. That was the collective value Bill Brown, one of the London-based reporters writing for the Glasgow *Evening Times*, put on Willie Henderson, Colin Stein, me, Willie Johnston and Alfie Conn.

If I blow the cobwebs off my cuttings book again, I find his article which begins as follows:

Rangers are an attractive lot. So West London is saying after seeing the Light Blues gain a well-earned victory . . . last night. After the match, a group of us – Scots and English – were speculating about the value that could be placed on the Rangers forward line. The figure we agreed upon was

£700,000 – £150,000 each for Willie Henderson, Colin Stein, Alex MacDonald and Willie Johnston – with Alfie Conn just a little behind at £100,000.

Poor Alfie. What had he done, or not done, to be marked down to just a hundred grand? As for me, well, in the estimation of these judges in the Chelsea press box, my worth had trebled since I signed from St Johnstone only three years earlier!

Anyway, the writer went on:

The wizardry of these boys had the Chelsea fans shouting for a helping of the same from their own lads. But, astonishingly, with all their known skills, Charlie Cooke, Peter Osgood and Peter Houseman simply couldn't produce the tricks of these skilful Rangers mites.

I would hardly have called Steinie a mite, or Alfie for that matter. But that's by the by, with the author continuing:

John Greig is a big man and he had a big game. A great player to have in your side, this fellow. Another is Davie Smith, whose tackling of the Chelsea forwards won praise from the terraces. And I'll have Sandy Jardine and Billy Mathieson in my team any day of the week. So there you are. Scottish exiles in London are grateful for the style Rangers put on. It was, by and large, a demonstration of the kind of Scottish football we are always talking about and which is all too rarely seen these days.

But, and there's usually a but, the journalist continued:

Now, having patted the backs of this fine Rangers lot, I have a criticism. It goes, I think, to the root of Rangers' troubles this season. Why should such a bunch of first-rate players find themselves trailing in the Scottish League? Simply, I think, because their forward line is too wee. I have seldom in my career seen such a tiny lot of frontrunners. Skilful, yes. But, when you take away Stein, who was in superb form last night, there's just no one to rise into the air for the ball. My English friends made a suggestion that really isn't as far out as it may seem. It is this – Willie Waddell should sell one, or even two, of those marvellous wee men for a fortune and use the money to buy, say, Rodney Marsh, the six-foot wonderman of that London side with the very Scottish name, Queen's Park Rangers. With another large lad of calibre up front, the Rangers would really be the tops.

Well, each to his own view of things, I suppose. Willie Waddell never did buy Rodney Marsh. I doubt if he even thought about it. And, if he had sold, say, Bud Johnston, would we have gone on to achieve what we did in Europe that season? Somehow I doubt that also.

Next up for us in the Cup Winners' Cup were Torino, against whom we claimed a creditable 1–1 draw in Italy. Who scored our goal? Wee Bud, of course. Our reckoning was if we didn't come out of the blocks quickly, we were likely to hand the initiative to Torino – and very likely suffer as a consequence. John Greig, especially, pledged that wasn't going to happen.

He was detailed to mark the opposition's supposed Wonderboy called Claudio Sala, and with us kicking off, he suggested I turn the ball straight back to him after Colin Stein knocked it to me. This I did, and with Sala having to challenge for possession, John almost broke him in two with a tackle. So the psychological advantage rested with us, before Torino had had a kick, and Bud put us in front after just twelve minutes. Of course, we sensed they would come back at us sooner or later, and so they did, with a second-half equaliser. Still, it was a good result for us, even if the return leg at Ibrox promised to be fraught enough.

The thing was, if Torino scored first they were liable to shut up shop and very possibly go through on account of that away goal. We had to be very disciplined, therefore, and not go charging forward lest we leave ourselves exposed at the back. In the event, more than half an hour passed before Peter McCloy had a save of any note to make. The Italians obviously had taken the view that if they didn't exercise caution and we got ourselves in front, there might be no way back for them. Here then was a game that had to be played with passion, but controlled passion. The crowd that night was 75,000. What an atmosphere – and what an outcome – as we won 1–0 by dint of the goal I scored shortly after the interval.

Tommy McLean deserved huge credit for helping set up the chance. He scampered past his direct opponent on the right flank and sent over a great cross towards the far post. Bud Johnston managed to get a touch on the ball before I, er, kind of bundled it over the line with my body. As one reporter attested, 'It was an undignified ending to such a glorious move.' But if I'd scored with a thunderous shot from thirty yards, the effect would have been the same. We were on our way to the semi-finals – and yet another meeting with Bayern Munich. They'd beaten Rangers in the final of the Cup Winners' Cup in Nuremberg in 1967 and the first round of the Fairs Cup in 1970. Might it be a case of third time lucky for us?

Willie Waddell was quite meticulous in planning for big occasions such as this one. He made sure we knew everything there was to know about opposing teams and, on an individual basis, the job each of us was required to perform against them. But sometimes you need luck as well. We certainly got at least as much as was our entitlement in the first and away leg against the West Germans. How we contrived to be only 1–0 down by the interval in Munich remains one of football's wonders. Bayern came at us every way imaginable, taking the lead through Paul Breitner midway through the first half. If I remember correctly, Gerd Muller had hit the bar beforehand with a header. We could do nothing other than try to hold tight at the back as Bayern bombarded us again and again.

One thing we didn't lack was stamina. Jock Wallace had built that into us with his tough training methods, so we could go the distance with anybody. Fighting spirit was another of our qualities, so were bristling to get out there for the second half and managed to equalise almost before it had got underway, with an own-goal by a guy called Rainer Zobel. Sepp Maier, the Bayern goalkeeper, almost certainly came up with another name for him as he diverted a low cross into the net. What it might have been, I don't know. I can't swear in German, only English. Willie Johnston actually ruffled the boy's hair in passing, as if to say, 'Well done, pal.' He shouldn't have done that but Bud, ever the wind-up merchant, was just being Bud.

Our confidence grew from then on and if there was the odd moment we thought we might actually win the match, we were both delighted and relieved to go home on the back of a 1–1 draw. Nothing could shake our self-belief for the return leg at Ibrox, not even the injury John Greig picked up in the intervening Scottish Cup semi-final with Hibs to put him out of contention. Ibrox was packed, with a crowd of 80,000, and what a roar went up when Sandy Jardine scored in the opening minute. Franz Beckenbauer, for once in his life, got himself into a fankle, giving the ball away to Derek Johnstone. Big Ba' promptly pushed it to Sandy, who scored with a curling shot into the top corner – with his left foot as well.

To say the Germans were a bit miffed would be a massive understatement. Beckenbauer, obviously unwilling to own up to the fact he'd squandered possession, rounded on goalkeeper Maier for not reacting as he might have done when the ball left Sandy's boot. But from our point of view, better was to follow soon enough, with the kid who had come in for Greigie, Derek Parlane, scoring midway through the second half after Colin Stein had re-directed a corner by Willie Johnston into his path. Bayern, gifted as they were, just couldn't come back at us – at least not in the manner we would have expected. It's not for me to make any excuses for them, especially after more than forty years have lapsed, but maybe the pitch didn't suit the likes of Beckenbauer. I can remember it being a bit bumpy and some of his supposedly measured passes slithering out of play.

So it was that we won 2–0, 3–1 on aggregate, to reach the promised land of the European Cup Winners' Cup final. Understandably enough, most of the plaudits went to young Parlane, still only nineteen. Among the others who shone that night were Colin Jackson, who had taken over at centre-half after Ronnie McKinnon broke his leg in Lisbon. If Bomber gave Gerd Muller a glimpse of goal, I don't remember it. But essentially, it was the all-round effort of the team which sustained us, as it had done in the first leg in Munich. A unique piece of history actually was written that night in Glasgow, what with Celtic playing the decisive leg of their European Cup semi-final with Inter Milan at Parkhead. It kicked off a bit later than ours, with the result that many Rangers fans had spilled into their pubs and clubs in time to see on television Celtic lose on penalties. As if they didn't have enough to cheer about!

7

HEROES ALL IN BARCELONA

Here's how NOT to prepare for a European final: do what a bunch of us did only a couple of days before Rangers met Moscow Dynamo at the Nou Camp in 1972. Sandy Jardine, Alfie Conn and I left the team's hotel in Castelldefels, near Barcelona, to go for an evening stroll. Well, it was a way of passing some of our free time, and before long, we came across this go-kart track. Anybody fancy a go? We all did. Our only instruction since arriving in Catalonia was to stay out of the sun in case we got heat stroke, and now the sun was going down.

Willie Waddell and Jock Wallace would have freaked out had they seen three of their players zipping around like maniacs. What if a couple of our karts had crashed into one another? What if someone's had rolled over? The possibilities for getting injured should have been glaringly obvious to all of us. Alfie went closest to having a painful mishap, when he lost control of the wheel and careered into a bale of straw. Honestly, Your Honour, we hadn't been on the sangria. We were just happy to be off the leash for an hour or two and acting like daft laddies. The sooner we screwed our serious heads back on, the better.

We'd left home on the Sunday prior to the Wednesday match, full of hope that we could become the first Rangers team to win a European trophy. The club had reached the final of the same tournament, the Cup Winners' Cup, in 1961 and 1967, losing out to Fiorentina and Bayern Munich respectively. We fancied we could make it a case of third time lucky, despite having performed uite poorly in domestic competition that same season. Nobody could say we'd had an easy run to Barcelona. Knocking out Rennes, Sporting Lisbon, Torino and Bayern had required a strong mixture of talent and teamsmanship on our part.

Moscow Dynamo hadn't had quite as tough a run, edging past Olympiakos of Greece, Eskisehirspor of Turkey, Red Star Belgrade and Dynamo Berlin, scoring ten goals to our thirteen in the process. Ok, they'd lost three fewer goals, six to our nine, but we didn't attach any great significance to that. Europe had brought out the best in our side. There was a strong camaraderie among us and we sensed within ourselves we had the all-round quality to make history on behalf of Rangers.

The manager had chosen wisely in selecting our hotel, which sat in peaceful isolation on a hillside several miles away from all the distractions that Barcelona had to offer. In saying that, none of us was particularly keen on occupying the room in which the famous actor George Sanders had committed suicide just a month or so earlier by taking an overdose of pills. The press guys who were with us could let their hair down a bit once they'd filed their stories. I dare say the veterans among them reminisced at the bar, if not in their actual copy, about Rangers' famous match against Moscow Dynamo at Ibrox in 1945. I wasn't even born then but knew all about how, in a 2–2 draw, the Russians had tried to work a flanker by sending on a substitute – without taking anybody off. It took Torry Gillick to make a quick head count and report the, er, discrepancy to the referee.

We knew we'd have problems enough in trying to beat eleven Moscow players, never mind twelve. Yet optimistic as we were about the outcome, it came as a bad blow to us when Colin Jackson went over on his ankle in training on the morning of the game. He had done so well since taking over from the injured Ronnie McKinnon and had been assured by the manager he would be playing. I felt sorry for Bomber, whose place went to Derek Johnstone. We all did. To miss the biggest game of his life must have been heart-rending. He ended up having quite a few swallies before we left for the Nou Camp, just to ease the pain of his disappointment. We pretty well carried him into the stadium when we got there.

John Greig had been nursing a foot injury for weeks, following a knock he picked up against Hibs in the semi-final of the Scottish Cup. He kept his worries pretty much to himself and, typical of him, elected to play with a heavy strapping on. Alfie Conn wasn't quite one hundred per cent either, although his injury had nothing to do with our madcap session on the go-karts. As for myself, I must admit to being a bit blinkered in the sense that I was most concerned about whether or not I would stay fit. Happily, I managed to do so, and couldn't wait to get in among the Russians.

Upwards of 25,000 Rangers fans had made the trip, while next to nobody came from Russia, which, of course, was still strapped into its communist straitjacket. Foreign travel, at least to the forbidden West, was something its ordinary citizens could only dream about. As a result, we had the huge majority of the crowd of 35,000 right behind us. I can't tell you how uplifting that was, and thankfully, we reacted accordingly by taking the lead midway through the first half when Davie Smith put Colin Stein through to score. Then, shortly before half time, again from a pass by Davie, Willie Johnston put us further in front.

If Moscow Dynamo weren't going to stop us, there was always the chance that the heat might. Willie Waddell had commissioned a special jersey to be made for us. It was lightweight and perforated, ideal for the conditions we expected. But he ditched it because it wasn't quite the right shade of blue. We ended up going into the game wearing polo-necked tops which were that bit heavier. Come half time, when we were leading 2–0, we changed to the kind of shirt we'd been wearing back in Scotland. It was heavier still, so the sweat was really dripping out of us after Wee Bud latched on to a long clearance by Peter McCloy in the forty-ninth minute to score his second goal, our third.

Not for a minute could we have anticipated being so comfortably placed in the match by that point. Maybe we slackened off a bit, maybe Dynamo upped the pace a bit by way of making a huge effort to turn the score around. Whatever the case, with just about an hour clocked, they pulled a goal back through a substitute called Vladimir Eschtrekov. It was game on, but somehow we had to hang in there. The Russians really showed their calibre in the time remaining and scored again, this time through Aleksandr Makovikov, with about three minutes left. The tension was almost unbearable by then and, like ourselves, our fans were in the grip of it.

Believe it or not, I've never watched the video of this epic match in its entirety, only bits of it now and again. So I can only say I THINK it was me who proceeded to give away a free-kick in the outside-left position. When the referee blew for it, hordes of our supporters spilled on to the park believing it was full-time. If I remember correctly, they came on again, probably for the same reason, as we continued battling to preserve what was left of our lead. One way or another, because of these hold-ups and the fact our nerves were jangling, it seemed a helluva long time before the final whistle went. When it sounded, the fans came on in their thousands.

Like us, they were expecting the trophy to be presented on the field, and who could blame them for wanting a close-up view? But such was the crush of bodies that we ended up being herded off the pitch towards the dressing room below. We were a bit worried about our safety, to be honest. Amid the melee, I spotted this big lad I'd known from my younger days, Stewart Daniels was his name. I'd kind of been brought up with him. 'Gonnae get me out of here?' I pleaded. I think I was lifted up and passed through the crowd. These fans could have killed me and other players with their kindness, all of them milling about while wishing to be part of one great celebration. So far as I was concerned, there was nothing sinister about that.

But what happened next, at pitch level, was unknown to us at the time. The fans and the police, dressed in their riot gear, really went at it in what the headline writers dubbed the 'Battle of

Barcelona'. I'd known long since that Rangers supporters were nothing if not passionate about their team, and also that the Spanish police could be very heavy-handed and prone to over-reaction. We were still in a daze in our dressing room when Willie Waddell and John Greig were led away to another room to accept the Cup. It was really only when we got back to our hotel that details of the rioting were fed back to us by the press.

All the wives came back with us to join the party. Then sometime after midnight I think it was, Willie Waddell said, 'Right, girls, you are going home.' To their own hotel, that is.

I remember saying to Beth McLean, 'If your Tommy gets up to any nonsense, I'll throw him in the pool.' She got all panicky, saying, 'Don't do that. He can't swim.' But, in fact, I don't remember too much nonsense involving anybody. Let's just say a good night was had by all.

I don't think many of us got too much sleep, if any. Everybody pitched in with a song, Greigie setting the scene with 'Big Spender'. More than a few drinks were taken. Rangers' first European trophy had been a long time coming and, regardless of the crowd trouble which still hadn't really sunk in with us, nothing could take the edge off the occasion so far as we were concerned.

The following morning saw some us still basking around the pool in the sunshine and talking about the game. Then on the flight home, I suddenly began to feel ill. Now, I'd had a few hangovers in my time, but this was something different. I'd even decided to sit near the front of the plane, rather than up the back with the rest of the lads. That wasn't like me. By the time we got back to Ibrox to parade the trophy, Donald Cruickshank, the club doctor, said, 'Take a look at yourself in a mirror, Alex. You've got sunstroke.' That's the curse of being redheaded. My face was ablaze. So I didn't mind at all that it was raining when we clambered aboard the lorry that took us around the track while holding aloft the Cup Winners' Cup for all our fans to see. It cooled me down.

Those scenes will stay with me forever and, amid the sea of faces on the terraces, I saw one I recognised instantly. It was

Bobby Shearer, our former club captain, wearing a white mac and looking as pleased for us as any other supporter. But there could be no escaping the backlash from the crowd trouble which, less than twenty-four hours earlier in Barcelona, had shamed the club as well as Scotland. 'Rangers WILL be Punished,' the back page of one of the Glasgow's evening papers warned. The accompanying report, which is in my cuttings book, testified: 'UEFA will take action against Rangers for the dreadful scenes which marred their great victory over Moscow Dynamo in Barcelona last night.'

It went on to quote UEFA secretary, Hans Bangerter, as saying, 'Action must be taken against Glasgow Rangers because of the behaviour of their fans. At present, I cannot say what form this action will take. But, be warned. Rangers will not go unpunished.' Another unnamed UEFA source promised a full investigation at the earliest opportunity. And what were the Russians saying about it all? The same article quoted their manager, Konstantin Beskov, as follows: 'The lives of my players were in danger towards the end of the game, and after it. From being 3–0 down, we pulled the score back to 3–2. Then the Rangers fans came onto the park. We were intimidated. Now we must protest.' Coach Lev Yashin, Moscow Dynamo's legendary former goalkeeper, went further by saying they would demand a replay.

As for the fact of our triumph and the football we'd played to achieve it, well, that appeared to have become a secondary consideration in this newspaper, as well as others. But Willie Waddell was quoted as being fulsome in praise of us players, in particular young Derek Johnstone, of whom he said:

He held us together in a sticky opening spell and then went on to play as if the game were a knock-about at our Albion training ground. He was tremendous. This boy is the finest prospect in Britain at present. The way transfer fees are going in England right now, I would not take a million pounds for him.

It was too soon for the manager to address the consequences of the riot, although he was obliged to do so soon enough. Rangers were banned from Europe for two years, but with Willie Waddell's statesmanlike intervention on our behalf, the sanction was reduced to one year and didn't bar us from playing the winners of the European Cup, Ajax, in a two-legged contest for the European Super Cup.

I seem to remember, before the home match, Jock Wallace just saying something like, 'Go out and enjoy yourselves.' We must have taken him too literally, with the result Ajax threatened to over-run us in what finished as a 3–1 win for them. I scored our goal that night and, along with Quinton 'Cutty' Young, who had joined us from Coventry, scored in the away leg, which we lost 3–2 to go down on a 6–3 aggregate.

Ajax were class back then, with Johan Cruyff to the fore. In truth, they were a team of great players, including the Muhren brothers, Gerry and Arnold. I recall becoming quite pally with one of them at the post-match banquet at Ibrox. So there was no shame in being beaten by them. Anyway, nothing and nobody could take the shine off our Cup Winners' Cup medals. Even now, forty years later, I can't be separated from mine. I still wear it on a chain round my neck. It is my finest treasure from all my time in football, and when I give it a polish, it is glittering testimony to how good a side we were back then and how well we played, for the most part at least, against Moscow Dynamo. Here are my snapshots of the team-mates who helped make that night, 24 May, the most memorable in Rangers' history:

PETER McCLOY: What a brilliant goalkeeper he was for us. About twice the size of me, so ideal for the position he played in. Those huge hands of his could get to just about every cross or shot, and he could kick the ball a mile as well. I'll never forget his clearance for our third goal in the Nou Camp. It went all the way forward from his penalty box for Wee Bud to score. The Russians kind of stopped, as if they didn't know how to deal with the situation. Bud had the ball in their net before they could wise up.

SANDY JARDINE: My mate who followed me to Hearts in the 1980s was class. I can't put it any better or more simply than that. We pal-ed about together from early on at Ibrox, maybe because we had the same sense of humour and were forever hitting each other with one-liners. He could run but never sold himself in the tackle. He was superb too at getting the ball into the opposition's box – more often than not by shaping to cross with his right foot, then jinking to send it over with his left.

WILLIE MATHIESON: A hardy boy who replaced Davie Provan in the Rangers team and made the left-back position his own for years to come. Willie could run the line, he could kick when he had to and could challenge strongly for the ball. Slide-tackling was one of his specialties. I always felt Willie was worth a Scotland cap but, for some reason, he never got one. We all knew his value; how good and reliable he was to have on our side. We always knew exactly what to expect of him. He was very consistent.

JOHN GREIG: Captain Courageous, wasn't he? Well named, as such, too. We always felt that bit better about going out onto the park if we knew he was playing. Whether he was fit or not, his presence could make the difference to us. There was something positively inspiring about him. The possibility of defeat never seemed to enter his head. We all knew he had a problem with his foot at the time of Barcelona but only he knew how big a problem it was. Still, it didn't stop him from pulling on the blue jersey.

DEREK JOHNSTONE: He was still just a kid at the time of Barcelona, but what composure he showed there when he came into central defence in place of Colin Jackson. Great in the air, whether he played at the back or front. I remember him better as a centre-forward, scoring a load of goals with his head. We used to call him 'Good Morning'. Why? Because, with Tommy McLean throwing crosses over to him from the right flank, he would convert them with just a nod of his head, like he was greeting somebody in the street.

DAVIE SMITH: He had so much skill it was untrue. He was another Beckenbauer, him. It didn't matter how big the game was – and none was bigger than Barcelona – he was never flustered. Sometimes he would take people on in his own box and we'd be shouting, 'Get rid of it', but Davie only got rid of it when he was good and ready. He did things the way he wanted. I recall later in our careers, when I was player–manager at Hearts and he was in the same role at Berwick, him taking us on almost single-handedly in a Cup tie.

ALFIE CONN: Like Derek Johnstone at the time of Barcelona, he was still maturing as a player, yet the occasion brought only the best out of him. Alfie was majestic in the way he ran at opposing defences and very composed if he found himself one on one with any goalkeeper. He had good pace and vision, and when he gathered the ball with a bit of space to move in, there was no getting at him. To put it in a nutshell, he was an all-round, great player – even if he wasn't the best at running back when the opposition were in possession!

TOMMY McLEAN: He could put the ball on your head – or any other place you wanted, in fact. I always thanked Wee Tam, as well as Scotland manager, Willie Ormond, for my one international cap because it was Tam who set me up for many of the goals I scored. He was a brilliant passer, as well as crosser. He used to get a bit of stick because he wasn't a tackler. But so what? He was everything else – and a great guy as well. Nobody knew the game better than he did either. It must run in the family, with Jim and Willie his brothers.

COLIN STEIN: I remember falling out with him the first time we played together. He spent the opening forty-five minutes shouting at me, 'Give it here.' Walking off at half time, I said, 'Who the f**k do you think you are, Martin Chivers?' Steinie buzzed the whole time he was playing, like he was wired up to something. The moon, maybe – I don't know. He was a runner essentially, and had the best pair of lungs at Ibrox. But he was a great goalscorer, as he proved yet again that night in Barcelona.

WILLIE JOHNSTON: Bud was electric, full of energy and always ready to burst forward. People thought of him as being essentially a winger, but he could be just as devastating when he came inside or pushed through the middle. Moscow Dynamo didn't know quite how to handle him, or where he was liable to turn up next. If his disciplinary record was a bit scary, it was mainly because of the abuse he took from opponents. It didn't matter how big they were, Bud wasn't afraid to take them on. I admired him for that.

What about some of the lads who for whatever reason never made the team that night? Colin Jackson was a big athlete, as brave as they come. He knew his capabilities and always kept things simple. Dead laid back as well, he was. Alex Miller was Mr Versatile and Mr Reliable rolled into one. Very steady and thoughtful. He gave Rangers everything he had. Derek Parlane, having scored a superb goal against Bayern Munich in the semi-final, came into his own in subsequent seasons. How can I forget either those good players like Andy Penman, Graham Fyfe, Jim Denny and a great one such as Willie Henderson, who starred in the earlier rounds?

I feel very privileged to have been an integral part of such a great achievement as winning the European Cup Winners' Cup. That entire season was one of my best for the club in terms of appearances and goals. I was approaching my prime and as things transpired, still had a host of domestic medals to come my way. By way of a postscript, let me add that our bonus for winning in Barcelona was £2,000 – almost half of which went on tax, it grieves me to recall. I swithered about buying a car from my pal Billy Clark, or putting an extension on the house, with the windfall. Eventually, I settled for the latter and just hope the family now living at the same address in Kirkintilloch are Rangers fans able to appreciate the extra space they have and how it was funded.

8

AN EYE FOR THE BIRDS

What a golfer I might have been – at 5'6" in my spiked shoes, Ibrox's answer to Gary Player, maybe – if I hadn't arrived at the decision quite early on in my career to preserve all the strength there was in my legs for playing football. I didn't want to leave it on any golf course. A lot of my team-mates, particularly the likes of Sandy Jardine, Willie Johnston and Willie Mathieson, were fast, and I wasn't inclined to lag behind them in training. Obviously, in the case of club outings, I would join in. It was either that or carry a team-mate's clubs for him, and I wasn't in to being anybody's caddie.

In my cuttings book, there's a picture of Sandy, Wee Bud and me standing back on the tee as Jim Baxter, wearing a Sam Snead hat, drives his ball straight down the middle. It won't surprise you to know that Jim, famous for his left foot, played golf left-handed. He wasn't bad at it either, although in my time with Rangers, nobody was better than Big Peter McCloy. That picture, by the way, was taken at Haggs Castle in Glasgow, and the event was the club's annual outing as we competed for the John Letters Trophy.

One time I was glad to dig out the clubs was after Rangers had lost a Cup final at Hampden. I was a bit down, as you might imagine, and my mate, Billy Clark, came to pick me up. I thought we were headed for a few pints by way of drowning my sorrows, but Billy ended up taking me to Cawder Golf Club near Bishopbriggs for an evening round, which I found to be very therapeutic.

But, generally speaking, when I was away from football, I preferred to spend some of my spare time by indulging what had been my boyhood passion for birds. See me and ornithology! I'm not sure if any of my colleagues could have told the difference between a swift and a swallow, but to me, it was no bother. My interest in our feathered friends was rekindled by a friend and near neighbour in Kirkintilloch. For fear of incriminating him by what I'm about to divulge, I'll just call him Auld Jock. On a Monday or Wednesday, when I had a day off from training, he and I would drive up to the Forth and Clyde Canal nearby and do a bit of spotting. Well, we did a bit more than that.

Jock was into breeding birds which he'd caught in the wild. He would mark out a square on the ground and put feeder down in each corner, as well as a bit of gluey stuff called DAK. Birds are nosey blighters. As we stood our distance, they would flutter down to sample the grub on offer, then become trapped by the DAK. He would grab them then and stick them in a cage. I know how cruel this might sound. Any bird lovers reading it might be tempted to report me to the some protection agency. But I was just a bystander, watching the Birdman of Kirkintilloch at work.

Once we got the birds back to Jock's place, he would use margarine to clean the DAK off them, then put them in his aviary in the hope they took a fancy to one another and started breeding. Some didn't, some did. They might be goldfinches, or bullfinches. Whatever, they were beautiful little creatures. I dare say Jock could have got the jail had the polis caught him at it. Come to think about it, maybe the pair of us would have ended up in court, although, like him, I didn't see the harm in any of this.

One day, when we were about our business at the side of the canal, I heard a horse approaching from a distance on the footpath. Was it a mounted polisman coming to rein us in, so to speak? No, it was an old adversary of mine, Willie Wallace of Celtic, out for a canter. I didn't know he was into horses, but then again, there was no way he could have known I was into birds. Suffice to say we tended not to talk about such things in the heat of an Old Firm game.

Still on the subject of birds, I can remember once when we were staying at Largs before a big game, driving with Sandy Jardine to Kilwinning, I think it was, to see Gordon McQueen's father's aviary. Sandy must have picked up from Big Go-Go, when they were on international duty together, that his dad was into birds. When later in my career I joined Hearts, I learned there were big bird shows in Edinburgh around the turn of each year. Unfortunately, because we were forever playing on 1 or 2 January, I never got to see them. Still later, I started to breed canaries and, at one point, had about fifteen of them in my own aviary.

So much for me and birds. Let me tell you now about a dog we had. A fantastic Afghan Hound, it was, bigger than me when it stood on its hind legs. For reasons that shouldn't be too difficult to discern, we called it Blue. It took a bit of looking after, I can tell you, but was great company about the house for maybe the first year and a half. Then Christine, all concerned, said to me one day, 'That dog went for me.' Eventually, it was growling menacingly at me. Neither Christine nor I could bear the thought of it turning on the children. Lisa had been born by then and, if I remember rightly, we had Nick as well. So I ended up taking Blue to the vet, who suggested I have it put it down. He duly jagged it in my presence.

I was left with only a lead and collar. I drove to the canal and sat there on the banking for about an hour, roaring and greeting. Eventually I threw the lead and collar into the water and made my way home, saying never again would we have a dog. I just couldn't bear the thought of parting with another, for whatever reason. But my resolution was broken soon enough. We got this Great Dane from a breeder in Dingwall. It was only a pup at the time and I'd to go to the station in Glasgow to collect it off the train.

We called it Danya, and as it grew bigger and bigger, it took more and more feeding. Not that I minded that, although I was never away from the meat market buying grub for it. Eventually, it just became too big for the house. What to do? Someone told me about this place near Coatbridge – a Catholic-run approved school which had a little farm – which might offer Danya a more suitable home. So I loaded the dog into the car and drove there to see the man in charge. My memory is that he was a priest, although I could be wrong about that. The first thing he asked me was would I do a question and answer session with the kids who were inmates. No bother, I told him.

Then, as we talked about him taking Danya, he asked me if I wanted a drink. 'No thanks,' I said, 'I'm driving.' He was in the throes of pouring a couple of glasses of whisky which he proceeded to top up with milk. At the end up, he sank them both. Then I said farewell to him and another faithful friend. If and when we ever got a third dog, it would be a smaller one. Lisa eventually persuaded us to get this toy poodle we called Tootsie. It followed me everywhere – and what a watchdog!

So much for my distractions off the field. Now it's back to the fitba. Where did I leave off? Oh, yes, the aftermath of Barcelona.

9

SCOTTISH CHAMPIONS AT LAST

See me and my big mouth? It didn't half get me into bother once when I was in discussion with Willie Waddell about a new contract. He'd invited me upstairs to his office to let me know what was on offer. Don't ask me now what the terms were, but very likely the deal was a ten per cent rise on what I was getting at the time. While I never considered myself to be greatly motivated by cash, I couldn't have been greatly impressed and said something to the effect, 'I think all the money is being made on the other side of this desk.'

Before I knew it, he was out of his seat and had me pinned against the wall, with his hands around my neck. I'm shouting, 'Whoa, whoa. Hold it! Hold it!' I'd said the wrong thing at the wrong time – and certainly to the wrong man. My remark was of the throw-away variety. I didn't intend it to be insulting but, looking back, I can see how he took umbrage at it. If I'd been a bit more diplomatic, maybe I could have left myself room for negotiation. In the circumstances, it was a wonder he didn't heave me back downstairs again, without any agreement having been reached.

Willie Waddell, although I respected him greatly and appreciated what he'd done for my career by that stage, was not a man to argue or fall out with. In saying that, he wasn't one to hold a grudge either. I can say that in the certain knowledge that, in my remaining years with the club, he never cast up that incident to me. But how about this for an intriguing postscript? A fan dug me up in a supporters club one night, saying, 'Do you know you're earning more than John Greig?'

My response was something like, 'Gie's peace. How can I be making more than John, the legend, the Rangers captain, the big-time Scotland international?' Yet he proceeded to show me copies of my contract, and John's, and so far as I could see, he was spot on. How he'd got his hands on such highly personal information, I have no idea. Take it as read that Greigie wouldn't have been best pleased had he found out. Quite rightly so. I was embarrassed, to say the least.

Willie Waddell had stepped up to the role of general manager in the wake of our triumph in Barcelona, with Jock Wallace taking over as team manager. We, the players, didn't see the change coming, although there were those who could recall Willie quitting Kilmarnock immediately after he'd led them to their one and only league championship in 1965. Maybe seven years later he didn't think he could better what we'd achieved in lifting the European Cup Winners' Cup.

Then again, because he always had Rangers' interests at heart, it's more likely he took the view there was a far bigger job to be done in giving the club a greater sense of leadership and not least of all overseeing the rebuilding of the stadium in the wake of the Ibrox Disaster. Whatever the case, Jock Wallace was tried and trusted by then. The players all related to him. They liked his methods, although in regard to those he applied in training, some of the lads found them more than a bit taxing.

Jock hungered for a challenge, and at the time, there could have been none bigger than trying to break Celtic's monopoly of the championship under Jock Stein. They'd won it seven times in a row by then. But who would have thought that shortly after we'd set out to prevent them making it eight we would lose such important players as Colin Stein and Willie Johnston? Steinie moved on to Coventry City, with Quinton Young coming to Ibrox in part-exchange, while Bud headed for West Brom.

What a turn this pair had done us in Barcelona, Steinie scoring once and Bud twice, in our famous 3–2 win over Moscow Dynamo. There were mutterings at the time that Big Jock thought they'd got a bit big for their boots, that they had become akin to prima donnas. Somehow I doubt if that was actually his view, but their way-going obviously gave him the opportunity to start rebuilding the team in his own, hardy image. In the event, nobody reflected it better than Tam Forsyth.

Tam, who was to become a Rangers legend, arrived from Motherwell in the autumn of 1972, virtually at the same time that Joe Mason signed from Morton. We were toiling a bit in the league by that point after a disappointing start. Our form in the League Cup was less than convincing also, in that we contrived to lose at home to Stenhousemuir in the return leg of a second-round tie. Still, we went on to reach the semi-final, losing to Hibs at Hampden. Then came the big turnaround, a 1–0 defeat by Hearts in the championship, giving way to a run of twenty league matches unbeaten. Celtic finished as title winners once more, but only by a point from us.

Derek Parlane had come into his own as a replacement for Colin Stein, and scored one of his nineteen league goals in a 2–1 victory over Celtic at Ibrox in early January. Cutty Young had done well too, pitching in with thirteen goals during the same campaign. But in his own, uncompromising way, Big Tam Forsyth had made at least as great an impression as anybody and was to see his name in lights as we ended that season 1972–73 by lifting the Scottish Cup that season for the first time since 1966.

Cutty, who had effectively taken over from Bud Johnston, set us on the road to Hampden by scoring in our 1–0 win over Dundee United at Ibrox in the third round. Then, with Derek Johnstone our marksman, we were held to a 1–1 draw at home by Hibs in the round that followed. Our games with Hibs around that time tended to be very difficult. They had a right good side. Yet we managed to beat them 2–1 in the replay, with Tam McLean getting both goals. Next up, in the quarter-finals, were Airdrie, who we beat 2–0. Derek Parlane and Cutty Young shared the goals in that game, and Derek got both as we beat Ayr United by the same score in the semis.

Who awaited us in the final? Celtic, of course, but we couldn't see any reason to fear them. Even after Kenny Dalglish opened the scoring, we still felt we had the beating of Jock Stein's team and were never behind again. Derek Parlane equalised before the first half had ended, from a pass by myself, while Alfie Conn put us in front shortly after the break. George Connelly, the Celtic player I admired more than any other, duly made the score 2–2 with a penalty. It must have been one of the best Old Firm games I was ever involved in – and what a finish Tam Forsyth provided on sixty minutes by scoring his most famous goal from all of about six inches out with the sole of his boot.

The big fella was beside himself with joy afterwards, and as my cuttings book tells me, was quoted as saying, 'I was up at the post for a free kick and thought the ball was going in after it came along the line. When I saw it hit the post, I was so excited I nearly missed. Then I just stabbed it over the line.' Aye, such is the stuff of which Rangers heroes are made. Tam wasn't exactly noted for his goal-scoring exploits but that less than spectacular effort guaranteed him his place in the club's history.

It was worth noting, by the way, that that was his thirtieth appearance for the club since his £45,000 move from Fir Park, and still he hadn't appeared in a losing side. I hesitate to say that I myself made a useful contribution to our cause on the same occasion, but if I refer once more to the family files, I find the following sentiments expressed by one man in the press box, former Rangers player, Doug Baillie. 'I told you last week – if it rained, Rangers would lift the Cup,' he wrote in the *Sunday Post*. 'The heavens opened . . . just in time for Rangers to turn on the style. And none more than Alex "Doddie" MacDonald, my Man of the Match.

'No wonder he was the player Jock Wallace made a beeline for on the final whistle. Big Jock lifted him clear off his feet and gave him a bear hug that Mick McManus would have been proud of.

Doddie richly deserves it, too. For he'd done the job which Big Jock set him – looking after Bobby Murdoch – and was never more than five yards from him, hustling the Celtic player in hurried passes. As I've always said, when Bobby's not doing it, Celtic aren't doing it. So much was Doddie on top of his job he had time to go up and have a pot at goal with a couple of headers, one off the post, the other sneaking past with Ally Hunter nowhere. Yes, it's Doddie for me.' Thanks, Doug. Did you get that brown envelope I handed in to your office? But thanks also to Big Tam Forsyth for making sure I got my hands on another medal.

No sooner had the following season 1973–74 got underway than we found ourselves facing Celtic twice more, home and away in the League Cup. We lost the first match 2–1 but won the second 3–1. That must have rated as one of my best Old Firm performances in that I scored our first goal and was credited with setting up the other two for Derek Parlane and Alfie Conn. Mind you, we took a bit of a pounding in the first half, what with Bobby Lennox putting Celtic in front and Kenny Dalglish hitting the post.

It was only after the break that we began getting a hold of the game, with my equaliser from what was described as 'a vicious volley' coming just before the hour mark. When not long afterwards Parlane put us in front, Celtic lodged a furious protest for offside. That was the cue for one of those spats which tend to characterise Old Firm games. I got involved with Jimmy Johnstone, and while referee John Gordon booked me, he sent off Jinky, who he had cautioned earlier. Even with ten men, Celtic still weren't beaten, Lennox hitting the bar and Peter McCloy having to tip over an effort by Harry Hood from the rebound. Fraught or what? It wasn't until four minutes from time that we could relax, Alfie scoring then after he'd had what we all thought was a legitimate goal disallowed.

Such were the rules at the time that both Celtic and Rangers qualified from our group for the later stages of the tournament, and we proceeded to reach the semi-finals by knocking out

Dumbarton and Hibs. As luck would have it, the draw then paired us and Celtic again, this time at Hampden. For reasons I never quite understood, Jock Wallace picked me at outside-left on that occasion. I wasn't greatly enamoured, to be honest, even though I scored a belter of a goal from a square ball by John Greig. I can see my shot yet, screaming into the top corner.

Not that it did us much good, right enough. Harry Hood ending up with a hat-trick for Celtic to give them a 3–1 win. It was never my way ever to question why I'd been picked out of position, but a couple of days later as we were walking from Ibrox to the Albion for training, I asked Big Jock why he'd put me down at outside-left. He came back immediately, asking, 'What's the problem? Do you no' want to play for Rangers?' My answer was, 'Of course I do. My granny would want to play for Rangers.' A pal of mine later expanded on that story by saying Jock quipped in a response of, 'Gie' me her phone number then.'

As it turned out, Celtic got the better of us in the league as well that term, winning 1–0 both at Ibrox and Parkhead. There was no stopping them winning what was their ninth successive title – by five points from us and four in front of Hibs. Considering we'd been knocked out of the Scottish Cup by Dundee at only the fourth-round stage, or second-round proper, and failed to qualify for Europe, none of us could take much credit for our domestic efforts. Come to think on it, with our European ban expired after Barcelona, we hadn't exactly distinguished ourselves in the Cup Winners' Cup either, losing out to Borussia Moenchengladbach at the second stage after starting with a win over the Turkish team, Ankaragucu.

Better luck next season? We certainly hoped so, as did all our fans. Rangers hadn't savoured success in the championship since 1964, Kilmarnock winning it the following year and Celtic every one in the interim. Jock Stein's side had evolved since his appointment as manager and, come the start of season 1974–75, arguably wasn't as strong as the one with which he'd set out. Still, we knew it would need a concerted effort by us if we were to break their momentum and with it their monopoly on the title. Imagine then our disappointment when we set out on the new campaign with a 1–1 draw against Ayr United at Somerset Park.

That result echoed the one from the corresponding fixture of a year earlier, when Ayr held us to a goal-less draw at Ibrox. But we put it behind us soon enough, beating Celtic 2–1 away in only our third match of the league campaign, with goals by Ian McDougall and Colin Jackson. Our confidence soared as a consequence and it wasn't until late November we actually lost in the competition, Hibs beating us at Easter Road. Then, just a few days before Christmas, we lost 4–3 at Airdrie. But again we showed our resilience, beating Ayr and Partick successively before playing Celtic at Ibrox on 4 January.

What a turn-up that was for us. We gave them a 3–0 doing, with goals by Derek Johnstone, Tommy McLean and Derek Parlane, to take over the league leadership on goal difference. The result could have been 4–0 for us had not the referee, John Paterson, chalked off an effort by myself just before half time. Picture the scene: a melee breaks out in the Celtic six-yard area. Ally Hunter, their goalie, goes to grab the loose ball as I lunge in to knock it over the line. But, in doing so, I show my studs and as I wheel away to celebrate, the ref's whistle sounds for a foul against me. I guess he was right, even if I didn't think so at the time.

Something wholly unforeseen happened after that: Celtic lost their way. To be more exact, they dropped twelve points out of a possible eighteen in their next nine matches. It was as if they'd become disorientated as a result of the thumping we'd given them in the first week of the New Year. We, on the other hand, dropped only a point to Morton, and another to Kilmarnock, before going to Easter Road on the last Saturday of March. Bear in mind the season still had a month to go, but there we were, needing only a point from the Hibs game to win the title. Who would have believed it? Colin Stein had returned to Ibrox only a few weeks earlier and it was he who scored our goal in the 1–1 draw that saw us installed as champions.

We'd broken Celtic's spell at last and, as you might imagine, celebrated wildly on champagne in our dressing room. I doubt if I've seen a happier man than Jock Wallace was around 4:40 p.m. that afternoon. A crowd of 38,000 had turned out for what registered as a famous day in the club's history. We sent the vast majority, upwards of 30,000 maybe, home in the very best of humour. It was quite some time before, with all the directors rounded up, we boarded our bus for the trip back to Glasgow. The driver had to make an unscheduled stop at the side of the motorway, somewhere around Harthill, for reasons I need hardly explain. Willie Waddell, I seem to recall, was first off.

All Big Jock's hard work with us had come to fruition, likewise all our application and dedication to duty. We were a team in the truest sense of the term, every one of us prepared to work for the common cause. Some critics didn't much fancy our style, believing it to be based more on physical power than finesse. But I would point to players such as Sandy Jardine, Tommy McLean and Bobby McKean and argue something to the contrary. We had quality all the way through the side in fact, starting with goal-keeper Stewart Kennedy, who went on to play for Scotland in the Home Internationals.

Derek Parlane excelled up front, claiming seventeen of our goals, including an eye-opening five in a 6–1 defeat of Dunfermline at East End Park prior to the turn of the year. Wee Tam McLean ended up with fourteen, as did Derek Johnstone, although he played many of his games in defence. Guys like Ally Scott, Jim Denny and Alex O'Hara, if used sparingly, all of them did us a turn when required, similarly Graham Fyfe, who had starred in the four-team Juan Gamper Tournament in Barcelona at the beginning of the season.

We had gone back to the Nou Camp then, intent on repairing the bridges that had been damaged so badly at the time of our Cup Winners' Cup triumph a couple of years earlier, and beaten Atlético Bilbao 1–0 in our opening game, with Sandy Jardine the scorer. Barcelona turned us over 4–1 thereafter to lift their own trophy. But what a performance Graham turned in and what a goal he struck in that match. The talk among our players later was that Barca actually wanted to sign him. Alfie Conn, soon to leave Rangers, had sussed as much from one of the opposition, but possibly to Graham's great disappointment, their interest wasn't followed up.

Those few days in Catalonia, by the way, marked our only competitive foray in Europe that season. As for the domestic cups in 1974–75, suffice to say we didn't make much of a mark in them either. But we ended up winning the First Division championship – the last before the tournament gave way to the Premier Division – and that more than compensated for all the disappointment which had gone before. I now had the full set of Scottish medals, plus a European one. It was at times like those that I felt like going back to my old stomping grounds in the city, looking up at the tenement windows and shouting, 'See, everybody, I've actually made it.'

10

MAKE MINE A TREBLE

This was the stuff of fantasy, the type of thing every schoolboy dreams about. I'd just scored what proved to be the winning goal – with a diving header, no less – in a Cup final. The occasion was the League Cup Final of 1975–76 at Hampden, with Celtic our opponents. Sixty-seven minutes had gone when Colin Stein sent Derek Parlane into the penalty box with a good pass. Derek managed to ride a tackle by Roddy MacDonald before slinging the ball across goal. Cutty Young promptly hung it up for me to launch myself in front of Danny McGrain and beat Peter Latchford.

From then until full time, I'm saying to myself, 'I hope naebody else scores. Please, make this the only goal of the game.' It was. We won 1–0, and I was over the proverbial moon. No kidding, I remember thinking that if anybody wanted to take me outside the ground there and then and shoot me, well, let them. Believe me, for an Old Firm player, scoring a Cup-winning goal against your greatest rivals . . . it just doesn't get any better than that.

Yet what a sickener I'd had only a few nights earlier, when we lost 2–0 to St Etienne away in the first leg of our second-round tie in the European Cup. I'd more or less gifted the French their second goal, scored only a minute from time, with a slack pass. So that fact was still weighing in my thoughts as we celebrated what was the eighth time Rangers had lifted the League Cup. 'I always enjoy playing against Celtic,' the papers quoted me as saying in the heady aftermath. 'Maybe it's the atmosphere, but usually I hit a good game. Even after our defeat against St Etienne, none of the lads were down. All of us felt we could beat Celtic, and the fact I got the goal maybe helped balance the books.'

That last remark, of course, was a reference to my faux pas in France, and I went on to admit, 'I blamed myself for what happened but felt sure if we won the League Cup it would be forgotten. We are by no means out of the European Cup just yet. There are still ninety minutes left in the tie, and if the boys go about their business with the same determination as we showed here at Hampden today, anything can happen.' What a bit of wishful thinking that proved to be. Although I managed to score late on against St Etienne in the return match at Ibrox, they beat us 2–1 to progress on a 4–1 aggregate. So much for our first crack at the European Cup since 1964–65 when Inter Milan put us out at the quarter-final stage.

We'd hoped to do so much better in the tournament after such a long absence from it. Yet in saying that, St Etienne were a class team and went all the way to the final at Hampden before losing to Bayern Munich. The opening round had us paired with the Irish side Bohemians, with the first leg played at Ibrox. I missed it through suspension but thereby, as they say, hangs a story. Here's what happened.

Rangers received a letter from UEFA prior to the game saying I was suspended because of two cautions I'd picked up the last time we'd been in Europe a couple of years earlier. The SFA confirmed this and therefore I had to settle for a spectating role as we beat Bohs 4–1 in front of our home crowd. Then, a few days later, it emerged there had been a clerical blunder. I had been booked only once, in the away leg of our tie with Borussia Moengladbach, so should have been free to play against the Irish side. 'We admit the error,' a UEFA spokesman was quoted as saying. 'It is embarrassing for us.' Jock Wallace was livid when he heard, saying, 'Though we won 4–1 against Bohemians, the communication from UEFA denied us the use of a valuable player. We accepted their decision because it was confirmed by the SFA.'

I was back in the side for the return match in Dublin, the build-up to which was especially tense but for reasons that had nothing to do with football. Newspaper reports suggested the IRA were out to get us, and nobody seemed more alarmed than my hotel roommate on that occasion, Graham Fyfe. We were allocated a room at ground-floor level, with Graham pointing to a bed in the corner, saying, 'I'm going to take that one because if any gunman looks through the window, he'll see only you.' Aye thanks, pal.

Next thing I know, Graham's pulling the furniture up against the window by way of protection. Then, come shut-eye time, I'm lying sleeping and Graham is having a nightmare. I wake up with him battering me. 'That's it,' I think, 'the IRA have broken in.' Tam Craig, our physio, must have heard the din and burst through the door, shouting, 'What's going on here?' Tam ended up giving Graham a sleeping pill. I didn't want one but have to say that every creak I heard in the pipes during the night left me wondering if our time had come.

The game itself I didn't enjoy one bit, partly because I was stuck out on the right side where I felt totally lost. The home fans proceeded to throw all sorts of things at us, abuse being the least hurtful. Our problems weren't confined to the ninety minutes either. On our way back through Dublin afterwards, one of the windows on our bus came crashing in. Jock Wallace was hit by flying glass and got a cut on his face. We were all crouched down, thinking someone had fired a bullet. But, in fact, it was a stone that had been thrown. As soon as we got to our hotel, I said to Fyfie, 'We're going to the bar for a couple of pints of Guiness.' Then we had another two. After sinking them, I looked at Graham, he looked at me. 'To hell,' we said, and ordered a third round. We might have been there all night had not Peter McCloy appeared, saying, 'C'mon, you pair, yer dinner's out.'

We couldn't get back to Glasgow quick enough, in the comforting knowledge that the 1–1 draw we'd got against Bohs was more than sufficient to see us into the next round on aggregate. Yet despite all the optimism we'd taken into the competition, we were out of it within a month or so and left to concentrate solely on domestic football. The big question confronting us around that time was whether we could add to the League Cup already won and, in particular, retain the championship. The inescapable conclusion was that Celtic were on the wane. They'd finished third, equal with Dundee United the previous season, eleven points behind us and four points adrift of second-placed Hibs.

Thereafter, they'd suffered the shocking setback of losing manager Jock Stein as a result of a car crash in which he was seriously injured. Sean Fallon, his assistant, took over and must have got an early sense of the difficulties confronting him when we beat Celtic 2–1 at Ibrox on the opening day of the league campaign, with goals by Derek Johnstone and Cutty Young. The new-styled Premier Division had come into being by then and comprised only ten teams playing each other four times. Then, within days of winning the League Cup, we went to Celtic Park and managed to get a 1–1 draw thanks to a goal by Derek Parlane.

We needed that result, what with Ayr United and Motherwell having beaten us in our previous two league games. By early December, we'd lost also to Hearts, Hibs and Aberdeen. But the last of these defeats proved to be something of a watershed in our season because we remained unbeaten between then and 24 April – a run of nineteen games – when we won the title with a 1–0 win over Dundee United at Tannadice. Derek Johnstone, who'd grown up supporting United, had the distinction of scoring on that famous occasion almost before the game had started. How's this for irony: Jock Wallace didn't even see Big Ba's first-minute goal. As we took the field immediately prior to kick-off, he'd hung back to visit the toilet. By the time the gaffer reached the bench, we were in front and counting down the minutes to when we could proclaim ourselves champions for the second successive year. I know there is no such thing as a meaningless Old Firm match, yet the one we played at Parkhead only a few days later and drew 0–0 meant rather less than most.

Celtic, in fairness to them and their stand-in manager, Sean Fallon, had led the title race in the first half of the season and, in fact, still held a slender advantage over us when we beat them 1–0, with another Derek Johnstone goal, at Ibrox on New Year's Day. But not even they could live with us thereafter, with the result we were six points better off than them at the finish. The statistics showed that while we scored fewer goals than Celtic over the course of thirty-six league matches they conceded more than us. In other words, our defence played a significant part in that triumph which, as every Rangers fan knows, wasn't our last of the season. The Scottish Cup Final against Hearts remained in the offing.

We'd set out in that tournament with a 3–0 win over East Fife at Ibrox, with yours truly managing to claim the first goal. Then came a resounding 4–1 win over Aberdeen, again at home, in which I got on the score sheet once more. By the time we hammered Queen of the South 5–0 away in the quarter-finals, there was a growing sense that our name might be on the trophy. That said, the side we met in the semi-final at Hampden – Motherwell – didn't want for optimism or, for that matter, talent. They were going pretty well in the league at the time and had an especially good attacking duo in Willie Pettigrew and an ex-Liverpool player, Bobby Graham. These guys represented a danger to any defence, even one as solid as ours.

As things transpired, they pushed into a two-goal lead against us, courtesy of Stewart McLaren and Pettigrew. Things looked ominous indeed for us, until Alex Miller scored with a penalty after the break. The game turned at that point, with Derek Johnstone scoring twice towards the end to send us into the final. Big Ba', having missed the East Fife game, had scored five times in three ties by then. That was good going by anybody's measure. Could he keep it up against Hearts? Of course he could – and, in the process, provide pub quizmasters with a question that has been asked a thousand times since.

Here it is: which player scored in a cup final before the actual kick-off time of 3 p.m.? Answer: Derek Johnstone. The game actually began a minute or so early and, with only forty-five seconds clocked, DJ had the ball in Hearts' net. What a sickener it must have been for the Tynecastle side who eight years earlier had finished runners-up to Dunfermline in the competition. The last time they'd actually lifted the trophy was in 1956. Our gaffer Jock Wallace recalled hearing about that triumph when he was away in Malaya fighting with the King's Own Scottish Borderers. Anyway, what promised to be a long afternoon for Hearts became longer still when I scored immediately before the interval. Derek Johnstone duly added a third goal before Graham Shaw pulled a meaningless one back.

So it was that for the third time in the club's history we'd won the Treble of the League Cup, Championship and Scottish Cup. Even though I didn't like champagne, I think I drank my fill in the heady aftermath of Hampden. It was the happiest possible ending to what, however way I looked at it, was my most rewarding season since signing from St Johnstone nearly eight years earlier.

Oh, and by the way, I'd had the further good fortune to have played for Scotland at Hampden just a month or so earlier. The game was a friendly against Switzerland and I was by no means a first pick. From memory, manager Willie Ormond lost eight players from his original squad of eighteen through one reason or another and ended up fielding five new caps, including myself, Alan Rough and Willie Pettigrew. Willie, with whom I was to play when I joined Hearts a few years later, scored in only the second minute to give us a 1–0 win. He went on to play in the Home Internationals at the end of that season, while Roughie proceeded to amass more than fifty caps. Me? Well, although I felt I acquitted myself well enough against the Swiss, I never re-appeared for Scotland but wasn't too despondent about that. In fact, any time thereafter I met Willie Ormond, I always made a point of thanking him for giving me the opportunity to play at international level. In the same way, I remained grateful to Rangers team-mate Tommy McLean for helping give me the platform with the service he provided at club level.

Scotland had been to the World Cup in West Germany in 1974 under Wee Willie, and more famously still, were to qualify for Argentina in 1978 under Ally MacLeod. I never gave myself much hope of making their squad, to be honest, although Jock Wallace fairly touted me as a candidate. 'I've already said that MacDonald is the most improved player at Ibrox,' he was quoted at saying in 1977. 'But he's also the best midfield player in the country. He gets a lot of goals from the midfield and can outrun any opponent. He wears down his marker in games to join up with the attack.'

The only other representative games I played in were for the Scottish League against the English League at Hampden in March 1976 – we lost 1–0 – and for a Glasgow Select against a Football League XI, again at Hampden, in May 1977. It was arranged to mark the Queen's Silver Jubilee and ended in a 2–1 win for us, with goals by Sandy Jardine and Kenny Dalglish. The strip we wore became something of a collector's item, comprising as it did the colours of all four Glasgow clubs – Rangers, Celtic, Partick Thistle and Queen's Park. If Third Lanark had still been in existence then somehow the designers would have had to incorporate theirs as well. Willie Ormond, my old gaffer at St Johnstone, took charge of our team, and I'll never forget an exchange between Kenny and him that took place in the dressing room beforehand.

Kenny said something like, 'Haw, boss, what do we say to the Queen when we shake hands with her before kick-off?' Willie, who was always great with the one-liners, instantly came back with, 'Just ask her, "Where's the party the night, hen?"' In truth, he said a bit more than that but if I tell you his full response, I doubt if I'll ever be invited to any royal gathering at Holyrood Palace.

Wee Willie was one of Scottish football's great characters, and a very good man-manager as well. I was much saddened when he passed away at a relatively young age in 1984.

11

FUN AND GAMES ON TOUR

How can I forget the name of Rioch? No, not Bruce Rioch who captained Scotland in the World Cup finals in Argentina and was among those players posted missing through injury on the occasion of my only appearance at international level. I'm talking, rather, of his brother Neil. He made a less than favourable impression on me when, in the wake of winning the Treble in 1976, Rangers headed across the Atlantic for a summer series of games in North America.

We were drawing 1–1 with his side, Portland Timbers, when he hacked me to the ground with a wild swipe. Only he knew what I'd done to deserve such treatment, but he couldn't have been prepared for what happened next. A gang of our players, led by Alex Miller and Tam Forsyth, literally chased him off the park. Then Jock Wallace, while obviously incensed by what he'd witnessed, sprang off the bench in a bid to restore order in a match we ended up winning 2–1 with a late goal by Alex O'Hara. In my book, there was no such thing as a friendly. Quite evidently, Neil Rioch was of the same outlook.

Yet in saying as much, we had a lot of laughs on that trip, starting on our flight from Glasgow to Vancouver the day after Scotland had beaten England 2–1 at Hampden in the Home International Championship. Big Tam (Forsyth) played especially well in that match, the highlight of his performance being a superb tackle on Mick Channon as the England player lined up to score an equaliser. Anyway, as our aircraft reached its cruising altitude,

John Greig thought he would have a laugh at Tam's expense by asking one of the stewardesses to say there was a call for him. Tam took the phone which, of course was just the inter-com, and found himself speaking to Greigie, who was pretending to be a reporter from a London-based newspaper and wanting to do a story about his Hampden heroics. It was the wind-up to beat any other. We were all up the back of the plane listening in.

At first, Tam was curious to know how this inquisitor had got his number, but Greigie got round that quite nimbly, saying that the top newspapers had contacts in all the airlines. That seemed to satisfy Tam, who became hooked from then onwards. Greigie, quite adept at putting on the English accent, proceeded to throw all sorts of questions at him and he, obviously flattered by the attention, answered them one by one. At the end, Greigie promised him a payment for his help and Tam asked that it be sent on to him at one of the hotels we were due to be staying. 'Take a look up the back of the plane,' John told him then. He did, to see all of us falling about with laughter. The penny had dropped, with a clang loud enough to be heard above the noise of the engines.

Our opening match against Vancouver Whitecaps resulted in a 2–2 draw. Then we were back on a plane again to face Seattle Sounders, hoping our old team-mate, Dave Smith, who had joined them, might be in opposition. In the event, Dave didn't play, but we quickly recognised Gordon Wallace, the former Dundee and Raith Rovers centre-forward, who was spending the summer with the American club. Another face familiar to us was Sounders' assistant manager, Jimmy Gabriel, who had played for Dundee, Everton and Scotland.

We felt like trailblazers, playing on artificial turf for the first time in the experience of many of us. Jock Wallace was well pleased by our performance, even if we let the opposition off lightly by winning only 1–0 with a headed goal by myself midway through the second half. I can remember making my way back to the centre circle and watching my scoring effort being replayed on a big screen. Again, this was something quite futuristic as far as we were concerned. The host club were into statistics in a big way too, and calculated that we made twenty-nine scoring attempts, or one every three minutes. One of them, by John Greig, was described in the travelling press as having 'broken the altitude record' for the Seattle Dome stadium.

There had been various attempts over the decades to popularise 'soccer' in North America. The mid-1970s were witness to another of them, but given the shortage of home-grown players, the teams tended to be very reliant on importing players from Britain or mainland Europe. The role of touring sides like ourselves was, if you like, to preach the gospel of football to a wider public, for the ex-pats still made up a fair proportion of the crowds. Certainly, there was no shortage of Scots in attendance that time in Seattle. They, like ourselves, would have appreciated the fact we took the field to the strains of a pipe band playing 'Scotland the Brave'.

We were no less pleased to hear Jimmy Gabriel say afterwards of Rangers, 'They made nonsense of the allegations they rely on strength. Anybody who understands the game was thrilled by what they did out on that field in strange conditions. They should have massacred us, and probably would have done on "real" ground.' He might have added 'if they'd had a decent night's kip, as well' because we'd hardly had time to put our feet up, never mind hit a pillow, since leaving Glasgow the previous weekend. The match against Portland Timbers came only twenty-four hours later, and three days on from then we drew 2–2 with Minnesota Kicks.

A whole four days after that, with suitcases full of dirty washing, we were back over the border to Canada to beat Toronto Metros-Croatia. At least we had some time there to look around and do our laundry. Some of us, like Alex Miller and myself, had relatives or friends in that area and got them to wash our shirts for us. We also had a few meals at their houses, which saved us dipping into our daily spending allowances. Skinflints, eh? Then having completed our schedule of five games in twelve days, it was back to Glasgow for the rest we'd truly earned after our historic Treble of the domestic season.

Join the Navy and see the world, they used to say. I saw plenty of it with Rangers, having gone right round the globe the summer before. Willie Waddell reckoned the effects of jetlag would be lessened if we went in a westerly direction, hence the reason our first stop was Vancouver, where we played and beat 4–0 a British Columbia XI. Graham Fyfe scored twice on that occasion, while Bobby McKean and myself shared our other goals. Then it was down to New Zealand, where we kicked off by beating Auckland 3–1 with two goals by Derek Johnstone, and another by yours truly. I got a kick on the sole of my foot in that game, without thinking too much about it. But in our next game, a 2–2 draw with a Canterbury XI, I cracked a bone in the same area. I actually heard it go and ended up in hospital.

Rae Simpson, our chairman, who was a surgeon, told me not to let the doctors put a plaster on it, only a crepe bandage. When I passed on this instruction to the medic in charge, he looked at me as if to say, 'You're in my hospital. I'll do what I think is best.' Just at that moment, Mr Simpson walked into the examination room and had a discussion with him. At the end, I was strapped with a crepe bandage. I think what Rae was trying to say was that if they put a stookie on my foot and leg, the calf muscle would start to wither, making my recovery time so much longer. He must have made a good call because within a week I was running about with a wee high-heeled shoe.

We were in Australia by that point, after a flight I was never likely to forget. I doubt if Ally Dawson, who sat beside me, will have forgotten it either. As we headed into this big, black cloud, Ally's knuckles were white as he clung on to the armrests on his seat. Jock Wallace saw this and told me to break his grip so that Ally could relax a bit. I wasn't exactly sitting comfortably either, I would have to say. My tour was effectively over, in the playing sense at least. I can recall saying to Big Jock when we were in

Sydney that I wanted just to go home. I was no use to the team, after all. There didn't seem much point in me hanging about, but he talked me out of the idea.

There were other things I could do on the club's behalf. Among them was going to a TV studio to give an interview. Willie Thornton came with me and asked to see the list of questions I would be asked. One was: 'Why don't Rangers sign Catholics?' Willie got it scored out. Another was: 'How much do you earn?' Again, Willie drew a line through it. At the end, I was given a bottle of champagne by way of a fee for answering only a couple of questions. The following day, I was off in my ambassadorial role again, this time to a school called Ibrox Park for a question and answer session with some of the pupils. At one point, I took off from round my neck my Cup Winners' Cup medal so it could be shown around the class. A while later, with the session just about to end, I put my hand to my throat and realised my medal hadn't come back to me, so had to say, 'Naebody gets out of here until it's handed over.' Eventually someone came clean and the medal was returned to me safely.

It remained my prize possession until I was mugged in Benidorm while on holiday earlier this year. Christine and I were on our way back from the Ibrox Bar in the town when a young guy jumped me from behind and ripped the gold chain from around my neck. He couldn't have known there was a medal hanging from it. I tried to chase him but I was never the fastest. I feel more embarrassed than anything else. There's no point in becoming depressed or resentful about something like that. But getting back to Australia, we ended up playing five games in almost as many days on that last leg of our world tour, in Sydney, Brisbane, Melbourne, Adelaide and Perth. Talk about gruelling. No wonder we lost two matches in the series. I wouldn't recommend that kind of schedule to any player. But the Rangers fans in exile seemed glad to see us and helped swell the crowd figures in at least a couple of the venues to more than 30,000. Throughout my time with the club, and regardless of where in the world we played, I never ceased to be amazed by the number of our fans who turned up. But then there are Rangers supporters clubs dotted all over. It doesn't matter how long these folk have been away from Scotland, they don't seem to lose their pride in the colours.

Besides competitive European ties and the tours I've mentioned above, my travels with Rangers took me to far-flung places like Israel and The Emirates. Closer to home, Scandinavia was a regular destination for pre-season matches. Likewise Germany. I remember once when we were in the latter and I was rooming as usual with Sandy Jardine, having a helluva job trying to sleep. So, come the back of six o'clock that morning, as I'm pacing the floor again, I decided to turn Sandy's watch on by a couple of hours. Now, Sandy was a boy for his breakfast. He never liked to miss it. I gave him a shake and said, 'Hey, it's about time we were downstairs.' We threw on our clothes and stumbled to the breakfast room. 'Where is everybody?' Sandy was saying. He thought they'd all gone training without us when, in fact, it was only about 6:30 a.m. I doubt if he was best pleased with me when I wised him up.

Football players are always game for a laugh, especially when the pressure is off. With guys like Cutty Young and Johnny 'Dingy' Hamilton in the company, the laughs were aplenty. Don't ask me where we were the time that this pair decided to make a punch for a party we were having. In went a dash of this, then a dash of that. I had a bottle of Pernod and tried to tell Dingy not to add it to the mix. He did – and ruined the concoction. All we could taste was the Pernod,which of course didn't suit everyone's palate. I often wondered after that how Dingy managed to get a parttime job working in Jim Baxter's pub near Paisley Road Toll. Maybe it was because Jim didn't do cocktails.

12

AND ANOTHER TREBLE, PLEASE

My time at Ibrox spanned almost twelve years, yet I could have been out on my ear after eight. Why? I walked out on the team at half time in a crucial match after taking the spur at something Jock Wallace said to me. The infamous occasion in question, which I referred to in the opening passage of this book, was a League Cup quarter-final against Clydebank in season 1976–77. What heavy weather we'd made of trying to beat them, drawing 3–3 at home and 1–1 away in what was a two-legged affair.

A decider was set for Ibrox, but it ended goal-less. So the teams had to face one another yet again, this time at Firhill. Anyway, during the first half of that game, Clydebank worked a throw-in movement involving my pal from our time of growing up together in the city, Jimmy Lumsden. I let Wee Lummie go by me, with the Bankies setting up an attack as a result. When we went in at the interval, Big Jock shouted at me something to the effect of, 'You should have kicked him.' Now then, contrary to what folk thought about me, I wouldn't have kicked my granny in order to win a match. I was no more inclined to kick my life-long buddy.

I lost the rag with the gaffer, pulled off my playing gear and changed quickly into my civvies. Then I headed for the door, saying, 'F**k you. You're trying to say I wisnae trying.' Then I headed for the car, which was parked close to the stadium, and never stopped until I got to the Kincaid House Hotel near Kirkintilloch, which was my local.

'Gie's a pint,' I said to the guy behind the bar.

'I thought you were meant to be playing tonight,' he said.

'I WIZ playing,' I told him, pulling up my trouser leg to show him the dirt on my knee.

It was then the owner of the hotel appeared and held up the (spoof) newspaper carrying the headline: 'MacDonald Joins Celtic'. But I've told you about that already, and how I reacted.

In the circumstances, and for all I knew, Rangers could have decided on the night to put me up for sale. I'd committed the unpardonable sin of deserting my team-mates, even though they'd finally overcome the Bankies 2–1 in my absence. I also had to answer to Wee Lummie, who I'd promised to give a lift home. But that could come later. I had to face Big Jock in the morning and didn't look forward to doing so. Quite how he explained to the press after the game why I hadn't reappeared for the second half, I've no idea. Maybe it was just assumed I'd been substituted, either because of injury or for tactical reasons, therefore nobody asked the question.

It was a rather sheepish Alex MacDonald who turned up for training the next day, half expecting to be pinned up against the wall of the dressing room and made to give a grovelling apology. One way or another, I sensed I could have done my career no good whatsoever. Give Big Jock his due, though. He just said to me outside the changing area in that gruff tone of his, 'Get yersel back in here.' He left me out for the following game, but I was back in for the next again, the League Cup semi-final against Aberdeen at Hampden.

What a going-over Ally MacLeod's side gave us. I wince even yet when I think of the scoreline: Rangers 1, Aberdeen 5. The fact I scored our goal was of absolutely no consequence. In saying that, Aberdeen were a good side at the time. They went on to beat Celtic 2–1 after extra time in the final, and partly on the back of that success, Ally was appointed manager of Scotland, in succession to Willie Ormond, before the season had ended.

By the way, among the players he proceeded to take with him on a pre-World Cup tour of South America in the summer of 1977 was Davie Cooper. This was the self-same guy who, having just signed for Rangers by then, had given us no end of trouble in that League Cup quarter-final saga before the turn of the year. From memory, Davie scored in three of the four games that Clydebank took us to. Quite obviously, Jock Wallace and Willie Waddell had earmarked him at the time as a potential Rangers player, and as we know, he turned out to be among the most popular the club had had in many a year. But let's track back here to the beginning of season 1976–77, one in which so much was expected of us after doing the Treble the season before.

Our opening league match was against Celtic at Parkhead, and having sped into a 2–0 lead with goals by Derek Johnstone and Derek Parlane, it seemed as if we were set to continue on our conquering way. But Celtic pulled us back to 2–2 and in the process helped set the tone for our challenge in the championship. Our opening eight games yielded only as many points, with Celtic proceeding to beat us 1–0, at Ibrox and Parkhead respectively, at our next two times of meeting. Back then, as now, the team with the better record in these Old Firm encounters tended to end up winning the title. We could only draw 2–2 when we played them a fourth time and they finished as champions, nine points in front of ourselves. What a come-down from twelve months earlier.

There was no accounting for our inconsistency. Derek Parlane did well enough, with sixteen goals in the campaign. Derek Johnstone pitched in with fifteen, while I, pushing from midfield, was next best with nine. Even so, while our respectively defensive records were pretty much on a par, Celtic outscored us by a quite sizeable margin, both home and away. We hadn't done ourselves any favours in the European Cup that season either, even if the first-round draw could have been a lot less kind to us. FC Zurich were our opponents, but we managed only a 1–1 draw with them, courtesy of an equaliser by Derek Parlane, in the first leg at Ibrox after falling behind in the opening minute.

A distinct advantage therefore lay with the Swiss for the return game. We simply had to score, to cancel out their away goal. What we couldn't afford to do though was lay ourselves open to being hit on the break. In the event, they scored in only eight minutes. Despite all our subsequent efforts, Zurich went through on a 2–1 aggregate. Looking back, we were especially naive in that tie. Our usual approach to European games was to let the opposition worry about us. We needed to wise up if ever we were to replicate the success we'd enjoyed in winning the Cup Winners' Cup in 1972. It was as if continental sides could see us coming, and by not taking the necessary precautions, their greater cunning tended to become our undoing.

Aberdeen seriously exposed the same weakness in us in the League Cup semi-final I mentioned earlier, and with our chance of winning the Premier Division title eventually slipping away, the Scottish Cup presented us with our only hope of redemption that season. Only Falkirk managed to score against us as we made our way to the final with successive wins over them, Elgin City, Motherwell and Hearts. Guess who awaited us at Hampden? Celtic, of course, and they fairly compounded our misery by winning 1–0. There is nothing about that occasion I care to dwell on. It rained heavily, our fans were relatively subdued, and the game turned on a moment's controversy midway through the first half.

Did Derek Johnstone handle the ball on the line then as my namesake and future colleague at Hearts, Roddy MacDonald, attempted to score with a header? Referee Bob Valentine thought so, and I would have to say many in the press agreed with him. Step forward Andy Lynch to score from the spot. At least my old team-mate at Ibrox, Alfie Conn, finished the match with a smile on his face. Jock Stein, back in harness after his car crash, had signed him for Celtic from Spurs a couple of months earlier in a £65,000 deal. Alfie's switch of Old Firm colours made a lot of headlines in the papers, although not nearly as many as Mo Johnston's many years later when Graeme Souness signed him for Rangers.

Our triple celebration of the previous season had all but faded from memory, doubtless causing manager Jock Wallace more than a little anguish. What could he, backed by Willie Waddell of course, do to ensure we got back to our winning ways? In came Davie Cooper, who had done so well against us in the League Cup saga I mentioned at the start of this chapter, his signing virtually coinciding with his selection by Scotland for their pre-World Cup trip to South America in the summer of 1977. Rangers paid £100,000 for him and, as events were to prove, it was money well spent. He is remembered to this day, and will be for a long time to come, as one of the club's finest players.

Gordon Smith joined us around the same time, in a £65,000 deal from Kilmarnock, and was to make no less of an impact in season 1977–78, which was about to unfold. But let's hear it too for a third acquisition, Bobby Russell, who arrived from Shettleston. Long gone were the days when senior clubs, especially the likes of Rangers, looked to junior football for talent. Yet it was probably the norm when Jock Wallace played, and Willie Waddell before him. Fair to say, they were given no cause to regret having turned the clock back, what with Bobby needing no time to adjust to the rigours of the senior game.

Straight into our team he went, along with Coop and Smudger, as Gordon Smith was known, thereby giving us yet another injection of skill and craftsmanship and helping set us for the successes which were to come. Bobby, in fact, scored in our opening league match away to Aberdeen, who had taken on my former Old Firm adversary Billy McNeill as manager in succession to Ally MacLeod. In saying that, we contrived to lose it 3–1 and indeed were beaten 2–0 by Hibs at Ibrox the following Saturday. In short, ours wasn't a very auspicious start to the championship campaign, and as I remember it, a section of our fans were heard to howl for Big Jock's blood. But not for long.

A 4–0 win over Partick Thistle at Firhill was followed by a 3–2 victory over Celtic at Ibrox, Gordon Smith scoring twice in both games. We were off on a run which didn't yield a defeat until Christmas Eve, when Aberdeen beat us by the numbing margin of 4–0 at Pittodrie. Hibs held us to a 0–0 draw at Ibrox on Hogmanay, but within the space of eight days, we went on to beat Partick 2–1 away and Celtic 3–1 at home. Those results saw us recover our momentum and take maximum points from all our Premier Division games until we lost 3–0 to Aberdeen at Ibrox in early March. It was clear by then, if not before, that they, rather than Celtic, were to be our closest rivals for the title.

Little did any of us imagine then that, with Dundee United soon to join the Dons as a force in the north-east of the country, we were witnessing the emergence of the so-called New Firm. We proceeded to drop a further six points in as many league games, two of them to Celtic in a 2–0 defeat at Parkhead, with the upshot being we were only a point ahead of Aberdeen with three matches remaining. Two were against Dundee United, at Tannadice and Ibrox respectively, the third and last against Motherwell at Ibrox. We managed to win them all, by 1–0, 3–0 and 2–0, and clinch the championship by two points from Aberdeen.

It's worth noting that of our four league games against them that term we lost three and won one (by 3–1 at home in mid-October). Contrastingly, in matches against Celtic, we won twice, drew once and lost once. They ended up in fifth-top place behind ourselves, Aberdeen, Dundee United and Hibs, having fallen off the pace early on by losing five times on the trot. Maybe we put the hex on them with that 3–2 win at Ibrox in September. We were actually 2–0 down in the first half, Johannes Edvaldsson having scored twice against us. But with Derek Johnstone moving up front thereafter, we became transformed and won well. Anybody who reckoned Jock Wallace didn't have a grasp of tactics would have been confounded by the Big Fella's expertise on that occasion. Jock Stein, his great rival, almost certainly was.

Of course, the championship title didn't come alone to us that season. We'd had the huge satisfaction too of beating Celtic 2–1 in the League Cup Final, with goals by two of our new players, Davie Cooper and Gordon Smith. Smudger had played wide left with Kilmarnock, but on coming to Rangers, he took up a more central role as an auxiliary striker, if you like. Exactly how effectively he performed in it was to be seen in an earlier round of the same competition against Aberdeen at Ibrox, when he struck a hat-trick in what resulted in a mind-blowing 6–1 win for us. Billy McNeill was moved to say after that game, one in which Bobby Russell starred also, that he couldn't recall a better performance by Rangers.

Our participation in the Cup Winners' Cup that season had ended by then, FC Twente of Belgium beating us 3–0 overall after we'd sneaked through on 3–2 aggregate against the Swiss club, Young Boys of Berne, in the opening round. What was it with us in Europe? Since Barcelona in 1972, we simply hadn't done ourselves justice on that front. Yet who at home could stand between us and the fulfilment of our ambition to finish season 1977–78 with a second Treble in just three seasons? With the League Cup and Premier Division title already secured, we could take absolutely nothing for granted as we prepared to face Aberdeen in the final of the Scottish Cup. Berwick Rangers, Stirling Albion, Kilmarnock and in the semi-final Dundee United had been our opponents in the earlier rounds, with a 1–0 win over Stirling at Ibrox registering as our narrowest.

Aberdeen hadn't lost a game since December and must have fancied they had the beating of us at Hampden. But their nerve obviously deserted them because we won more easily than the 2–1 outcome suggested. I got our first goal that day, with a flying header. A photo in the family cuttings book shows me diving to meet the ball square on, with the Dons' international full-back, Stuart Kennedy, powerless to get in the way. Derek Johnstone added a second, and it wasn't until near the end that Aberdeen struck, through a recently signed defender from lower league football in England, Steve Ritchie, who pulled a goal back.

Happy days indeed, and yet another outstanding Hampden memory for yours truly. From having won nowt the previous season, we were hailed once more as the all-conquering heroes of Ibrox. I hitched a ride on Big Peter McCloy's back at one point as we paraded the cup on the pitch. Jock Wallace, whose head a few fans had called for earlier in the season, was given his own ovation as he ran on to to join our celebration. Here's an odd thing, though. When the Manager of the Year announcement was made the following week, the recipient was . . . Billy McNeill. How could that have been, when Big Jock had just cemented his place in Rangers' history by winning his second Treble? It turned out the votes among the press were cast some time earlier, before Rangers had won the title, never mind the Scottish Cup. Jock couldn't have been best pleased. As for Big Billy, maybe he was just a tad embarrassed.

But that was only a minor postscript to a memorable season for Rangers. Far bigger issues were to envelop them and other top Scottish clubs before long.

13

'IS YER GRANNY OK, KID?'

For months, all of Scotland had been agog at the prospect of Ally MacLeod's team participating in the World Cup finals in Argentina. The hype stoked up by the media was something else, with John Greig a beneficiary of it. Sixty-five thousand fans turned out for his testimonial game between Rangers and the national side at Ibrox shortly before the end of season 1977–78. We ended up winning 5–0 and, fittingly, Greigie scored two of our goals. But the result was hardly meaningful and did nothing to dull the nation's sense of anticipation of what was to come in South America.

So, with us having completed our second Treble in three seasons, the back pages of the papers were cleared for the remaining build-up to the great event on the far side of the world. Day after day, the headlines focused solely on Ally and his squad – until, that is, two momentous things happened at club level to divert the public's attention. The first was Jock Wallace's resignation from Rangers, the second was the way-going from Celtic of his great rival, Jock Stein. Who could have seen either event coming?

Our Big Jock quit little more than a fortnight after we'd lifted the Scottish Cup at Hampden – and only a few days before some 30,000 Scotland fans congregated there to give the national squad, including my club-mates Sandy Jardine, Tam Forsyth and Derek Johnstone, a hearty send-off to Argentina. I remember being stunned by the news and was still trying to take it in when, with the World Cup not yet underway, the other Big Jock stood down from Parkhead.

All the medals I'd collected by that stage in my career at Rangers I owed in no small way to Jock Wallace. He'd turned Rangers into winners, initially as a coach under Willie Waddell, then subsequently as team manager in his own right. I was certain to miss his presence both at the training ground and in the dressing room, even if I needed no introduction to the man appointed within a day or so as his successor, John Greig. One of Jock's great strengths was man-management. He was great at getting everybody together. I can remember us once being abroad one pre-season, I think it was, and him saying, 'Right, after training tonight, we'll meet in that bar across the road from the hotel at nine o'clock.'

It saved everybody going their separate ways and helped turn us into a unit. The side effect was that he knew where everyone was and could be sure no one was getting up to any nonsense. That particular time, Derek Johnstone must have saved us a fortune on the collective drinks bill. With every round ordered, the barman would stick another tab in front of us. There was quite a pile eventually, but without Jock noticing, Derek removed some and stuck them in his pocket. What is it they say . . . you can take the boy out of Dundee, but not Dundee out of the boy?

Another aspect of Jock's way with people was that he had a word for each and every one. I can recall this one morning before training at Ibrox when he saw me looking a bit glum. He followed me into the dressing room, asking, 'What's wrong, kid? Yer granny ok?' It was his way of showing that if you had a problem of any sort you could always speak to him about it. He was portrayed in the papers as something of a fighting man, and understandably so, in that he'd spent much of his National Service in the Malayan jungle battling the 'commies', as he used to call them. But with us, he didn't lose his temper very often, if at all. He was too big for that. Tactically, he wasn't bad either. There were a few occasions going into games when some of the older players would change things from the way Jock had suggested. But that was just us reading things according to how we assessed our ability rather than the way he assessed it. He was actually quite a deep thinker about the game.

Nobody could be quite sure at the time why Jock left Rangers so suddenly for Leicester City. As clubs, they didn't begin to compare, and at the time, Leicester were in the English Second Division. My reading of the situation was simply that he'd been tapped and made a good offer. Maybe he turned to Rangers – Willie Waddell in particular – and said, 'Can you better that?' The answer was, 'No,' so he threw in his keys and walked away. A good friend of mine, Ibrox historian David Mason, later confirmed this to have been the case in his book *Rangers: The Managers*.

As for Greigie taking over, I don't think any of us had a problem with that. I certainly didn't. Everybody respected him for what he'd achieved as both player and captain. They knew how solid his commitment to the club was. Whatever he told us, we were expected to do. He never had to suffer any backchat from those of us who had been his team-mates for so long – certainly none from me.

The transition from player to manager, which he'd been asked to make literally overnight, couldn't have been easy for him. Nor could he have been enamoured with the start we made to the new season, with only one win (4–1 at home to Motherwell) in our first nine matches in defence of the title we'd been so proud to win those few months earlier. Give Greigie his due, though, we made a far quicker and better impression in Europe than we'd done for some time, with no less formidable a side than Juventus awaiting us in the first round of the European Cup. Ok, we lost the away leg by 1–0, but everybody agreed we did well to hold the Italians to that score in front of a frenzied crowd of 70,000 in Turin. Sandy Jardine played at sweeper on that occasion, helping keep us secure at the back after we'd fallen behind in only the eighth minute.

Going on 45,000 fans turned up for the return match at Ibrox. What a din they made to help propel us to a 2–0 win which took us through on aggregate. The new manager had instilled in us the need to be patient, with a newspaper report of the next morning attesting: 'Rangers waited for the breaks, they forced the Italians into making mistakes and snatched the chances which come so rarely against such teams.' Juventus, by the way, were a side comprising no fewer than nine players from Italy's World Cup squad, yet we got ourselves in front of them after only seventeen minutes. Here's how the goal came. Tommy McLean slipped a free-kick to Bobby Russell, who in turn fed the ball to Alex Forsyth, who hadn't long joined us. Alex, a bit off balance, tried a shot, which was blocked. Gordon Smith followed up with another effort, one which Dino Zoff could only parry, before I stepped in to score with a header.

Smudger headed our second goal, on sixty-eight minutes, after Bobby Russell had picked him out in the penalty box with a good ball. What a result was in the offing. Juventus came on strongly towards the end, as was to be expected, but couldn't break us down. Never before, apparently, had Rangers come back to win a European tie after losing the first leg. So there we were, making club history as we progressed to the next round and a tie with another highly rated set of opponents, PSV Eindhoven. Like Juventus, the Dutch were bolstered by a fair number of World Cup players – in their case, guys who had finished as runners-up to the host nation, Argentina, in the tournament. It took a great performance by their goalkeeper, Ton Van Engelen, to hold us to a 0–0 draw at Ibrox and the odds seemed to be stacked against us in the return.

PSV's record at home suggested they were as good as invincible there. No European side had ever beaten them on their own patch. The chances of us being the first appeared to be reduced the more when they took the lead in the opening minute and held it until half time. Imagine my relief, and Rangers' relief, when I managed to score quite early in the second half. PSV promptly hit back before Derek Johnstone claimed our second equaliser. Unbelievably, we were as good as through, but just to make sure, Bobby Russell struck a superb goal in the dying minute, from a great ball by Tommy McLean, for a 3–2 win. This was the same Bobby Russell who less than eighteen months beforehand had

That's me, aged about sixteen, in the middle of the front row of the Glasgow United team for whom I played before joining St Johnstone.

Here I am aged about fourteen, standing back row, one in from the right, after picking up a medal with Tottenham boys' club side who played in Glasgow.

Off on a training trek up Kinnoull Hill (near Perth) with St Johnstone, led by manager Willie Ormond. I'm to his right, with the number 1

Me and my dog, Blue.

On our marks: Willie Waddell putting us through our paces with Rangers.

Tommy McLean about to shake hands with the Queen before the match at Hampden to mark her Silver Jubilee in 1977. I'm next to do the honours.

Is it a bird? Is it a plane? No, it's me scoring with a flying header in the League Cup Final against Celtic in 1975.

Celebration time after I score for Rangers against Juventus in a 2-0 win at Ibrox in 1978.

All smiles at Hampden after we beat Aberdeen in the Scottish Cup final of 1978 to secure the

Showing off a glittering array of trophies in the Blue Room at Ibrox.

Back at Ibrox after Barcelona, and just about to parade the European Cup Winners' Cup in front of the fans.

Up I get to score our first goal against Juve at Ibrox. Gordon Smith running behind

There are a few sore heads in this picture. Taken at our hotel outside Barcelona the morning after we won the Cup Winners' Cup.

A Barcelona old boys reunion at Ibrox. Don't see Sandy Jardine. Maybe he took the photo.

Me in a tussle with my wee pal from
Ibrox, Tommy McLean, after I'd
moved from Rangers to Hearts.

Here I am in a pensive
mood during a game
with Hearts.

On parade at Tynecastle in readiness for season 1983-84.

Sandy Jardine and I must be wondering how we can put some

'V' for Victory – we hope – as the Hearts boys pose at Tynecastle circa 1986.

A penny for my thoughts in the Hearts dugout.

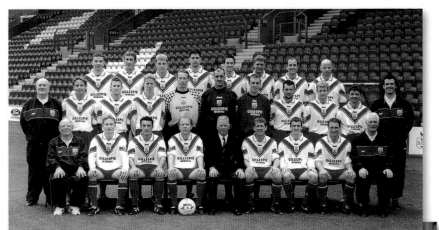

Lining up with Airdrie after we'd got the keys to our new stadium in 1998.

Next stop Hampden, as the Airdrie lads prepare to leave our hotel at Seamill for the 1992 Scottish Cup final with Rangers.

I'm in good company here, with Ally McCoist of Rangers, after we'd been presented with monthly awards at Turnberry.

The sing-song can wait as Rod Stewart, referee Bill Innes and I prepare for kick-off in a charity match at Firhill.

Rangers Great Bob McPhail and me showing off some silverware

Wee Doddy Easy Ranger

Great to be back on the saddle of a Harley while attending a Rangers fans' convention in Florida.

Checkmate? Impressionist Jonny Watson about to meet his match at chess while we're on a charity assignment in Cuba with Dukla

been plying his craft at junior level with Shettleston. What an important player he turned out to be for us in that brief timespan. He was a fine passer of the ball and, as he showed on that momentous occasion in Eindhoven, he could be no less poised in front of goal. I could never quite get my head round the fact he never played for Scotland, Sure, he was slight of build, but then again so was the man to whom many people likened him: the revered John White of Spurs, who won twenty-two caps in the early 1960s before losing his life in a tragic accident on the golf-course when, taking shelter from a storm under a tree, he was struck by lightning. Anyway, with Bobby's valuable assistance, we were through to the quarter-finals of the Champions Cup for the first time since 1964–65. Not since our run to Barcelona in 1971–72 had we had European football to look forward to after Christmas. We couldn't wait for March when we were paired with Cologne.

Unfortunately, a harsh Scottish winter conspired against us, causing a pile-up of domestic fixtures and leaving us stretched for personnel by the time we played the first leg in Germany. We ended up losing 1–0 over there and in the return leg at Ibrox fell behind early in the second half. We just didn't have the wherewithal to turn the score around, Tommy McLean's eventual goal for a 1–1 draw being, as they say, too little, too late. Maybe we could derive some solace from the domestic competitions, starting with the League Cup Final, which was scheduled for the end of March. We'd beaten Celtic 3–2 in the semi-final as far back as mid-December, with our Alex Miller and their Tommy Burns sent off in that match, and keenly anticipated returning to Hampden to face Aberdeen.

Alex Ferguson had taken charge of them at the start of the season, replacing Billy McNeill, who'd gone back to Celtic as Jock Stein's replacement. This then was to be Fergie's first final in management, the first of goodness knows how many, we came to learn, as he guided the Dons to unprecedented success before doing likewise with Manchester United. Aberdeen actually took the lead through Duncan Davidson, then controversy took a hand in proceedings. At the time of my equaliser, goalkeeper Bobby Clark was lying injured. The Dons players all protested that play should have been held up so Bobby could get treatment. But that was a matter for the referee and not them to decide. I did what I had to do in the circumstances, by putting the ball in the net. Big Doug Rougvie was sent off subsequently after an incident involving Derek Johnstone, and Colin Jackson headed the decisive goal in the last minute.

Our dismal start to the championship season, which I touched on earlier, included a 3–1 defeat by Celtic at Parkhead, and we could only draw 1–1 with them at Ibrox in November. What with the winter proceeding to play havoc with our fixtures and the fact Ibrox was undergoing renovation, we didn't play them again until May – at Hampden. I managed to score on that occasion, giving us a 1–0 win, but we messed up badly later in the month when we went to Parkhead for the teams' fourth, and last, league meeting of the campaign, losing 4–2. Celtic took the title as a result, despite having Johnny Doyle sent off after I'd put us in front and Bobby Russell scoring later. We'd actually played Hibs in the Scottish Cup Final by that point, drawing 0–0, and a first replay yielded the same result. So a week after squandering our chance of winning the championship, we faced Hibs a third time.

The crowd was only 31,000, a drop of 20,000 from the first game and 3,000 or so down from the second. But those fans who stayed away missed a whole lot more excitement than was generated in the previous two games, what with Derek Johnstone scoring twice for us and Tony Higgins and Alistair MacLeod getting goals for Hibs. So the match spilled over into extra time, when Arthur Duncan had the misfortune to deliver us a 3–2 win by knocking the ball into his own net. Needless to say, we were delighted to retain the trophy, but what an effort it had required. With Partick Thistle having taken us to a replay in the semi-final, we'd had to play no fewer than nine games. That was four more than the previous year when we'd beaten Aberdeen in the final. Fair to say the close-season, long overdue, couldn't come quickly enough

– even if we hadn't quite forgiven ourselves for blowing the title that fateful night at Celtic Park.

What might the following season, which was to be my last at Ibrox, bring by way of rewards? Well, it kicked off quite brightly for us in what was a new, if short-lived, tournament called the Drybrough Cup. Having beaten Berwick Rangers and Kilmarnock in quick succession, we faced our oldest rivals, Celtic, in the final at Hampden and won 3–1. A young namesake of mine, John McDonald, scored our first goal and Sandy Jardine the second, but it was our third by Davie Cooper that remains implanted in people's memories. I can see him yet, flicking the ball over the heads of four Celtic players without letting it touch the deck, then stroking it into the net. Coop, in that famous instant, took Hampden's collective breath away. And not for the last time either. The season after I left, with Dundee United having held Rangers to a goal-less draw in the Scottish Cup Final, he gave a sensational display in the replay which 'we' won 4–1.

14

THE END IS NIGH AT IBROX

With season 1979–80 underway, I could reflect on almost eleven years with Rangers. Hadn't they been fruitful too, with no fewer than twelve winners' medals coming my way? At the time of my signing from St Johnstone in November 1968, the club were becoming ever more anxious about Celtic's domination of the domestic scene. In the event, it took us until 1975 to break their monopoly on the league title, which had stretched to nine successes in a row by then. But we'd claimed it on two more occasions since, in 1976 and 1978, the years in which we won the Treble.

Poor Davie White, the manager who'd shown sufficient faith in my ability as a kid to pay £50,000 for me, had been sacrificed in Rangers' failed attempts to thwart our Old Firm rivals, likewise Scot Symon before him. Some good players, Alex Ferguson among them, had had their Ibrox careers cut short too as a result of the hex Celtic held over us. Remember, it was their 4–0 win against us in the Scottish Cup Final which did for him. He should have stopped Billy McNeill from heading the first goal, or so the critics said. I ask you. Big Billy was one of the best in the business in these situations. Not many players could compete with him in the air.

Fergie has claimed subsequently that the fact he was married to a Catholic further undermined his time with Rangers. That's not something I can comment upon, simply for the reason I knew nothing of anybody plotting against him for any reason. Anyway, he moved on, first to Falkirk, then Ayr United, before quitting as player in the early- to mid-1970s. Alex opened a pub around that time near my old stomping ground of Kinning Park, and my mother-in-law, Isa, and brother-in-law, Tommy, both gave him a hand out in it.

But the pull of football was too strong to keep him stuck behind a bar for long. Into management he went, briefly with East Stirling before moving to St Mirren. Then, having joined Aberdeen in 1978 and given up the pub, fate decreed that Fergie was about to start haunting Rangers – and his old pal from their playing days together at Ibrox, John Greig. Within the space of a month in 1979, his Dons side beat us three times: 3–1 in the Premier Division at Pittodrie and 3–1 and 2–0 in the League Cup, which by then was being played on a home and away basis in its earlier rounds. Given how Dundee United were beginning to shape up at the time under Jim McLean, Scottish football was witnessing the rise of the so-called New Firm as a rival to the Old.

I dare say I could have tipped that Fergie would make a good manager, if not the great one he was destined to become both in Scotland and England. In our relatively brief spell of being together at Ibrox and on the various occasions we lined up in opposition to one another, I could see he was nothing if not competitive – a bit like myself, if you like. This quality assuredly rubbed off on Aberdeen players like Willie Miller, Alex McLeish and Gordon Strachan. He implanted in them, and others, a winning mentality, not least by kidding them into thinking that everybody, from referees to the press, wished them no favours.

Still, having won the Double of Scottish Cup and League Cup in John Greig's first season as manager and suffered a near-miss in the championship, there was no way we – or Celtic, for that matter – could have sensed Aberdeen would make such a profound impression as the one which followed by winning their first title since 1955. We kicked off well enough in the league, beating Hibs 3–1 at Easter Road with goals by myself, Davie Cooper and Bobby Russell. Then came a 2–2 draw with Celtic at Ibrox, a result which didn't exactly set any alarm bells ringing in our heads, even though Celtic had been 2–0 down at one point and had Roy Aitken sent off. But our subsequent 2–1 defeat by Partick Thistle signalled the start of a woeful spell for us, one in which we won just four games out of a dozen. The month of December saw us arrest our poor form sufficiently that we strung three victories together, against Kilmarnock, Morton and Dundee United. We hit a similar, good spell in February. But before and after, oh, dear, we fell far short of the fans' expectation.

Aberdeen duly lifted the title, a point ahead of Celtic and eleven points in front of us, as we languished in equal fourth position alongside Dundee United. Maybe it said something about the legacy Fergie had left behind at St Mirren that they actually finished third top. Our away form had been especially poor, what with twelve games out of eighteen lost and two drawn. Like I said earlier, Aberdeen had knocked us out of the League Cup on a 5–1 aggregate in the third round and reached the final, only to lose to Dundee United. There was a further sign of the New Firm's emergence. As for our European challenge that season, suffice to say we hadn't shown quite the same spark as we had in the preceding one.

The preliminary round of the Cup Winners' Cup had us paired with Lillestrom, who we could only beat 1–0 at home, but a goal by myself, and another by Derek Johnstone, saw us win the away leg 2–0. Next up were Fortuna Dusseldorf, with me and Tommy McLean scoring to give us a 2–1 win over them at Ibrox. Over in Germany, where Peter McCloy played a starring role despite his sight being impaired through a first-half injury, we drew 0–0. So it was a case of so far, so good. A subsequent 1–1 draw with Valencia in Spain, with Wee Tam our marksman, was better still. But they were too strong for us in the return at Ibrox, winning 3–1 with a couple of great goals by Mario Kempes, who'd helped Argentina win the World Cup in 1978. So it was that we were left looking to the Scottish Cup as a means of salvaging a degree of consolation from our season.

Consolation, did I say? I was in need of commiseration come the second half of that season, in that my senses were telling me I might be falling out of favour with John Greig. He'd signed Ian Redford from Dundee for £210,000, and while I played in our 2–2 draw with Clyde as the Cup got underway, it was to be the only tie I started in the tournament. Come February in the league, I began to find myself nominated as a substitute, if at all. Some of us in the team, Sandy Jardine, Alex Miller and Colin Jackson, for example, weren't getting any younger. Me? I was coming up thirty-two, and while I didn't think I'd lost anything, the manager appeared to have his doubts as to how much I still had to offer.

I can recall around that time taking a bit of stick for not tackling with quite the same gusto as before. But I felt my game had moved on a bit. Rather than launch into a challenge and risk being caught out, I thought it better to stand up to an opponent. That, by the way, was a philosophy I was to take with me into management. 'Stay on your feet,' I would tell my players at Hearts and Airdrie. But whether I was doing things to John Greig's satisfaction was another matter. He was the boss – even if, latterly, I didn't always appreciate his style of man-management. Thereby hangs a story, as they say.

Sandy Jardine and I liked to get to Ibrox early for games so that we were away from any distractions. We'd have a bit of grub, change into our gear, and go play heidie tennis by way of a warm-up and keeping the eye in. This became routine and didn't mean I took the fact that I would be playing for granted. Imagine, though, how I felt on the occasion of one night game when I went back into the dressing room to hear Greigie read out the team and make no mention of me. My cheeks must have been glowing with embarrassment as I picked my civvies down from the peg and went into the physio's room to get changed. I would have felt better about being left out if Greigie had taken me aside beforehand, in training maybe, and given me even a hint of what he had in mind. It was time I took stock of my situation.

Hadn't I always said as a kid that just to play one game for Rangers would be enough for me? They could free me after that. Well, there I was, having played around five hundred matches for the club I grew up supporting. Maybe I should be looking to move on, even though nobody was forcing me towards the door. So I asked Greigie – a couple of times, as I remember it – about the chances of the club letting me go. I remember him saying the directors were thinking about it, but as the end of the season approached, nothing appeared to be happening. That's when I decided the best thing to do was to go straight to the top with my request.

By that, I mean write a letter asking to be released and hand it to the chairman, Rae Simpson. This I did one time we were playing Partick Thistle at Firhill.

He said to me, 'No, no. You'll have to give your letter to the manager.'

I told him, 'No, Mr Simpson. I'm giving it to you.' But the next thing I heard was that Greigie had said to the board he still needed me, for the Scottish Cup Final, I assumed. By the way, despite our lamentable form in the league particularly, we'd done well to get to Hampden again.

After beating Clyde in a replay, we'd knocked out Dundee United, Hearts and Aberdeen in succession. The Hearts result was especially impressive. We beat them 6–1, with my near namesake John McDonald scoring twice. From memory, I don't think I even made the bench for that one.

Anyway, with Celtic awaiting us in the final, we went down to Troon to do our preparations. In one of our practice games, Sandy Jardine was winding up Greigie to pick me for the big game to come. Every time I scored, Sandy was shouting, 'Great goal, Doddie!' Every wee pass I made he was giving it, 'Well done, Dod. Well done.' It got to the stage I had to say to him, 'Gonnae shut up? You're putting me aff.'

It turned out Sandy could have saved his breath. I didn't play at Hampden, not even as a substitute. That, in case anybody needs reminding, was 'The Riot Final', where we lost 1–0 in extra time to a deflected goal by George McCluskey. Fans invaded the field at full time and knocked hell out of one another. It was as a result of those shocking scenes the government imposed a ban on taking alcohol into matches. I could have picked better circumstances in which to bring the curtain down on my Rangers career, if indeed that infamous occasion did prove to be the end for me. In the event, I didn't have long to wait before being told I was free to leave. Assuming some club came in for me, that was. But were there any takers out there?

Close-season speculation involved me, initially at least, with Partick Thistle and I wouldn't have minded a move to Firhill. Other Rangers players had gone there before me, George Niven being a prime example. One of the papers saw fit at the time to write:

> If Alex MacDonald signs for Partick Thistle, it will be the end of an Ibrox era and there will be sighs from thousands of Rangers fans. To them, Doddie was a hero, a grafting, tireless stalwart who typified all they feel is Rangers. He had never the flair of a Baxter, the magic of a Henderson, but he symbolised what former manager Jock Wallace called "the true Rangers spirit, the real Rangers character". For MacDonald gave his all for the club in every game he played. He played it hard and he played it for ninety minutes. Thousands of Rangers fans will now feel that Rangers won't be the same without Alex MacDonald.

Kind words, but no sooner had they appeared in print than John Greig phoned me to say Hearts were interested. Things took off from there. Bobby Moncur, who was their manager at the time, came to speak with me at my house – I was living in Kilsyth by then – and brought with him his chairman, Archie Martin, who turned out to be a great guy, easy to speak to. We duly negotiated and I decided I would sign for them. So I phoned Greigie back and told him the news.

He said, 'Fine, we'll give you two weeks' wages . . . tax-free.'

I went, 'Aye, thanks very much.' After nearly twelve years at Rangers and helping them win two Trebles, as well as the European Cup Winners' Cup, that was the sum of my parting gift from Rangers: two weeks' wages, tax-free. I think Rangers got £35,000 from Hearts, which was only £15,000 less than what they'd paid St Johnstone for me in 1968.

There had never been any question of Rangers giving me a testimonial match, even though other clubs were in the habit of doing so with players after they'd served ten years. John Greig's own benefit game in 1978 against Scotland was the first they'd sanctioned since Davie Meiklejohn's about half a century earlier. I think they took the view that it was an honour to play for Rangers and their players were better paid than most, if not all, in Scotland anyway. Who was I to argue? I'd never been greatly motivated by money and regarded it as a privilege indeed that I'd had the chance to pull on a blue jersey over such a long period. Looking back, my view hasn't changed a bit. Everything about being with such a big and famous club was a pleasure, so far as I was concerned.

Don't get me wrong. It was a blow at the time to leave Ibrox. But how lucky I'd been in the first place to cross their threshhold and claim a place in their dressing room. I could remember so well the day after I'd signed, standing nervously outside the stadium and asking myself, 'Is this real, or am I just imagining it?' It was this same laddie who'd grown up near Ibrox, climbed over the wall to kick a ball about on the hallowed turf, dodged school to watch Willie Henderson and others play heidie tennis in the tunnel. Definitely, I had to be dreaming. Yet as I walked away that day in the summer of 1980, it was with a record of having played five hundred and seventy-nine games for the club and scored a hundred and twenty goals. That was fact rather than fantasy.

What had been the highlights of my time with the club? Obviously beating Moscow Dynamo to win the Cup Winners'

Cup in Barcelona in 1972 was uppermost in my memory. Not far below was scoring the only goal of the game against Celtic at Hampden in 1975, which saw us lift the League Cup and lay the foundation of the first of our two Trebles under Jock Wallace. In all, my haul of medals came to twelve: three Championships, four Scottish Cups and four League Cups, plus the European one. Not bad for a boy from Kinning Park.

Yet my first couple of seasons had been less than memorable because of the nervous tension which affected me. I loved training. Yes, even under Big Jock. But in those early days, I found I left most of my strength on the practice pitch and had nothing left for a Saturday game. Only when Willie Waddell took over at Ibrox, by which time I was beginning to feel a bit more confident, did my career begin to prosper. Players like Willie Henderson and Alex Willoughby were of particular help during my settling-in period, offering me encouragement on a regular basis, and Sandy Jardine became like a blood brother to me. Did he and I have some laughs!

Just about everybody on Rangers' books when I arrived was an internationalist, and trying to match their standards was quite a challenge for me. In saying that, and because of my in-built enthusiasm and stamina, I could hold my own with anyone on the training ground. Occasionally my competitiveness there would get me into bother with team-mates. There was the time, for example, after some argument or other, I ended up giving Gerry Neef a Glasgow kiss. Oh, and I could recall having a scrap too, with Big Orjan Persson. But, generally speaking, I got on pretty well with all the guys around me.

There were some characters among them, Big Ronnie McKinnon being one. Once, when I was still with St Johnstone, I passed him in Buchanan Street in Glasgow and thought he looked a million dollars in this fancy suede coat he wore. At that time, I was buying any gear I had out of Burton's for £1 down and a £1 a week until it was paid off. When finally I joined Rangers, Big Ronnie still wore the same coat, only it had big stains on the shoulders where his kids had been sick. This was the guy who, when he took off his shirt before training, would be wearing a Superman t-shirt underneath. He used to take some ribbing, but nothing ever got to him. Ronnie and Colin Jackson probably were the two most laid-back guys I'd come across in football.

I wouldn't say there were cliques as such at Ibrox, but John Greig, Davie Smith and a few others were pretty close, while the guys I got involved with were the likes of Sandy Jardine and Alex Miller. Come a match day, though, everybody pulled together. That was one of Rangers' greatest strengths in my time: we were a team, in every aspect, with Jock Wallace having been an expert at getting us to bond. I had great respect for him. He was a man's man and always looking out for your welfare. If anybody could get the best out of Wee Doddie, it was Big Jock. Which reminds me: I don't think I've explained so far how I came to be called Doddie.

In those early days, I used to strip beside Erik Sorensen. He could reach the peg for his clothes quite easily, while I had to jump up to reach mine. He started to take the mickey this time about me being one of the little Diddie people. Diddie became Doddie, and like it or not, I've been such with the handle ever since.

15

CULTURE SHOCK AT HEARTS

'Hearts, Hearts, Glorious Hearts.' Hearing that theme song ring out from Tynecastle made a change from the one I knew by heart: 'There's Not a Team like the Glasgow Rangers'. But it was no less stirring. Hearts are endowed with a glorious tradition. It was part of the attraction that moving from Ibrox to Tynecastle held for me. If as a kid growing up in Glasgow in the 1950s I hadn't seen much of them, I could hardly have failed to notice how strong they were in that era.

Their rise to prominence began when they beat Motherwell 4–2 at Hampden in 1954 to lift the League Cup for the first of four times between then and 1962. Then in 1956 they won the Scottish Cup with a 3–1 win over Celtic at the National Stadium. I think their name was on the trophy from early on in that competition, when they thrashed Rangers 4–0 at Tynecastle. By 1958, they had won the League Championship for the first time in more than half a century and were to repeat the feat in 1960.

I would always argue with those who said, maybe still say, that Hearts are just Rangers in maroon jerseys. Their fans didn't like the Glasgow clubs, and I'm not aware anything has changed on that score. In my experience, they would try to wind up Rangers by singing Celtic songs and vice versa. They were very much their own people and, rightly, proud of Hearts' lofty place in the history of the Scottish game. What great players the club had in those bygone days. The Terrible Trio of Alfie Conn, Willie Bauld and Jimmy Wardhaugh were folk heroes. Likewise Davie

Mackay, Alex Young, John Cumming and a whole host of others.

Of course, the intervening years had been less kind to the club known (on one side of the capital at least) as Edinburgh's Darlings. They'd been relegated from the Premier Division in 1977 and 1979, winning promotion within a season in each case. Money, or the lack of it, was the root of their problems. But at least they were back where they belonged – in the Premier Division – by the time I joined them in time for the start of that 1980–81 season. The challenge of trying to keep them there appealed very much to me. Furthermore, I was pledged to prove to myself, as well as others, that Doddie wasn't a spent force at thirty-two.

I was also determined to look the part on arrival for my first day of duty in these new surroundings. In fact, I can see myself yet, dolled up as I was in a black and white herringbone jacket, dark trousers with the crease just so, plus collar and tie. I don't mind saying I would have turned the heads of shoppers in Princes Street had I been standing in Austin Reed's window. So you can imagine the shock I got when other players duly arrived in tatty old denims and casual shirts. As I tuned in to some of the conversations going on among them, I heard one ask another, 'Where were you last night?' Then came the reply, 'I was at a party. In fact, I'm no' long back.'

This other guy – I can't remember his name either – came in with a bag stuffed with goodies, including crisps, chocolate bars and bottles of Coke which he proceeded to set out for team-mates to buy by way of topping up whatever they'd had for breakfast. I got the sense that if he didn't make it as a footballer, he had it in him to become a business tycoon. All the while, as we stripped for training, somebody's transistor radio was blaring out pop music in the background. As I said to Sandy Jardine when I called him later in the day, it was brilliant – like I'd walked into a disco. In truth, the whole scenario was unreal, totally alien to me after – what was it by then? – about fourteen years in professional football with St Johnstone and Rangers.

So we then went to the training ground, it was pouring with rain, and our coach, Tony Ford, said to me, 'Alex, I want you to move down to the far end of the field and clip balls into the goal-keeper.' So much for my keeness to get right into the hard work, but I did as I was told, possibly with a pensive look on my face.

This player, Crawford Boyd, came up to me then and asked, 'What are you thinking about – spending your signing-on fee?'

I looked him straight in the eye and replied, 'Naw, I'm thinkin' about what the f**k am I doin' here.'

Almost nothing about my introduction to Hearts was what I expected, or what I was used to. Even the training was different, with the result being that I began to pick up hamstring problems. That was worrying, insofar as I'd been pretty lucky with injuries until then. Still, things might have been worse. I could have got on the end of one of manager Bobby Moncur's challenges in the bounce games we played. He would come quite late to the training ground as a rule, presumably because he had other things to be getting on with in his office at Tynecastle. But he always made sure he was in time to play in the kick-abouts.

'How many caps have you got, eh?' Bobby would ask as he went about smacking people. He had played sixteen times for Scotland during his successful career with Newcastle United and obviously was quite proud of the fact. I could see my own career coming to a premature end if he played rough with me. Then again, given that he knew Doddie to be a fiery character, maybe he stayed out of my way. For all that, I had a pretty good working relationship with him and Tony Ford. Tony did pretty much every-thing on the training field. I remember once asking Bobby if the boys could do some shooting practice. 'See Tony,' he said. Tony's influence stretched to the dressing room even, in as much as he was the one who pinned up little notices with sayings like, 'If you don't train hard, you don't play hard.' Neither he nor Bobby had anything to worry about with me on that score.

What I learned soon enough was that one of my old Rangers team-mates, Alfie Conn, who arrived at Hearts shortly before I did, had been largely instrumental in my joining them. Apparently, Bobby had asked him who he could sign to stiffen up his midfield, and Alfie had said, 'Why don't you go for the Wee Man, Doddie, at Ibrox?' Not only did Bobby accept Alfie's advice, he wanted to make me captain pretty well straight away, but I wasn't keen on the idea.

I told him, 'Hey, I'm just in the door, and anyway, you've already got a very capable captain in Big Jim Jefferies at left-back. If you want, I'll be your captain in midfield. All you'll need then is another captain up front.' To my mind then, as now, you can't have too many leaders in your team, but Bobby let it be, for a time at least.

A couple of months later, when I think Jim Jefferies may have been out injured or suspended, the manager came back to me and said he wanted me to take over. So I said to him, 'Ok, if you want me to be your captain, I'll be your captain.' To this day, I have the feeling Big JJ didn't take too kindly to being ousted from the role, although if he'd known me better, he would have realised I never went looking for it. No way, that wasn't my style. Much good the change of skipper did us though, as we stumbled through the season and ended up being relegated for the third time in four years.

I'd made my club debut in a 3–2 defeat by Partick Thistle at Firhill on the opening day of the championship season, by which point Airdrie had already knocked us out of the Anglo-Scottish Cup on a 6–3 aggregate. The East of Scotland Shield got underway within a few weeks, and if I remember rightly, it was in a tie with Berwick Rangers that I must given Bobby Moncur some cause to wonder why he'd signed me. The game was decided by penalties, with the manager instructing me to take the first of them.

'But I've never taken a penalty in my life,' I protested.

'Why not?' he asked, with more than a hint of disbelief. 'Well,' I told him, 'I've always just stuck to what I'm good at.' That was one of my maxims as a player and I carried it into management, both with Hearts and Airdrie. I used to say to the players, 'Don't get up in the morning and look in the mirror thinking you're Pelé. Just do what you're good at.'

At the risk of getting ahead of myself here, and just for the record, I actually broke my penalty duck the following season when we went to play Rangers in a closed-door game at Ibrox. We were leading 2–0 when I pushed through on my old colleague, Peter McCloy, who promptly pulled me down. Penalty! I opted to break the habit of a lifetime and take the kick myself. If I may say so, I made a right good job of it too. For years after that, every time I saw Peter, I took great delight in recalling how I'd beaten him from the spot.

Now then, where was I before going off on that tangent? Oh, yes, talking about our bad start to season 1980–81. We finally managed to beat St Mirren in late August, and Kilmarnock in early September. But our third league win didn't come until we met Killie again, this time in early December. One of my few consoling moments in that long interim came when playing Rangers at Ibrox.

We took a good support through with us to Glasgow – big enough to fill the two decks of what I still call the 'Celtic end' – and we didn't need half their encouragement as we battled to avoid a hefty defeat. Rangers were actually leading us 3–0, then I pulled a goal back. The Hearts fans gave out an almighty roar of appreciation, but you can imagine my surprise when the Rangers fans did likewise. They hadn't forgotten me, obviously. Their cheers, coupled with those of our own support, had the hairs on the back of my neck sticking up. It can't have been often, if ever, that a visiting player had got such a rousing reception for scoring at Ibrox. I felt quite proud.

Ayr United had knocked us out of the League Cup by then, our 4–0 defeat in the away leg being especially painful. Just for the record, a teenager by the name of Gary Mackay played as a substitute on that occasion. He, like myself and other older players, wouldn't have wished to reflect upon it with anything other than a feeling of shame. After the turn of the year, we made a quick and inglorious exit from the Scottish Cup, with Morton beating us 3–1 in a replay at Tynecastle. Unfortunately, our form in the

Premier Division hadn't picked up any. Nor would it do so until, by some quirk of fate, we beat Rangers 2–1 at home with an own-goal and another by Frank Liddell.

Could we possibly avoid relegation? A 6–0 trouncing by Celtic at Parkhead seemed to suggest we couldn't, and despite beating Killie and Airdrie in the run-in, we were consigned to the First Division once more. But that seemed like the least of Hearts' worries at the time. Their financial position had worsened during the course of the season and a new owner was being sought. Chairman Archie Martin tempted the Edinburgh bookmaker and well-known Hibs fan, Kenny Waugh, to make an offer. His was countered by one from a certain Glasgow businessman with Edinburgh connections, Wallace Mercer.

I hardly need remind Hearts fans of who eventually won that battle for control at Tynecastle in the summer of 1981. Mr Mercer took over in a blaze of publicity and, throughout what became his historic tenure of the club, continued to make banner head-lines. He was nothing if not a good publicist. Archie Martin, who had helped attract me to Hearts in the first place, was in an unten-able position. By supporting the bid by his bookie friend Kenny Waugh, he had backed the wrong horse. Alex Naylor took over from him, but from the outset there was no question that the reins were in the hands of Mercer.

Manager Bobby Moncur didn't last much longer either, it tran-spired. He and Mercer never gelled, and within a matter of weeks, the man who had signed me a year earlier was off to Plymouth Argyle. That left the question of who might replace him. My old gaffer at Rangers, Jock Wallace, was approached but no deal could be struck with him. Jim McLean, making his name at Dundee United, was sounded out also, but preferred to remain at Tannadice and brick by brick build the side that won the championship a couple of years later. So Tony Ford, who Moncur had brought with him from England, was appointed to the job.

The pressure was on Tony from the start. He had to get Hearts back in the Premier Division within a year, and players like Stewart

McLaren, who was a real battler; Henry Smith and a namesake of mine, Roddy MacDonald, formerly of Celtic, were brought in to help. Not that Tony had much say in any signing policy. Wallace Mercer took control of that side of things, as he did with all others. Where did he find the energy, while looking after his business interests at the same time? But it was evident to me that Hearts' future well-being rested at least as much with their young players as any of us older ones. Gary Mackay, Davie Bowman and John Robertson, of course, proved to be the pick of these kids.

Gary and Davie both had broken through in my first season with the club but were still novices who used to get my gear for me every morning before training. I used to wind them up with one-liners, and while Bow laughed, Gary would just look at me. Then, when they went outside, Gary would say to Davie, 'Is he serious? What does he mean?'

He didn't share my sense of humour, and furthermore, seemed to be a bit intimidated by me. I'll go further still, in fact, by saying I don't think he liked me one bit. Why? Apparently my aggressive style when playing for Rangers against his boyhood heroes, Hearts, used to upset him. He'll tell you himself how, shortly after I arrived from Ibrox, he looked through me in the corridor at Tynecastle when I said good morning to him. I pulled him up about it, saying he didn't have to like me but he could at least show me a bit of respect. It was the way I'd been brought up as a player. If, in my younger days, I'd blanked a senior player like Gary blanked me, I'd have got a kick up the backside for my troubles. But he soon came to realise that as well as being his colleague, I was in a position to pass on valuable experience to him.

Davie Bowman was that bit in front of Gary in terms of his physical development, hence the reason he played in more games during season 1980–81 season. Wee John Robertson had yet to make an appearance by then, but fair to say, the fans would get to see plenty of him before long. In the meantime, they gave their support to John's older brother, Chris, who always had a good few goals in him. Clearly, it was a family trait and one Chris remained intent on displaying as we warmed up for the following term with three matches in the north-east of England.

It was on that trip, when we played North Shields, Whitley Bay and Blyth Spartans, that I first clapped eyes on our new goal-keeper. He came strolling through the hotel where we were staying, with his frizzy hair and fancy shirt. I turned to John Brough, our first-choice goalie at the time, and asked, 'Who the hell's he?'

'That's Henry Smith,' John informed me.

If my first impression of Henry was that he looked more like a pop star than a fitba player, I was to learn better soon enough.

Willie Pettigrew and Derek Addison joined us from Dundee United within a couple of months of the season getting underway, but their signings were to cause a bit of brouhaha. Basically, Hearts couldn't afford them and fell behind with paying the instalments of the combined fee which, from memory, amounted to £165,000. The upshot was that, until such time as they honoured their debt, they were banned from the transfer market. All of this embarrassment could have been avoided had Wallace Mercer managed to sell either myself or another of Bobby Moncur's signings, the full-back Peter Shields. St Mirren had come in for me – I can't recall who was after Peter – but neither deal materialised. It would have been around that same period Aberdeen reportedly also made a move for me.

Gordon Strachan was out injured at the time, and Alex Ferguson needed a ready-made replacement to tide him over. I was struggling for fitness myself, as it happened, because of a nagging knee problem. The specialist told me there was a slight problem with a cartilage but I was as well playing on with it, just to bring the damage to a head, as it were. So I played on – and nothing happened. The problem never got any worse. One way or another though, I missed quite a few games as we struggled to make the desired impression in the First Division. I was back playing when, in October, we managed to draw 2–2 with Motherwell at Fir Park. Willie Pettigrew scored both our goals on that occasion, against the team with whom he had come to such prominence in the mid-1970s.

But I was out again the following month when we suffered the indignity of losing 1–0 to East Stirling at Tynecastle. So things went on, not very satisfactorily from either the board's point of view or Tony Ford's. Something had to give, and it did, after we'd been held at home to a 1–1 draw with Queen's Park in early December. Tony lost his job.

What with Bobby Moncur's early departure under Wallace Mercer, here was further evidence to suggest the club's new steward wasn't a man who shied away from taking a difficult decision. In saying that, Tony possibly saw it coming. From my days with Hearts, I have bound copies of each season's programmes. In his notes for that fateful Queen's Park game, he wrote: 'With seventeen league games played, I feel the time is right for an interim report on how things are going at Tynecastle.

'First of all, let me say I am not satisfied with our position in the League . . . during the last few matches, we have let slip a number of points which, at the end of the season, could be crucial. Now it is going to take a lot of hard work from myself and the players, not just to win the championship but to win promotion. We have not been scoring enough goals, which is very evident when you look at the league tables. We have created a great number of chances in most games, the only thing lacking has been the end product. However, I would hope that in the not too distant future these chances will be converted into goals.'

Had we beaten Queen's Park then, who knows, Tony might have got a stay of execution. But a goal by Willie Pettigrew on that occasion wasn't enough to see us through, or save Tony for at least another match day. Who would take over from him? If I felt sure at the time the club wouldn't be short of candidates, you could have knocked me down with one of the cleaner's feather dusters when the man they picked was . . . me.

16

ME, A MANAGER?

Tony Ford hadn't long left Tynecastle before I was called into the boardroom to be hit with an announcement which left me as stunned as I might have been by one of Stewart McLaren's tackles.

'Alex MacDonald,' Wallace Mercer, seated there among his directors, intoned. 'We want you to be the next manager of Hearts.'

Once I'd recovered from the shock, I said, 'Wait a minute here, this is Heart of Midlothian. You've got to get somebody with experience, and I don't have any experience.' In truth, I'd never seen myself as a manager. Right from the outset of my playing career with St Johnstone, I'd never looked beyond kicking a ball for a living.

I proceeded to stammer, 'I don't think I could do it . . . hmm, I just don't know.' Then I got a hold of myself – well, enough of a hold of myself to continue. 'Right, ok. Let me think about it.'

So I went home and said to Christine, 'You'll never guess, they want me to be the new manager.' When I saw the look of shock on her face, I added, 'No, I couldn't believe it, either.'

Then she said, 'Take it. Take it.' If she'd said the opposite, I'm not sure what I would have done.

Anyway, I went through to Edinburgh the next day and said, 'Yeah, I'll take the job.' With those few words, and for better or worse, I'd sealed my own fate for virtually the next nine years.

No sooner had I done so though than I learned that Wallace Mercer had approached no less an authority than Jock Stein about the advisability of appointing a player–manager. Jock, who was the Scotland manager at the time, apparently had cautioned him against making such an appointment, saying more or less, 'It can't be done.' I don't think he meant that I, Alex MacDonald, couldn't do it. His tack was simply that nobody could do it successfully, or it shouldn't be asked of anyone. Playing was playing, with managing a different matter entirely. The two should not be mixed, especially by a club of Hearts' standing.

Contrary to Jock Stein's considered judgment, there I was then, Scotland's first player–manager, or 'player–coach' as I was tagged for the first few months after my appointment. It would be another four and a half years before my old club, Rangers, saw fit to make a similar appointment with Graeme Souness. All of a sudden, and for the first time since coming into senior football with St Johnstone, I had to think of more than myself. Hearts must have had around thirty players on their books at that time and I had to begin thinking for, and about, all of them. Talk about being thrown in at the deep end! I could only hope I didn't end up floundering.

A lot of good luck messages came my way, among them one from Jock Wallace. Willie Waddell wished me well too and was quoted in the papers as saying, 'Doddie is a thrawn, wee so-and-so. He'll prove he's up to the job.'

The first person I turned to in the hope of appointing him as my assistant was an old pal from Ibrox, Tommy McLean. Sandy Jardine was still playing for Rangers at the time. Nobody knew more about the game than Tommy did. I felt he could organise the front players while I looked after the others, but he had something else on the go at the time – he was about to become John Greig's assistant, in fact – and knocked back the chance to join me at Tynecastle. Still, I had Walter Borthwick *in situ*. He'd come to Hearts as a coach shortly before me and was a great guy to have around. Wattie knew his stuff and proved to be a good ally as I got to grips with the huge challenge that I'd been given so unexpectedly.

In saying that, we were a while waiting to play our first game since the change over. The winter of 1981–82 played such havoc with our fixture list that we went nearly six weeks either side of Christmas without playing competitively. I lived on black coffee and Fisherman's Friends during that long hiatus, the coffee to keep my adrenalin flowing and the lozenges to soothe my throat after so much shouting in training and fending off the inevitable cold brought on by the bad weather.

You can imagine then how I welcomed a call from Ibrox, with John Greig saying, 'Doddie, do you fancy bringing a team through to play us in a closed-door game? I want to use some of my fringe players. You use whoever you fancy.' John didn't need to ask me twice. We were through to Glasgow at the toot for a game that allowed us to get some of the rustiness out of our joints – and me, as I mentioned earlier, to pot the first penalty I'd ever taken. Would Peter McCloy ever live it down? Not if I could help it. As the temperature began to rise, we managed also to fit in the East of Scotland Shield final against Meadowbank at Tynecastle, winning 5–0, with four goals by Willie Pettigrew. One competitive match, one trophy. What a start.

Peter Marinello was with us by then, as Tony Ford's last signing. He'd made quite a name for himself with Hibs in the late 1960s before going to Arsenal, supposedly as London's answer to George Best of Manchester United. Maybe the burden of expectation that weighed on him at Highbury was too big for any young player to bear and it was within a relatively short time – three seasons or so – that he moved on to Portsmouth. Here he was, coming towards the end of his career. Exactly how much he had left to offer us, I would find out soon enough.

So far as I was concerned, everybody was on trial when, on 30 January, we met Motherwell at Tynecastle in what was my first league game in charge. Motherwell were leading the table at the time and promised to be difficult opponents for us. In the event, by way of underscoring the improvement we had to make, they went away with a 3–0 victory. It was in the programme for that match, under the headline of 'Alex MacDonald Talking', I wrote:

As you will readily understand, it is quite an amazing transformation to find yourself a player with Hearts one day – one of the lads, as it were – then to find yourself player–coach the next.

I am naturally hoping the transition will be effected as smoothly as possible [but] obviously it is a hard task that faces us. I'm not going to make any rash claims. That would be foolish, and anyway, it's not my style. However, there is one thing I can say with every confidence. And that is that myself, the players and indeed everyone at Tynecastle, are going to do everything possible to meet the challenge ahead and provide what has been expected from Hearts teams throughout the years. It is a great club which deserves greatness, and one promise is that we will all do our best to make it so.

Starting with trying to pick up more momentum in the First Division and fulfilling our quest for promotion back to the Premier. I was picky about which games I played in, although fitness concerns sometimes dictated whether I appeared on the park or on the bench. I sat on the bench for that Motherwell match which, the adverse scoreline apart, remains in my mind because of a sickening clash of heads involving two players, our own Derek Addison and an opponent by the name of Tony O'Hara. Play had to be stopped for going on five minutes, and while Derek required four stitches in his wound, the Motherwell boy needed fourteen. The sight of them being carted off was not for the squeamish.

One of my earliest decisions was to appoint Stewart McLaren as captain. He had good experience and, a bit like myself, had a real competitive streak in him. Wattie Kidd, another player I came to value, showed the same kind of zeal. Roddy MacDonald had settled in well since arriving at the start of the season too, and I could see us beginning to make some headway as we beat East Stirling, managed at the time by a friend of mine, Martin Ferguson; Falkirk; Queen of the South; and Ayr United in successive matches.

But there was the odd upset also, like our defeat by Forfar in the fourth round (or second-round proper) of the Scottish Cup. They beat us 1–0 at Tynecastle, their scorer being a guy called Steve Hancock, who had been on Hearts' books as a youngster. I was quoted at the time as saying that in my whole career I couldn't remember a more frustrating occasion and that the result was a stain on Hearts' record.

Much of what was happening behind the scenes didn't interest me. Even when Alex Naylor resigned as chairman, my gaze remained focused on playing matters. Wallace Mercer was very much the man in charge of board matters, and had been since his arrival, although he had a sound adviser in a fellow director and former player, Bobby Parker, and a first-class secretary in Les Porteous. I'd got on well with Les from the time of starting out with Hearts as a player and had taken it upon myself on occasion to go to him with various requests on behalf of team-mates. Les, in turn, would transmit these to the board. Maybe it was partly the result of Les bringing me to the board's attention in this way that they asked me to take over. It was certainly a possibility I thought about when asking myself over and over again, 'Why me? Why did they want Alex MacDonald as manager?'

But back to our gradual improvement on the pitch and our resultant climb up the table. Having been well down it before the turn of the year, we had got ourselves in fourth-top place, then second, albeit a long way behind leaders Motherwell, who were doing so well under a great adversary of mine from our Old Firm days, Davie Hay. Willie Pettigrew's goals were a tonic for us. He scored a hat-trick in a 5–1 win away over Queen of the South, and when we beat Clydebank by the same score at Kilbowie, he banged in four. Chris Robertson was still getting his share as well, setting an example that his brother John, who had begun to emerge, would surpass soon enough.

A feeling of excitement, not to mention expectation, was beginning to grip the fans by then. It really did look as though we could win promotion at the first attempt, and as we went into a midweek game against East Stirling, I wrote in my programme notes, 'If we win our next four games, including tonight's, we'll be back in the Premier Division [as runners-up to Motherwell].'

It turned out we beat the Shire 2–0, with a penalty by Paddy Byrne and a later goal by Gerry McCoy. I promptly did my sums again and calculated that we needed only four points from our remaining three games to go up in Motherwell's slipstream. But that was when the gremlins started ganging up on us.

Those three games, by the way, were against Dumbarton (home), Kilmarnock (away) and Motherwell (home). I had to sit out the last two because of suspension, but what happened to us in the one with Dumbarton was something I couldn't get my head round. We were actually leading 1–0 at half time, only to end up being thrashed 5–2. That result obviously lifted Killie, who by then were our closest rivals, and we could do no better than draw 0–0 with them. So we were left needing to beat Motherwell on the last day if we were to fulfil what we hoped would be our destiny. Were we up to the challenge or not? I still fancied we could prevail, especially if Motherwell took their foot off the gas, as we willed them to do.

'If we win today, Hearts will line up alongside Celtic, Rangers and Aberdeen in the Premier Division next season,' my programme notes confirmed. 'Before the Dumbarton match, I had hoped today would be a tension-free gala day, with Hearts promoted and Motherwell, the deserved champions, providing the opposition. But results over the last two weeks have been somewhat disappointing. Two points dropped at home to Dumbarton and only a point taken from Rugby Park has resulted in today's situation. The mathematicians have been working their calculators hard and conclude a point would probably be enough to send us into the top flight today, even if Kilmarnock thrash a few goals past Queen of the South.

'However, I prefer the clear-cut approach. Two points for Hearts today mean promotion, and that's what I want. I want victory for the players who have battled for promotion and I want victory for the supporters who have given us their backing through thick and thin this season. Nobody is under any illusion about the task that faces us. Motherwell come here as champions, and in their last visit to Tynecastle, they beat us by 3–0. They clinched the Championship in style, scoring bags of goals and providing spectators with genuine entertainment. While Motherwell, managed so capably by David Hay, deserve admiration, we won't be overawed.'

Talk about famous last words. Motherwell stuffed us by the same score as those few months before, 3–0, while Killie won to pip us by a point. To make matters worse, the occasion at Tynecastle was scarred by crowd trouble, which resulted in more than a few Hearts fans being arrested and three policemen injured while trying to quell the trouble sparked by sheer frustration.

Wallace Mercer was upset, although no more than me or the players. A few tears were shed in our dressing room afterwards, I can tell you. Nothing like as many as on the last day of season 1985–86, right enough, but I'll have a lot more to say later about that far crueller twist of fate.

17

SUPPORT ARRIVES FROM RANGERS

And then there were two – soon to become three – former Rangers players at Tynecastle. By that I mean Sandy Jardine joined me in time for season 1982–83 getting underway, with Willie Johnston arriving a few months down the line. Some cynics referred to us as Dad's Army, more so, I dare say, when the likes of Jimmy Bone and Sandy Clark came in later. But these guys were seasoned professionals with great track records. To my mind, it was vital we had them around the place, not least for the experience they could pass on to younger players.

I knew Sandy Jardine was coming to the end of his time with Rangers and pressed Wallace Mercer into bringing him to Hearts as my assistant. We'd been together at Ibrox for the duration of my career there, Sandy having made his club debut about a year and a half before I joined them. We'd been roommates more often than not on tours and for away games in Europe and could read each other's minds when it came to football, if not other things.

So, even before news of Sandy's release by John Greig had become public knowledge, Wallace did a deal with him to join us at Tynecastle, where I felt quite certain he had a lot to offer. He may have been thirty-three at the time, about nine months younger than me, but he was a very fit thirty-three. Jock Wallace's training had underpinned his physical condition for a long time to come, as Hearts fans were to discover. I hardly had to sell the club to him. He'd supported them as a kid, after all, when he was growing up in the capital.

The one thing I stressed to Sandy was that the Tynecastle support would sooner see an Edinburgh guy (him) than a Glasgow guy (me) in charge. Ours was to be a shared responsibility, and if Sandy took over from me at some point, fair enough. Don't forget that I had never seen myself as management material, mainly for the reason I'd never looked beyond being a player, and I was still feeling my way into the job. To be sure, it was big enough to demand the full attention of both of us.

By way of reminding myself what the challenge meant to him, I need only refer to our first home programme of the season in which Sandy wrote, 'Hearts are a club I have dreamed of playing for. I was born only a few miles from the ground, and from the age of seven I was a regular at Tynecastle. So taking on the role of assistant manager and helping out Alex MacDonald is [something] I'm looking forward to. My duties will obviously include playing and coaching, but I'm here to help the manager in all aspects of the job and I'll be learning all the time. The set-up at Tynecastle is excellent and everything is geared for Premier Division football by the end of the season.'

Those last few words encapsulated the task in front of us: we had to get promotion after missing out so narrowly and disappointingly those few months earlier. Bud Johnston, when we brought him in that September, was every bit as keen as the rest of us to show the task could be fulfilled. Yet his recruitment aroused a few adverse comments, the essence of which was, 'Not another ex-Rangers player.' Needless to say, after his clearance had come through from Vancouver Whitecaps, Bud wasn't long in winning the critics round. Who was least surprised about this? Sandy Jardine and I, of course.

Bud's reputation for getting sent off, to say nothing of the ignominy he had to bear on being sent home from the 1978 World Cup finals for taking a pill he shouldn't have done, tended to cloud most people's judgment of him. But we knew, having been his team-mates at Ibrox, that he was dedicated in training and a good guy to have about the place. The fact he had turned thirty-five was incidental. Youngsters like David Bowman, Gary Mackay and John Robertson wouldn't have been long in recognising as much. We set up a wee tearoom for the players to gather in before training, and as the kettle boiled in the background, these lads soon were hanging on Bud's every word.

Wee Robbo, by the way, struck his first league goal for us in a 3–0 win over Alloa just a couple of months into the season. The first of many goals, it was to turn out. A programme note from a couple weeks later said, 'John, who is top of the Under-18s scoring charts, certainly took the Alloa game in his stride and may well have scored a hat-trick. Well done, we all hope it's the start of something big.' Alloa, like ourselves, were tucked in behind the First Division leaders St Johnstone at the time, but it was our progress in the League Cup as much as anything that had the fans rallying round us. Who would have believed we might reach the semi-finals to play Rangers over two legs?

This was quite a fillip for the club, and we were nothing if not professional in our build-up to the away leg at Ibrox, taking our whole first-team squad through to Glasgow to watch Rangers play a European tie against Cologne. I said at the time, 'The big stadium, the lights, the atmosphere will be as near as dammit to what we can expect when we go there, and I don't want anybody overawed.'

Each of our players was challenged to assess the man who was liable to be his direct opponent, while Sandy Jardine, Wattie Borthwick and I concentrated more on Rangers' all-round style of play in the hope of finding way to curb them.

It turned out we lost 2–0 to them away, their goals coming late on from Jim Bett and Davie Cooper. But given where we were in our development as a team, that wasn't a result we should have been ashamed of – far from it, in fact. Needless to say, the miracle we required to turn the score round in the return match at Tynecastle didn't happen, Rangers scoring twice (through Bett and Derek Johnstone) to our once (Derek O'Connor), to go through on a 4–1 aggregate.

Still, there was a sense of anticipation growing in and around Tynecastle where, within a few weeks, no less than Dynamo Kiev would come to play a friendly. They were Soviet champions at the time and had in their squad a former European Golden Boot winner, Oleg Blokhin. Also included was the less well-known – at least until he came to Scotland to play his football with St Johnstone – Sergei Baltacha, who had appeared for the Soviet Union in the 1980 Olympics. Great stuff and great experience for our players, especially the three kids, Bowman, Mackay and Robertson, who all played that night.

The fact we lost 2–0 was neither here nor there. The fact we'd been able to bring such attractive opponents to Tynecastle was further evidence of Wallace Mercer's determination to raise our profile. He represented the new breed of people becoming involved in football. He looked upon the game as being more a business than a sport and must have been the first of his kind to refer to fans as customers. Right at the start of 1982–83, his second season in charge, he had organised the club's first ever Open Day, which pulled in some five thousand people to watch a bounce game involving old players and see the current batch train. It was his way of trying to engage with Hearts', er, clientele – or to put it more simply, sell the club to a wider audience. Very much involved in that venture also was a new director Wallace had brought on board, Pilmar Smith.

Pilmar was a successful bookmaker and a Jambo through and through. He also happened to be a big Labour man, which put him at the opposite end of the political spectrum to Mercer, who could have been Mrs Thatcher's emissary in Scotland. In that sense, they made for the oddest of odd couples, yet they got on well. Pilmar also had a sense of humour, and when I recall an incident involving him, maybe it was just as well. He drove this big fancy car, a Merc maybe – I really can't remember. He caught me admiring it one day and asked if I fancied a drive. When I said yes, he threw me the keys, so off I roared for a tour of the Gorgie area.

It so happened that, around that time, the people marketing all things good about Glasgow had designed a sticker bearing the logo 'Glasgow Smiles Better'. I duly stuck one of these on the bumper of Pilmar's motor and it was days before he, such a solid Edinburgh citizen, actually noticed and ripped the thing off. Needless to say, he took a bit of ribbing from everybody around Tynecastle.

But I'm digressing here. It's back to the fitba and our ongoing bid to win promotion that term. As December approached, we'd lost only two league matches, 1–0 to Raith Rovers at Starks Park and 4–2 to Airdrie at Tynecastle. Our results over the forthcoming holiday period were going to be crucial to us, and with no little credit due to Willie Pettigrew, we came through it unscathed.

Great marksman though Willie was, I used to get a bit frustrated with him insofar as he didn't always score in the games that mattered most. But I couldn't quibble with his contribution up to and beyond the turn of that year, when he potted six goals in a run of five matches, which yielded a win for us in each case. These were against Clyde, Ayr United, St Johnstone, Airdrie and Partick Thistle. If a bit of inconsistency began to nag us thereafter, the flow of goals from another source, Wee John Robertson, kept us in the chase for what we all believed was our rightful, if not overdue, return to the Premier Division.

Wee Robbo bagged his first hat-trick for Hearts in a 3–0 win over Queen's Park away in late February, then another in a 4–0 victory over Partick at home. What a run the kid was on, even if results weren't always to our liking. For example, towards the end of April, after losing to league leaders St Johnstone at Perth, we could only draw successively with Clydebank, Alloa and Dunfermline. Yet in the last of these games, a 3–3 draw, Robbo helped himself to all our goals. So it was that we went into our second-last fixture of the season against Dumbarton away in the knowledge that a win would see us promoted, as runners-up at least.

Again, Robbo did us a real turn, scoring twice in a 4–0 win in which Derek O'Connor and Gary Mackay got the other goals to spark wild celebrations among our travelling support. Wattie Kidd had another reason to be jubilant, in that that historic game was his 250th for the club. Over 9,000 fans turned out for our one remaining match against Hamilton Accies at Tynecastle, knowing if we won and St Johnstone lost at home to Dunfermline, we could go up as champions. Suffice to say we did what we could to make it happen, winning 2–0 with goals by Willie Johnston and Derek O'Connor, but my old team, the Saints, won 1–0 to assure themselves of the title.

When I look through my compilation of programmes, I laugh when I see the one for that match against the Accies. It's like the Wallace Mercer Edition, with Message from the Chairman emblazoned across the front cover. Here is what he had to say – ok, some of what he had to say. I'd be labouring things a bit to give you the full text:

I am writing this short note on the Monday morning [after the Dumbarton game] and still cannot believe that the dreams and ambitions which were thrust upon me in May 1981, when the board decided to support my takeover proposal, have come to fruition. It has been at times an onerous task and there have been many doubts along the way . . . but, without the ambition and energy generated by the players, and the tremendous support from shareholders and the club supporters, the task probably would have been impossible. Hearts is more than a football club, it is an institution, and not even I realised the patient was indeed sick and a bold initiative was required from everyone.

In hindsight, the failure to achieve promotion last season was a great benefit to the club; it made the players work harder, it gave our youngsters a year to mature, the signings of Sandy Jardine and Willie Johnston increased the number of winners, and allowed me time to re-structure the board and attract new directors of the calibre of Douglas Park and Pilmar Smith. Having now obtained the opportunity to play in the highest division, it is our joint responsibility to ensure the financial resources are made available to the manager and Sandy Jardine to enable them to keep the best young players and strengthen the team.

Believe me when I say there's more – much more – where that came from. Wallace was never stuck for a thousand words to say, or in this case, write. But it pleased me that in waxing about our achievement, he highlighted how important the signings of my two former team-mates from Ibrox, Sandy Jardine and Willie Johnston, had been. Without their combined influence, both on and off the field, we could have foundered. Sandy had converted to sweeper and appeared in no fewer than sixty games, including four in the Scottish Cup in which we reached the quarter-final, only to lose 4–1 to Celtic. Fate didn't half conspire against us in that game at Parkhead, by the way.

Peter Shields broke his leg and Wee Bud got sent off, supposedly for aiming a swipe at Davie Provan while taking a throw-in. These two blows knocked the stuffing out of us, and the fact I scored in what was my 100th appearance for Hearts offered little consolation. I remember thinking around that point in the season that, between the league, the League Cup and Scottish Cup, we'd played so many games, our legs could buckle beneath us. Happily that didn't happen. Even Wee Bud, despite turning thirty-six, managed to last the pace and played in more than thirty matches. Indeed, he had enough energy left over to go spend the summer in Hong Kong, playing for South China Sea. Me? At thirty-five, and after clocking up around fifty games, I just looked forward to a decent break, if the business of management would allow one.

As for the three kids, Dave Bowman, Gary Mackay and John Robertson, they had started fifty-eight, thirty-seven and twenty-five games respectively, and the experience gained in the process was to prove invaluable to them and Hearts. Wee Robbo ended up our equal top scorer with Derek O'Connor that season, with twenty-two goals – pretty good going considering he didn't get his first goal until October. Willie Pettigrew, who was to move on to Morton within a few months, finished just behind them on twenty. But while it was pleasing to hear the chairman pledge we'd be given money to strengthen the side, Sandy and I couldn't help wondering where it might come from. I dare say Wallace Mercer himself had no better an idea.

We'd been banned from the transfer market as a result of problems arising from our difficulty in meeting the payments due to Dundee United for Willie Pettigrew and Derek Addison. Derek has moved on to St Johnstone, in time to help them win the First Division title, in fact. But that hadn't eased the club's relationship with the bank to any appreciable degree. Hearts, rich in ambition, remained virtually skint in terms of actual cash available. As and when we began to bring in players thereafter, it was like shopping from a Kay's catalogue. You know, £1 down and £1 a week thereafter. I couldn't remember it ever being that way at Rangers!

Among the first guys we brought in was young Malcolm Murray from Buckie Thistle. I think the fee was supposed to be £2,000, but about five directors went to watch him in a game against Queen's Park, just to be sure the club weren't about to waste their money. We ended up paying £1,000 on the basis we'd play Buckie in a friendly at some point. That's how tight the money was, and how careful Hearts had to be in spending it.

Still, there wasn't a man among us at Tynecastle who didn't look forward to the challenge of being back in the Premier Division. It had been hard work all round in actually getting there and promised to be at least as taxing, if our stay wasn't to be a short one.

18

PUTTING CRAIG LEVEIN
IN HIS PLACE

Sandy Jardine and I knew we'd found an emerging star in Wee John Robertson, all 5'5" of him. He was one of the few players at Tynecastle who could rightly call me Big Man. But he wasn't yet nineteen as Hearts prepared for the rigours of the Premier Division in 1983–84 and needed an experienced hand to take some of the weight off him as well as assist his development. Who was available? Jimmy Bone fitted the bill at least as well as anybody. Jimmy had enjoyed a good career since helping Partick Thistle win the League Cup with a famous win over Celtic at Hampden in 1971. He'd played for Scotland on a couple occasions and knew the game inside out.

The fact he'd been freed by St Mirren a few months earlier, at the age of thirty-four, didn't put us off him any. In the sense he was available for nothing, and it made him an even more attractive proposition. The word on the grapevine was that Hibs were in the market for his services, albeit in a coaching capacity. Consequently, when we heard he was on the way back from Hong Kong after playing there during the summer, we left a message for him at Edinburgh Airport saying to call us before he spoke to anybody. Jimmy duly phoned and was taken by our suggestion that he join us at Tynecastle and continue as a player.

So it was that our so-called Dad's Army got another willing and very able recruit, one who joined us in time for our pre-season warm-up games in the north of Scotland and made an instant impression in the Premier Division by scoring the only goal in our opening match, against St Johnstone away. In fact, Jimmy went on to establish a Hearts record for the Premier Division by scoring in each of our first four league games that season. These included a derby against Hibs at Tynecastle, which we won 3–2, with Wee Robbo scoring the other two goals. Jimmy, by that early juncture, was proving to be a valuable player in his own right, as well as someone who could act as Robbo's mentor.

Donald Park, who had been with Hearts during the 1970s, came back to Tynecastle at the same time as Jimmy arrived, and having just turned thirty, was a relative youngster. George Cowie, more youthful by far, joined us around then also, and was to be another very useful acquisition. But it was towards the end of that year we made a signing that was to have a greater and more lasting impact than pretty well anyone during my time in charge at Tynecastle. Let's hear it, folks, for Craig Levein.

Sandy and I had taken note of him when he played against us, for Cowdenbeath, in the League Cup in the opening month of the season. We could see he had various qualities, good pace among them. Various clubs were said to be monitoring his progress, but so far as we knew, none of them had made an actual move to buy the lad. Could we beat them to it? Equally to the point, could Wallace Mercer possibly rustle up the £35,000 or so it might take to bring Craig to Hearts? As they say, where there's a will, there's a way.

Craig arrived for signing talks with his dad, and so far as his personal terms were concerned, we did our best to look after him by adding a bit on top of whatever it was he wanted. We took the view that it wasn't the directors' money we were spending. It was the fans', and in Craig we reckoned we had found a player who could become a real crowd-pleaser.

I can't recall the actual terms offered Craig, but I can remember the case of another player we brought in at the same time. This young lad, whose name escapes me, started out by saying, 'Me and my dad were talking last night and we felt, well, how to put this . . . ?' Eventually, once he got his tongue untied, he got to the point and said, 'That I should ask for £60 a week.'

Sandy and I said to him, 'No, we're not going to give you that. We'll give you £80 instead.' You should have seen his face.

But getting back to Craig Levein, he wasn't with us long when I went into the players' tearoom one morning and found him scattering salt over this table. 'What the hell are you doin'?' I asked.

'It's ok, gaffer,' said he. 'I've lost one of my contact lenses and this is the best way to find it.'

What had we signed, I wondered! Our idea with Craig was just to break him in gently, but injuries meant we'd to push him in quicker than intended and he performed at least as well as we could have hoped. Maybe that wasn't surprising because on top of being a good, young player, he was a clever guy who took on board what we were trying to tell him . . . a future Scotland manager, indeed.

In saying that, Craig always had something to say for himself. I recall once, quite some time after he'd settled into the team, we were training at Murrayfield and he was hitting me with his one-liners. I motioned him to come closer and said, 'See that ball there? Sit on it while I speak to you.'

Well, he was a lot bigger than me, wasn't he? Better I looked down at him than up. So he sat on the ball and I told him, 'See when you have your own team, you do whatever you want. But so long as you're playing for my team, you'll do what I want. If not, you'll end up sitting in the stand.' I think I made myself clear enough and he got the message.

Gary Mackay, Dave Bowman and Ian Westwater had played for Scotland in the World Youth Championship in Mexico by the time Craig came to the club, so he knew he was in good young company. John Robertson, meanwhile, had appeared for the Scottish Under-18s side in the European Championships held far closer to him in England and scored twice in a 4–2 defeat by the host nation. These kids were making good progress then, with Robbo feeling the benefit of the sprint training given him by George

McNeill. Sandy Jardine, as far as I recall, got George and Bert Logan involved with the players. He'd known them, I think, from his young days at Ibrox when he and Willie Johnston used to do the professional sprint circuit. Among the things they introduced was a routine with a speedball, which was great for building upper-body strength.

So, while Hearts of that time weren't exactly brimming over with finesse, we didn't want for fitness. We had even introduced the players to the sands at Gullane, where Sandy, Willie Johnston and I could remember being hammered by Jock Wallace when we worked under him at Rangers. Nor did we want for determination. How could we, with so many battlers in our team? But no less importantly, we weren't short of confidence in that first season after promotion. Beating St Johnstone and Hibs in our first two league matches went some way to ensuring that was the case, these two results helping bring the players closer together.

Even a 3–0 defeat by Rangers at Tynecastle in the League Cup didn't do any obvious damage to our self-esteem, for within three days, again at home, we beat them 3–2 in the league, with goals by Robbo, Jimmy Bone and myself. The League Cup was a bit of sideshow so far as we were concerned. Consolidating in the ten-club Premier Division was our priority, and as Christmas approached, we were sitting in fifth place. So far, so good, although Rangers had beaten us 3–0 at Ibrox by that point, and Aberdeen 2–0 both at Pittodrie and Tynecastle. Just for the record, Craig Levein made his debut in that Rangers game. Despite the score-line, he did ok.

The fact we'd managed to draw 1–1 with Hibs at Easter Road and with Celtic at Parkhead helped sustain the belief we could finish the season in a respectable position, and a subsequent 1–1 draw with Hibs, this time at Tynecastle, went some way further to ensuring we could keep our heads held high in Edinburgh. Dundee duly gave us a going-over right enough, by 4–1 at Dens Park, and likewise Celtic, by the same score at Parkhead. But in between those times, we drew 2–2 with Rangers at Tynecastle.

The Scottish Cup was underway by that point, and while we beat Partick Thistle 2–0 at home in the third round, we lost 2–1 to Dundee United away in the fourth. There was no shame in that. United were one of the teams sitting above us in the league at the time, and of course, the reigning champions.

Aberdeen appeared to be running away with the title, so we were quite pleased to hold them to a 1–1 draw at Pittodrie in early spring, then draw 0–0 with Rangers at Ibrox the following week. Next up were Hibs at Easter Road, and we valued the point we took from a goal-less draw there. But we got something of a fillip around that time from beating Arsenal 3–2 in a challenge game at Tynecastle. Among the top players in the Londoners' squad were Tony Woodcock, David O'Leary and a certain Charlie Nicholas. It was important – particularly for the young players in our team – that they had the chance to compete against that calibre of opponent.

In the event, we beat them 3–2, with Wattie Kidd, Jimmy Bone and Gary Mackay our scorers. The countdown to the season's end was underway by then, and looming large before us was the prospect of finishing high enough in the table to claim a place in the UEFA Cup. A 1–0 defeat by Aberdeen at Tynecastle threatened to undermine our cause, but we recovered well enough to draw 1–1 with both Celtic and Dundee at home before winning 1–0 at Motherwell in our last game. Time for us, and the fans, to dust down the passports. We were headed for Europe and, as it turned out, a mouthwatering tie against Paris St Germain. Who would have believed it?

Possibly not even Wallace Mercer, who wrote in the programme for the Dundee match, 'I wish to congratulate the players, and also the supporters, both of whom have worked hard in their different ways to enable us to contemplate being in European competition for the first time in many years. This season has enabled us not only to consolidate in the Premier Division, but to progress, and you can be assured that your directors will be working during the summer recess to assist that progress by re-investing further funds in the playing staff.' Sandy Jardine and I were especially gratified to read that last bit. It gave us immediate licence to start looking round the transfer market for likely signing targets.

But the final bit of the chairman's parting message for the season had particular relevance for myself. It read, 'I also look forward to every genuine Heart of Midlothian supporter turning out for the Alex MacDonald Testimonial match against Rangers, which will not only be a fiesta occasion but a final way of thanking the players, and Alex, for their assistance in enabling Hearts to get into Europe.' The event in question, which attracted a crowd of just under 18,000 (the actual attendance was 17,853), took place at Tynecastle on a Tuesday night in the middle of May. I was thirty-six by then and probably more nervous than I'd ever been before a game.

My testimonial committee, chaired by Jim McLean of the *Scottish Daily Express*, had done brilliantly to entice Kevin Keegan into playing for Hearts. What a coup, just so long as the former captain of England didn't take my place! Kevin, twice European Footballer of the Year, had just led Newcastle United to promotion, and at the relatively young age of thirty-three, announced his retirement. He ended up playing for seventy-three minutes against Rangers and provided something of a masterclass, for some of our younger players especially. One of the photographers covering the game later gave me a set of pictures of Keegan, each of them showing by way of his hand-signals how he wanted the ball delivered to him. I pinned them up on the wall of the dressing room to illlustrate how things should be done.

That game, by the way, marked my 142nd appearance for Hearts in four seasons. The old legs weren't done yet, thanks in no small way to the training I'd done in my younger days under Jock Wallace, who was back in charge of Rangers. My old gaffer was complimentary to me in the match programme, saying:

From the first moment I cast my eyes on Alex at Ibrox, I knew we had a really special player. He was asked to do a lot of work and his response was quite magnificent . . . the wee man used to run himself into the ground for Rangers and played his part to the full, as we won the European Cup Winners' Cup, League Championships and Scottish Cups. Over the years, we had our ups and downs, but we never lost our mutual respect for each other.

One great thing about Alex is that he was always a great listener and had the ability to transform those hours and hours of talking into his play to make him a better player. Alex is still playing away with Hearts and a credit to the game. He has everything going for him to become a great football manager. The team of MacDonald and Sandy Jardine has done really well for the Hearts, and there's no happier man than me to see that. I'm delighted to be bringing Rangers to Tynecastle to play for Alex. He thoroughly deserves this special night, for he has made a great contribution to Scottish football in general.

Wallace Mercer was no less generous in his comments in the same publication, acknowledging his own background as a bluenose as he said:

During my time as a Rangers supporter, Alex was the work-horse in midfield who, week in, week out, seemed to defy the manager in dropping him. He was never a classical player in terms of skill, but through guts and determination, retained his place in the team and eventually transferred to Hearts of Midlothian. He could have taken the 'easy road' and played for a couple of years, then retired; however, on assuming control at Tynecastle, I continued to be aware of his inspirational qualities and promoted him from club captain to player–manager.

His ability since then to continue playing and also attract other fellow professionals of a similar attitude to the club has assisted Heart of Midlothian. I therefore wish supporters from Rangers FC and Heart of Midlothian tonight to enjoy the occasion and to recognise one of their own and to congratulate Alex for being the only manager still to play at the highest level in the Premier Division. The club have recently signed Alex for a further three years. My board and I are taking the view that the characteristics which have established him as a player for many years can be cultivated and extended to enable him to continue . . . contributing in a managerial capacity and transmitting to younger players the drive, will and ambition which is necessary to earn their living as professional footballers.

Bobby Brown, the man who gave me my first break in senior football by signing me for St Johnstone, had a piece in the programme too. In it, he admitted:

I haven't been surprised by his success in the game. Even back in the Sixties, you only had to look at him to know he was going places. He could never be described as a speed merchant, but the first thing that struck you was his confidence. Not cocky, but he had a lot of skill and an old head on young shoulders. He wasn't overawed in the slightest, and his control and composure in tight situations was excellent. But perhaps the thing which shone through above all his other attributes was he could see and read things quicker than a lot of older players. I haven't been surprised at the successful start he's made as a manager . . . and I'm sure he'll do even better in the coming years.

I would have been flattered at the time to read comments such as these, but as ever in my experience of the game, nobody would have needed to tell me there was little point in dwelling on the past. Far more important was the future and what Sandy and I could still do for Hearts.

In the season just ended, we'd achieved what we'd set out to do by finding stability in the Premier Division. Getting into Europe was something of a bonus, but the greater challenge facing us all at Tynecastle was trying to build on the foundations we'd laid, and with luck, bring a measure of distinction to this great club that the chairman invariably referred to as Heart of Midlothian. Doing so didn't promise to be easy, not when we were competing for prizes along with the so-called New Firm of Aberdeen and Dundee United, as well as the Old Firm of Rangers and Celtic.

19

MY FALL-OUT WITH MO JOHNSTON

Football does funny things to people. Why, it can even make them fall out with their friends. I remember once taking Hearts through to Glasgow for a game against Rangers. Among those on the opposing bench, in his role as coach under John Greig, was my long-time pal from our time together at Ibrox, Tommy McLean. Now, I've mentioned in an earlier chapter that I thought so much of Wee Tam as a guy and a fitba man that I wanted to join me at Tynecastle. That was when I was given the job as player–manager.

Anyway, I was playing that day when I saw Tam shout something about us from the touchline. I responded with a hand signal, telling him to quit mouthing.

We went up the tunnel at full time and he was by my side, going, 'You shouting at me, eh?'

I said by way of reply, 'Tam, what are you on about?' I reached our dressing room and headed straight for the shower area. Lo and behold, Tam was still with me, and still whining.

'You were taking the piss out of me, weren't you?' he said.

I told him, 'Tam, away and gie's peace.'

I went back into our dressing room and Wattie Borthwick and John Binnie were complaining about all the abuse they'd been getting from the Rangers bench.

I told them, 'Hey, does that no' mean we were doing well? What are you upset about?'

Petty stuff, but tension can bring out the worst, as well as the best, in most of us, myself included.

Several years later, by which time I'd stopped playing, we found ourselves up against Rangers once more at Ibrox. Mo Johnston hadn't long joined them, amid much controversy about him being their first Catholic signing in modern times. I need hardly remind anyone that a lot of Rangers fans weren't best pleased to see him in a blue jersey. Many Celtic fans were upset also, in that he had been poised for a return to Parkhead before Graeme Souness convinced him to cross the Old Firm divide.

Mo, in this particular instance, wasn't having his best game ever, so much so that Souness decided to substitute him. The disappointment was etched on his face. That much was quite clear to me from where I was standing, right on the corner of our technical area. Mo duly ran past me, and looking for somebody, anybody, to vent his annoyance at, he threw me a scowl and said something which sounded to me like, 'You old bastard.'

I promptly asked him who he thought he was talking to, before adding as many a Rangers fan might have done, 'You shouldn't be here anyway, you . . . ' I left the sentence unfinished.

Come the end of the game, when we were back in our dressing room, there was a knock on the door. It was our chairman, Wallace Mercer, asking if he could have a word with me. I followed him out to the tunnel and he said I'd been accused by Rangers of calling Mo Johnston a Fenian bastard.

I said to him, 'Mr Mercer, I don't call anybody in a blue jersey a Fenian bastard, simple as that.' The way I worked it out was that Mo had complained to Graeme Souness, who had complained to David Murray, who had complained to Wallace Mercer. You couldn't have made it up, but that was the end of the matter.

Needless to say, as a way of working off my frustrations, there were occasions when I got myself involved with referees. For instance, the time Hearts were playing at Kilmarnock, with Alan Ferguson the match official. He and one of his linesmen were finding themselves at odds with each another over a couple of decisions. I was falling about the bench, shouting in a mocking fashion, 'I don't believe this.'

A couple more bad decisions went against us, so I started chanting, 'Fergie, Fergie.' He kept running past the dugout, hoping to see who was winding him up. Sandy Jardine, meanwhile, was telling me to shut it, otherwise I could land myself in trouble. So on it went, with me greeting yet another bad decision with yet another 'Fergie, Fergie' chant, and Sandy telling me once more to be quiet.

At full time, as our players were coming off the pitch, I walked over to Henry Smith and told him, 'Look, I'm going to start bawling here, but what I have to say has nothing to do with you, ok?'

Then, with Alan Ferguson within earshot at this point, I let rip at Big Henry, saying, 'You effing diddy, every time we come here, we don't get this, we don't get that. It's always the bloody same.' I think I'm right in saying this was an old Jock Stein tactic: dressing down an innocent target when the intended victim of his rant was, in fact, the referee.

Having got things out of my system and made sure Mr Ferguson had heard every word of my tirade, we headed for the dressing room, where Sandy Jardine said to me, 'Dod, you'd better calm down and watch yourself.'

Just then, there was a chap at the door. Someone opened it, and there was one of the linesmen saying Mr Ferguson wanted to see both Sandy and me in his room.

Here we go, I thought. At the very least, he's going to challenge us about who was giving out with the sarcastic 'Fergie, Fergie' chants from the bench. Sandy whispered to me, 'I told you, Dod, you're for the high jump.'

So we went to the ref's room and he took Sandy in first. Sandy came out after a time, looking none too pleased and complaining, 'You'll never believe this. He's reporting me to the SFA. You'll get the same treatment, guaranteed.'

So I went in then – and got off with a warning.

That scenario, well, the bit about shouting at Big Henry as a way of getting at the referee, reminds me of another match which left me fuming about decisions going against us. It was at Celtic Park, although I can't remember the actual official in charge.

I waited inside for the ref at full time, and as he approached, I turned to this picture hanging on the wall and started hollering, 'It's always the same with us at this place. We get f**k all.' I dare say the ref would have liked to have done me there and then, but he couldn't. I was shouting and jabbing my finger at a photo on the wall, not him.

The next thing I knew, Billy McNeill was hanging his head out of the Celtic dressing room and snarling, 'What are you going on about?'

But once you get these things out of your system, you do your best to forget about them. In that case at Parkhead, I was in Big Billy's room half an hour later having a drink with him. Well, I did say at the start of this chapter that football does funny things to people, even those of us who should know better.

Maybe it was as well I got out of management when I did, otherwise I could have ended up being certified. Yet despite the regular bouts of tension that went with the job at Tynecastle, I was revelling in the challenge it presented as Hearts went into season 1984–85. In particular, I was invigorated by the prospect of them being back in Europe for the first time since 1976–77, when they'd lost both home and away to Hamburg in the second round of the Cup Winners' Cup.

Fair to say, Wallace Mercer was excited too. The club had come a long way during the three years of his stewardship, and if not quite awash with money, we were starting to pay our way. Put it another way: at least the Sherriff's officers had stopped banging on the door of Tynecastle. We'd had a few visits from them prior to Wallace's arrival. In truth, I hadn't paid that much attention to how he'd managed to get us out of the financial morass he'd inherited. My focus was solely on the playing side of the busi-ness. But I do recall he was into all sorts of fundraising schemes, which included a deal with a builder to give away a house in a prize draw. Wallace became big on in-house hospitality also, and

I remember counting no fewer than eleven places he'd created within the stadium where people could get a drink.

The effect of our improving relationship with the bank was that we could afford to improve our squad that bit more, hence the likes of Brian Whittaker and Kenny Black joining us from Celtic and Motherwell respectively in the summer of 1984. Another arrival then was a wee guy who went on to make a bigger name for himself in Scottish rugby, Gary Parker. Sandy Jardine and I watched him play for the reserves one time, and when he lashed in a goal, we turned to one another and said, 'This lad will do for us.'

Brian Whittaker, a good bloke who was to become an agent before dying at a tragically young age, gave us cover both at full-back and in central defence, while Kenny Black, a really combative character, could switch between full-back and midfield. I'd actually tried to get him a year or so earlier when I heard he was leaving Rangers. One morning at home, while I was in the middle of shaving, Christine answered the phone and shouted to me, 'It's Kenny Black for you.' He was on to tell me he'd decided to join Motherwell instead of Hearts, but thanked me for our offer. I duly thanked him for calling and wished him all the best. But when I hung up, I let out a curse about the frustrations of the transfer market. Still, the fact we'd got him eventually was pleasing.

The more experience we could muster, the better prepared we might be to cope with the rigours ahead, especially in the UEFA Cup in which we found ourselves matched with Paris St Germain. They were a relatively new club, founded as recently as 1970. But they'd been quick to establish a decent reputation for themselves and had a number of international players, including the winger Dominique Rocheteau, who Sandy and I remembered from his time with St Etienne in the mid-1970s. We soon made it our business to find out all we could about them and PSG paid us the respect of coming to watch a couple of our games at Tynecastle. Mind you, if their coach at the time had taken the word of France's top football publication, *L'Equipe*, he might have headed for

Newcastle instead. Why do I say this? Well, *L'Equipe* responded to news of the draw which paired Hearts with PSG by reporting that our 'English-style ground with wooden stands' was situated on the banks of the River Tyne after which it was named. What a faux pas.

We ended up taking 2,500 fans to Paris for the first leg of the tie, where Wallace Mercer had booked us into a top-class hotel just outside the city. He did like to do things in style, didn't he? Unfortunately, our best-laid plans to hold the French side unraveled all too quickly, as they thrashed us 4–0. Who knows, had Gary Mackay accepted a chance to make the score 1–1, we might have held up a lot better, but in truth, PSG were far too good for us on a night when their Yugoslav striker, Safet Sušić, struck two terrific goals. It was a hugely disappointed Hearts team who trudged off at full time, yet while the supporters must have shared our hurt, they contrived not to show it. In fact, they seemed reluctant to leave the stadium, and I was asked to go back out and give them a wave of thanks for getting behind us.

Sandy and I, while realising we had next to no chance of overturning the scoreline in the return leg at Tynecastle, did our best to lift the players' spirits. In the event, we recovered a bit of our pride by holding the French to a 2–2 draw, with John Robertson scoring both our goals. It was, as managers are wont to say, 'a learning experience'. Yet, to the team's credit, we showed no sign of any hangover and proceeded to beat Rangers 1–0 at Tynecastle only three days later, with Robbo our scorer again. That was our best performance of the season to date. In fact, it was only our third victory in the championship, the other two having been against Hibs away and Dumbarton at home. Happily, we proceeded to string a few more decent results together thereafter and pull ourselves up into mid-table.

In saying that, we'd done pretty well in the League Cup, beating East Stirling, Ayr United and Dundee in the earlier rounds before facing Dundee United over two legs in the semi-final. They ended up beating us 2–1 at Tynecastle and 3–1 at Tannadice, yet within seventy-two hours of that second defeat, we beat them 2–0 in the league at Tynecastle. Funny game, football. It was thereabouts we made our next significant signing, Sandy Clark, who joined us from Rangers for £35,000. From memory, it was one of our directors, Douglas Park, who fixed that deal, which was done on the 'never, never'. Sandy had had a good career by that point, first with his local team, Airdrie, then with West Ham, and therefore had great experience to offer. Goals weren't long in coming from him – one in a 3–2 win over Morton at Cappielow and two in a victory by the same score over St Mirren at Love Street.

Sandy, big and powerful, helped take the weight off John Robertson, who was emerging rapidly as a goalscorer almost without peer in Scotland. I've no doubt Robbo had learned a lot from Jimmy Bone, who was to leave us after the turn of the year and become player–manager of Arbroath, and playing alongside Sandy proved no less beneficial to him. Another player, much younger than Jimmy, who departed Tynecastle around the same time, was Davie Bowman. Coventry City had come in with a £170,000 bid for him, and who were we to stand in his way? I was pleased for the lad, who along with Gary Mackay, had fetched my kit and polished my boots when I first arrived at the club. The fee we got was more than enough for us to bring in Andy Watson from Leeds and Neil Berry from Bolton.

I like to think that, in some small way, I had aided Bow's development. In the event, he didn't stay that long at Highfield Road – a season and a bit maybe. But his next move, to Dundee United, where he worked under Jim McLean, really brought the best out of him and he won a handful of Scotland caps during his time at Tannadice. Craig Levein, meanwhile, was displaying more and more signs of maturing into a very fine player for Hearts, his speed alone helping set him apart from many other defenders in the country. Just to prove how quick he was, Craig actually won the professional footballers' 1985 New Year sprint at Meadowbank. Working under our sprint coaches, George McNeill and Bert Logan, had brought that extra yard out of him.

We were all pleased for him, but not half as pleased as we were that, with his assistance, we beat Hibs 2–1 at Easter Road in the festive derby. Gary Mackay, who'd had a worrying spell of injury earlier in the season, gave us the lead in the first half of that match. If memory serves corrrectly, Gary's goal could have been one of several for us before the break. Sandy Clark scored our second shortly after it, and we looked to be cruising until Willie Jamieson scored for Hibs.

Inconsistency may have been a problem for us that season, but not in games against our Edinburgh rivals. We'd beaten them 2–1 away early on, with Craig Levein and Derek O'Connor our scorers, and drawn 0–0 with them at Tynecastle thereafter. Then, towards the end of the season, we drew 2–2 with them at Tynecastle, but really should have won. Goals by Robbo and Sandy Clark had us 2–0 in front, only for Joe McBride to score twice near the end. Still, six points from a possible eight from these games wasn't bad. If only we could have played the Hibees every week, we'd have been up there challenging Aberdeen for the title they eventually won for the second year in a row.

They'd beaten us 4–0 at Pittodrie in September – a sore one that – and 2–1 at Tynecastle in December. Trust us to draw them in the quarter-final of the Scottish Cup when, after a 1–1 draw at Tynecastle, they edged through on a 1–0 scoreline in the replay at their place. That result heralded a disappointing run-in for us, one that yielded only a single victory (against Dumbarton) in our next six league games. But at least, we managed to beat the German side, Eintracht Frankfurt, by 3–1 in a friendly. Sandy Clark put us in front in that game at Tynecastle. Then, after conceding an equaliser, Brian McNaughton restored our lead after a shot by John Robertson had come back off the bar. Who scored the decisive goal? Wee Robbo, of course.

We had only three league games left by that point and, mathematically, were still in with a chance of finishing fifth-top to secure a place in Europe for the second season in a row. But the wheels came off the bogie, as they say, as we lost 3–1 to Rangers at Ibrox, 3–0 to Aberdeen at Tynecastle and (whisper it) 5–2 to St Mirren at Love Street. At the end, it was St Mirren who claimed the last remaining spot in the UEFA Cup. Given how well we'd done the previous term – against everyone's expectation at that – this was an inglorious finish for us. Celtic in particular had given us a hard time, with four wins out of four in our games with them. Their 5–1 win at Tynecastle before the turn of the year was especially numbing, and the old Rangers man in me grieved at that result.

I still got a hard time from their fans, as I was reminded in the minutes leading up to one of our games at Parkhead. I'd been having a slight problem with an injury and the physio suggested I go out ahead of the rest of the players to do a little warm-up. This I did, but as I made to come back inside, I managed to trip over the wooden edging that surrounded the pitch and ended up face down on the track. You should have heard the stick I got from the Celtic supporters as I dusted myself down and headed, red-faced, for the dressing room.

20

THE SEASON THAT ENDED
IN TEARS

For how much longer could my ageing legs keep me going as a player? By the summer of 1985, when I'd turned thirty-seven, they'd kept me upright for twenty years in senior football. But there was no point in kidding myself on that I could still do the amount of running I used to do. In short, the pain in my calf muscles was killing me. Way back when I took over as player–manager of Hearts, my left leg in particular had started to give me gyp. If I could have undergone surgery to ease the problem, I would have signed up at the earliest opportunity to have the operation. As things turned out, I just had to rely on physio-therapy to keep me anything like match-fit. That eventually meant me going on a regular basis to see a rugby specialist down in the Scottish borders, and I can recall clinging to the ceiling as he ground his thumbs into my legs in his attempts to get rid of what-ever was the problem.

On reflection, maybe I'd done as well as I could reasonably have expected by appearing in the number of games I did in season 1984–85 – more than thirty, including Cup ties. But I had to wonder if the team really needed me for the season that was about to begin. The younger lads were getting faster and fitter, while I couldn't say the same for myself. As things transpired, maybe they didn't need me. For it was in 1985–86, when my playing contribution was limited to one appearance as a sub, we went so close to writing a glorious chapter in the club's history.

So close, did I say? Heart-breakingly close, in fact, with the last eight days leaving all involved in a state of absolute anguish at the thought of what might have been.

There we were, on 3 May 1986, within ninety minutes of winning the League Championship for the first time since 1960, only for fate to conspire wickedly against us. There we were a week later, within ninety minutes of winning the Scottish Cup for the first time since 1956. Again, we were thwarted cruelly by providence. Edinburgh lads like Gary Mackay and John Robertson could have dined out for life had we become the first Hearts team ever to win the Double. I dare say all of us could. Still, as we and the fans dried our tears, nobody could knock us for the effort which went into trying to make the near unimaginable actually happen.

Yet despite a worthwhile pre-season tour of West Germany in which we won four of our five matches and drew the other, the portents suggested we were to be blighted by the inconsistency of the previous term. By this I mean that, having drawn 1–1 with Celtic at Tynecastle in our opening match in the Premier Division, we lost the next by a thumping 6–2 to St Mirren at Love Street. By early September, we'd lost 3–1 to Rangers at Ibrox, beaten Hibs 2–1 at Tynecastle, and lost 3–0 to Aberdeen at Pittodrie. The one truly encouraging sign for us during that early spell was the form of a player we'd signed from Celtic in the summer for only £35,000, John Colquhoun.

Sandy Jardine and I had enquired about the availability of another Celtic winger, Davie Provan, only to be told he wasn't available. But, on reflection, we did very well indeed to get Wee John, who in the seasons to come proved an invaluable asset to Hearts and a great favourite with the support. John actually scored in what was his competitive debut for us, that 1–1 draw with his old club I mentioned earlier. He even scored for us in the doing we got from St Mirren, as well as in the win over Hibs which followed. We could hardly have expected such a good goals return from someone who was essentially a wide player.

The need to find someone like him – a player who could get the ball into the opposition's box, if not their net – had become something of a priority since Willie Johnston's departure a few months earlier. But without having limitless funds to dip into, it was important we stocked up in other positions also. Hence a midfielder, Ian Jardine, arrived from the Cypriot team, Anorthosis, around the same time and a striker-cum-defender, Colin McAdam, from Adelaide City that bit later in the season. This is not to forget a kid we picked up from our own doorstep, Scott Crabbe, who'd been playing with Tynecastle Boys' Club. I might be understating the case just a bit by saying Scott looked like he could emerge as a decent attacker. We put him in the care of reserve-team coach John Binnie, who helped turn him into a real scoring talent.

Ian Jardine soon began weighing in with a few goals, one in a 2–1 defeat at Motherwell, another in a 1–1 with Dundee at Tynecastle. Little could we have fancied that the second of those matches, in early October, was to mark the beginning of a momentous run by us in the championship. Yet I felt the actual turning point in our season came a week later, when we beat Celtic 1–0 at Parkhead, with a goal by John Robertson. Robbo actually was carried off in that game with what appeared to be a serious neck injury, but fortunately for him, and us, the problem eased far quicker than we feared it might. The confidence within the team began to soar from then onwards, with consequences none of us could have imagined. Put it another way: having started the season as 200–1 against to win the title, the odds became ever shorter thereafter.

If you believe footballers are motivated by money, then it couldn't have been a bad thing that the chairman, Wallace Mercer, had introduced an innovative bonus scheme which was to pay big dividends on a monthly, roll-up basis. Come the turn of the year, and more especially, the run-in to the season, the players' wives must have been delighted with the size of the wage packets being brought home to them. Ok, we had our share of draws in the interim, but the trick was to remain unbeaten and our guys were getting good at performing it. Take the month of December by way of an example. It yielded 1–1 draws with Dundee away and Celtic home, then a 1–0 win over St Mirren away and a 2–0 win over Rangers away in which John Colquhoun scored twice. That sequence of results made for a happy festive season.

By the way, we'd already beaten Rangers 3–0 at Tynecastle in November, with two goals by Sandy Clark and another by John Robertson, and were to beat them again in late January, this time by 3–2 with Gary Mackay, Robbo and Colin McAdam the scorers. Was it possible we could keep going and actually win the title? None of us at Tynecastle dared even think about such a possibility for fear we might lose our collective nerve. We'd moved to the top of the table by late December, which was some going after being near the foot of it after the first quarter of the season. What had brought about the change in us? Well, one important factor was the sound link that had developed between Sandy Jardine and Craig Levein in central defence. We'd also made a conscious effort to improve our possession play.

All the while our unbeaten run was continuing, to the point that, when we won 2–0 against Motherwell at home in mid-March, it had stretched to twenty-one matches. That equalled the Premier Division record held by Rangers. Consistency of selection was a big help. I liked nothing better than to say to players in the dressing room before a game, 'Same team as last Saturday.' We'd set out promisingly in the Scottish Cup by then, but without shouting it from the rooftops of Gorgie, our primary aim was to do as well as we possibly could in the league. Beating Hibs 2–1 at Easter Road further underpinned this ambition, as did our subsequent victories (by 3–0 and 3–1) over St Mirren and Rangers at Tynecastle. Still we were at the top of the table, and with only four games to play. The countdown to our destiny had begun.

Dundee United were our closest rivals at that late stage in the season, five points adrift but having played two games fewer. Imagine our delight, therefore, when we beat them 3–0 at Tannadice in early April, with two goals by Wee Robbo and another by Sandy Clark. Bring on Aberdeen, who when we met them at Tynecastle had dropped into fourth place, two points behind United and Celtic, and like them by then, with just the one game in hand. The excitement surrounding the fixture was such that television claimed it as the first in the Premier Division to be screened live. Sandy Jardine and I weren't too enamoured either by that prospect or the fact the game was shifted from its designated Saturday spot to the following day, Sunday 20 April, to accommodate the cameras.

Our feeling was that the added hype might get to our players who, after all, were far less used to being the focus of the nation's attention than Aberdeen. There was also the fear that a lot of our fans might prefer watching from the comfort of their front rooms rather than actually turning out to give us their much-needed backing. In the event, a crowd of 19,000 was counted. But there was no doubt that the tension affected the way we played. Aberdeen looked conspicuously more relaxed and could easily have taken the lead before the interval. That they didn't was a blessed relief to us as we laboured on into the second half with the belief we'd do well to claim a goal-less draw. Then only fifteen minutes from time, Aberdeen got a penalty from which Peter Weir put them in front.

Game over? Not quite. Just five minutes later, as John Robertson jostled for possession, the ball broke to John Colquhoun, who prodded the equaliser past Bryan Gunn. The gods were on our side it seemed, with 1–1 being the final score and keeping us three points in front of Dundee United, who had played the same number of games as us by then – thirty-four – and four in front of Celtic, who had played only thirty-three. Could we possibly hang on? The whole country was asking the question, especially after we ground out a 1–0 victory over Clydebank at Tynecastle the following Saturday with a great strike by Gary Mackay.

Let me just digress for the moment and say it was on the back of that goal that Gary became a late pick by Scotland for the match against Holland the following midweek, one which was to see them complete their preparations for the World Cup finals in Mexico. He and John Robertson, who was named in the original squad, never got off the bench in Eindhoven, but could take no small measure of pride from this richly deserved recognition by the man in temporary charge of the national side, Alex Ferguson. But for the slight leg strain he'd been carrying for a few weeks that forced him to withdraw, a third Hearts player, Craig Levein, would have received the same honour.

Now, where was I? Yes, talking about Hearts being on the very cusp of greatness, one game away from winning their first title in twenty-six years. With Dundee United losing 2–1 to St Mirren at Tannadice on the day we beat Clydebank at Tynecastle, and Celtic winning 2–0 against Dundee at Parkhead, it was they who had become our closest rivals for the title. These results left them four points adrift of us, and a few days later, they closed that gap to two points by winning 2–0 at Motherwell. As if any Hearts fan needs reminding, this left us needing only to draw our last game – against Dundee at Dens Park – to be proclaimed champions. Alas, in the build-up to that climactic occasion, the gremlins moved into Tynecastle and began undermining our chances.

John Colquhoun, Neil Berry and Kenny Black were stricken by a flu bug and told to stay away from training for a couple of days. By taking this measure, we hoped to contain the infection. But later in the week, Brian Whittaker and George Cowie were similarly affected, and come the day of the Dundee game, I got the call saying Craig Levein was the latest victim and couldn't travel. This was serious, even if Sandy Jardine and I weren't inclined to admit as much publicly. We kept our worst fears to ourselves, not least for the reason our many years in football had taught us that excuses count for nothing. Only results matter.

Roddy MacDonald came in for Craig Levein, and given how well he'd done for us in the past, we didn't doubt that his experience would be invaluable on such a crucial occasion as this. Neil Berry and Brian Whittaker seemed ok to start the game, although, as things turned out, we had to replace Brian with another of our ailing players, Kenny Black, at half time. We were hanging in by that point, our game still being goal-less. What we didn't want to hear was that Celtic were banging in goals against St Mirren at Love Street. Sandy and I had tasked our club scout, Ian Cruickshanks, to attend that match, and by means of a walkie-talkie device, or maybe it was the original mobile phone, keep us informed of how it was unfolding.

Needless to say, Ian didn't bother calling after the interval. What he would have had to say could only have intensified the tension gripping us at Dens where, to our horror, substitute Albert Kidd proceeded to put Dundee in front with a seventy-third-minute goal. Our historic unbeaten run, having stretched to twenty-seven league games and thirty-one in all, suddenly appeared to be in jeopardy and all of us knew how bitter the consequences would be if we couldn't come up with an equaliser in the short time remaining.

Kidd duly scored again, with just two minutes left, to seal our fate with a 2–0 win for his side. Coupled with Celtic's 5–0 victory in Paisley, this result meant we had lost the title on goal difference. I could have wept. In fact, once we reached the dressing room, I did weep – along with everyone else.

If I'd been a year younger, with the ability to foresee how the last seventeen minutes of that game would unravel, I'd have thrown myself on as a substitute and kicked every ball which came my way into the stand. Those Hearts fans who had made the trip to Dens with such high expectations were as distraught as the rest of us. In truth, I've never quite come to terms with how the title was snatched away from us in such dire circumstances.

A few years back, I was asked to do a bit for a TV series reflecting on the occasion. Eventually, I had to hold up my hand and tell them to stop. The episode was just too painful for me to talk about.

Among the first things to hit me at the time was that, with our Scottish Cup Final against Aberdeen only a week away, I'd to try and lift the players' spirits. But I couldn't do it because I started to fill up with tears. I went into the toilet, spoke to myself, and resolved to try again. Still, I couldn't do it. I felt like Robert the Bruce telling himself to try, try, try again. Finally, I was able to tell the players to think about what they'd achieved in taking the title race to the last day – and with a big day at Hampden looming, what they could achieve still. Much good it may have done me, or them. Everybody was so cut up. I went home that night and got wellied.

Getting to the Cup final was a feat in itself, given that we'd set out by beating Rangers 3–2 at Tynecastle in front of a capacity crowd of 27,500. That game produced all sorts of drama, starting with Sandy Clark and his direct opponent, Craig Paterson, clashing heads and having to retire hurt. Then Ally McCoist put Rangers in front, but not for long, as Colin McAdam, who'd come on for Sandy, equalised shortly after the break with what was his first goal for Hearts. Gary Mackay proceeded to give us the lead, then Ian Durrant pulled us back to 2–2. By the time Derek Ferguson got sent off for a retaliatory foul on Gary, Rangers probably would have settled for a replay. But John Robertson denied them that hope with a late winner.

Henry Smith was hailed as a hero for us in the next round – against Hamilton Accies – on a heavily sanded pitch at Douglas Park. Four times the tie had been postponed because of bad weather, and when it finally got underway, we were caught as cold as the night, with John Brogan scoring for them in only fifteen seconds. Wee Robbo, fortunately, equalised within three minutes, and Gary Mackay put us 2–1 in front midway through the second half. Thereafter, it was Hamilton against Henry, with our goalie defying them time and again. And so to the quarter-finals in which we played St Mirren at Tynecastle. They lost their goalkeeper, Campbell Money, with a head knock shortly after John Colquhoun had put us in front, and David Winnie, an outfield player, had to take over.

The switch obviously affected the quality of the contest, and early into the second half, we were 4–0 in front, with two goals from Robbo (one of them a penalty) and another by Kenny Black. We were free-wheeling from then onwards – maybe a bit too easy-oasy for my liking, for I recall being a bit irked that we allowed Frank McGarvey to pull a goal back. A more professional approach was demanded from us come our semi-final tie against Dundee United at Hampden, and it was to that end we took the players away to a hotel in Irvine for a couple of days' preparation. These occasions are often nervy ones, with nobody wanting to miss out on a final. But a first-half goal by John Colquhoun helped settle us a bit and eventually saw us through by a 1–0 margin.

It was hard to get our heads round the fact that we'd reached out first final since the 3–1 defeat by Rangers ten years earlier. How could I forget that occasion, given I was in the opposition and scored one of their goals? Still, with our league challenge on-going, we didn't have the time or inclination to focus on the prospect until the days following the deep depression which had set in after losing the title at Dens Park. This time we chose to do our preparation at Seamill, which, back then, was Celtic's traditional hideaway before big games. Fortunately, the flu virus that had taken such a heavy toll of players the previous week had passed on. We just had injuries and a collective wounded spirit to contend with. How might we cope? The answer wasn't long in coming.

Aberdeen took the lead in only five minutes with a goal by John Hewitt, from whom Henry Smith was to make a great save before the interval. But we weren't out of things during that spell – far from it, in fact. Wee Robbo went agonisingly close with a lofted shot, while Gary Mackay sent a drive just wide. Sadly for us though, the second period began as the first had done, with Hewitt scoring to put Aberdeen 2–0 in front. Still our guys weren't beaten, and it was only after we'd hit the bar, with an effort by Neil Berry as I remember, that Peter Weir struck Aberdeen's third to finish us off 3–0. Alas, that wasn't an end to our misery. Walter Kidd, who'd been doubtful beforehand with a burst blood vessel in his foot, got himself dismissed for throwing the ball at an opponent. His was an act of frustration rather than malice, and pretty well summed up how all of us felt after an eight-day spell which had left us on our knees.

We went back that night to an Edinburgh hotel for what we'd hoped would be a celebration, but in the event, became more like a wake. Good on the fans, who were waiting to meet us and doing their best to lift our morale. Sandy Jardine and I headed for one of the rooms for a beer. Well, it would be a start to drowning our sorrows. Then, just as we were saying we'd have to go down and try to get things going, there came a knock at the door to tell us the chairman needed us in attendance before he could start his speech. All the wives and girlfriends had arrived by that point, and while we did our best to get into a party mood, it was difficult going on impossible to let our hair down.

What had promised to be Hearts' most memorable season in years, possibly their entire history, couldn't have come to a more miserable end, and neither Sandy nor myself were much consoled by the kudos that came to us on an individual basis. Sandy was nominated Player of the Year by the Scottish Football Writers' Association for the second time in his great career. The presentation took place at a dinner in Glasgow the night after we'd lost the league, and I think he had to be dragged away from a darkened room at home to receive it. As for myself, I was voted Manager of the Year, and among those who congratulated me on getting the award was Jim McLean of Dundee United.

'Well done,' he said, before adding something to the effect that, 'at least you haven't girned too much about the way things turned out.'

It made me feel a bit guilty about some of the tricks we'd played on him at games involving our teams at Tynecastle. I could recall once when he was watching from the stand, we got somebody to play about with the network of the walkie-talkie system he was using to communicate with his people on the bench. Poor Jim ended up speaking to himself. Then, on another occasion when he was in the stand again, we locked a door leading downstairs to the dressing room so he couldn't be there waiting for his players come the interval. No kidding, MI5 had nothing on some of us managers.

21

LANDING A KICK
ON WALLACE MERCER

Quite the biggest story to break in Scottish football in the latter half of 1986 was Alex Ferguson's move from Aberdeen to become manager of Manchester United. Nobody could say he hadn't earned it after a phenomenal eight-year reign at Pittodrie, which yielded three League Championships, four Scottish Cups and one League Cup. This is not to forget the Dons' greatest prize of all, the European Cup Winners' Cup that they lifted in 1983 before going on to win the European Super Cup.

But who would take over from him? I'd been over in Arran one Sunday with my pal Billy Clark, playing in his brother Arnold's golf outing, and got home to find Sandy Jardine sitting in my front room waiting for me.

'What's happening?' I asked, surprised to see him. Sandy proceeded to say Fergie had been on the phone saying he had recommended him to the Aberdeen directors as his successor. 'Brilliant, absolutely brilliant,' said I. Then Sandy asked me if I would fancy going with him. But I sensed he wasn't in any hurry to leave Edinburgh, his home city, and also that he shared my belief we could build on what we'd achieved to date at Hearts.

So it was agreed between us he would speak the next morning to Wallace Mercer. This he did, with the upshot he was appointed joint-manager of Hearts alongside myself. His step up was no problem for me. We knew each other so well, after all, and had been pals and colleagues so long, both at Rangers and Hearts.

The fact Wallace Mercer hadn't consulted me beforehand wasn't a problem either. He would have known anything he arranged with Sandy would be ok by me.

How might it have worked had Sandy opted for Pittodrie? Well, I dare say I could have been his assistant, or co-manager. It would have been immaterial to me, but with Sandy having made his decision to stay on at Tynecastle, it was academic also.

Earlier that year, when Hearts still were pushing to win the league and Scottish Cup, there had been talk in some of the papers that Sandy and I could be in line to take over at Rangers. Come the end of the season, with the World Cup finals in Mexico in the offing, Rangers plumped for Graeme Souness to take over from Jock Wallace in the role of player–manager. So much then for the rumours about me and Sandy going back to Ibrox, although had there been an actual offer made, I dare say the pair of us might have been tempted to accept it.

But regardless of what might have been, there was an ongoing challenge to be met at Tynecastle as season 1986–87 got underway. A heavier expectation than usual was weighing on Hearts, for the obvious reason of how close we'd been to achieving success on two fronts only a few months beforehand. The intervening summer break had been long enough for us to put our abject disappointment pretty well behind us and re-focus on the job of making Hearts that bit stronger. Freshening up our squad seemed the least we could do to that end, hence the arrival of Wayne Foster from Preston North End, who was to become a firm favourite with the fans.

Another recruit was a player who I shouldn't name out of respect to him. Let's just say he had scored quite a few goals for a rival club. The chairman invited him to his house for signing talks and insisted that I be present. So, with the three of us sitting round a table, Wallace started to talk money. The longer he went on, the more the money went up. I finally booted him under the table, as if to say, 'Hey, you're going over the top here.' He promptly looked back at the player, saying, 'Oops, my manager's kicking me.' Gee, thanks, Wallace. The guy finally signed for us but didn't fit in well as we'd hoped, and within a couple of months, the club accommodated his request to be released from his contract.

We'd played our first derby of the season by that point, and what a boost we got from the result, a 3–1 win, with goals by Ian Jardine, Sandy Clark and John Robertson. Hibs fans had been making merry since the summer about how the previous season had ended in such crippling disappointment for us. Come the day of the game at Easter Road, as our lads wandered out to inspect the pitch, they copped for an earful of jeers from the Hibs supporters already gathered. If anything, the mocking reception we got made us even more determined to put on a show. Now, I was never one for gloating in victory, but I made an exception in this case.

When the team came into the dressing room at full time, I let out with a chorus of 'Can you hear the Hibees sing – no-o, no-o.' Some of our guys probably thought I'd taken leave of my senses, but I invited them to join in. Some did willingly, others a bit reluctantly. We even left the door open so that our chants could echo throughout the building for all to hear. I felt a bit better after that. It was my way, our way, of letting Hibs and everybody else know Hearts were still in business and resolved to put behind us all the anguish we'd had to endure over the close-season.

Manchester United, still under Ron Atkinson's managership, duly played us in a friendly at Tynecastle, one which ended 2–2. A fortnight or so later, we met Dukla Prague in the opening round of the UEFA Cup, and with goals by Sandy Clark, Wayne Foster and John Robertson, beat them 3–2. But that result wasn't good enough to sustain us overall in the tie, the Czechs winning 1–0 on their own patch to go through on the away goals rule. A worse fate had befallen us in the Skol Cup by that juncture, with Montrose twice surging forward on the break to knock us out of the tournament with a 2–0 victory. Dundee United, who were early leaders in the championship, beat us 1–0 at Tannadice a few days later, although subsequent results stablised us in the upper half of the table.

These included a 1–0 win against Aberdeen at Pittodrie, with Sandy Clark our scorer, and a 4–0 victory over Motherwell at Tynecastle in which John Colquhoun, Sandy, Wayne Foster and John Robertson got our goals. Then, by way of showing we weren't going to be pushed around by the team Graeme Souness was in the early throes of re-fashioning, Neil Berry earned us a 1–1 draw with them at Tynecastle. But a couple of weeks later, during which time we'd lost 2–0 to Celtic away and drawn 0–0 with St Mirren at home, we were hit by a serious setback with Craig Levein suffering a knee injury which was to keep him out for what seemed like an eternity.

Forgive me if I jump ahead of myself here by recalling how, the following year I think it was, we tried to sign John Brown from Dundee. What a player he could have been for us and what a player he turned out to be for Rangers once Souness signed him at the start of 1988. The deal was as good as completed to bring John to Tynecastle. All that remained was for him to undergo his medical at an Edinburgh hospital. The chairman decided to accompany him for that and came back with an anguished look on his face.

'What's the problem?' I asked.

'The specialist says he can't guarantee five years out of one of John's knees, so I've called off the deal.'

To which I said, 'But tell me the player whose knees you can guarantee five years out of? Remember Craig Levein.'

Craig was a big athlete, as fit and strong as anybody at the club, but unknown to all of us, his must have been an accident waiting to happen. It occurred in a reserve game at Hibs when, without so much as anybody putting in a tackle on him, he just keeled over with what proved to be ligament damage. Rest rather than surgery was prescribed, and almost a year elapsed before he managed to play again. Sadly, within a matter of months, in a game against Rangers at Tynecastle, Craig collapsed again with a recurrence of the same problem. There was no avoiding surgery this time and a complicated operation it was too, rendering him inactive for another year.

The fact he made it with Scotland to Italy for the 1990 World Cup finals was testimony to the character he showed during his two long spells on the sidelines. As a player, I was pretty fortunate to avoid any long-term injury but took my hat off to any guy who had to slog, sometimes for months on end, in the gymnasium before coming back. Craig had my utmost admiration for the way he managed to cope. I don't doubt for a minute that were it not for those setbacks at a crucial stage of his career, he could have earned himself a move to a bigger club than Hearts. Rangers and Spurs had been interested, and I certainly remember Alex Ferguson talking admiringly of him.

That would have been in September 1989, after Craig had returned a second time. Fergie brought his team to Tynecastle then for a friendly, as Ron Atkinson had done those three seasons earlier, and spoke with me about him afterwards. I had always told Craig that if anybody made a bid for him, he would be told, but no bid by Fergie ever materialised.

But back to his initial injury, which occurred in October 1986. Our consolation was that Roddy MacDonald was available to come in. He was a good pro from the old school, always ready to do his bit when called upon. We were sitting fourth-top in the table at the time, behind Dundee United, Celtic and Rangers, and believing we could make up the leeway.

Losing 3–0 to Rangers at Ibrox in November didn't set us back that much because the following week at Tynecastle we beat Celtic 1–0 with a goal by Neil Berry. That was us into December, which is to be remembered for the fact we registered our biggest victory in years then, 7-0 against bottom-placed Hamilton Accies at home. Believe it or not, Wee Robbo only scored twice on that occasion, the other goals being shared by Sandy Jardine, Roddy MacDonald, John Colquhoun, Neil Berry and Gary Mackay. The Scottish Cup was in the offing, and the players looked forward to competing on that front as well, maybe to make up for having lost the previous season's final to Aberdeen. It was to prove a gruelling, if exciting, experience for them.

The opening round saw us paired with Kilmarnock at Tynecastle and draw 0–0. The replay at Rugby Park ended 1–1, with Wayne Foster getting our goal. Needless to say, it was a tired Hearts team that faced Rangers at Tynecastle in a league game just a few days later, and despite a brace by Robbo, we ended up losing 5–2. That result, by the way, put an end to a record we'd been proud to hold in that it was our first league defeat at home in thirty-two games spanning twenty-one months. It also gave us cause to sense, if not admit publicly, that the title was likely to be beyond our grasp. Rangers, in their first season under Graeme Souness, won it eventually after being pushed a fair bit of the way by Celtic.

Our focus of attention promptly swung back to the Cup – and a third game with Killie, again at their place. There was no messing with us this time, not after Gary Mackay had put us in front. Kenny Black duly increased our lead, and while Killie pulled a goal back, Wayne Foster struck late on to see us through with a 3–1 win. Bring on Celtic, who as nobody at Tynecastle could have forgotten, had deprived us of the title we craved less than a year earlier. Both teams really went for it in the tie at Tynecastle, and we did well to win it 1–0 late on, when from just outside their penalty area, Wee Robbo slammed in a free-kick. That was us into the quarter-finals in which we had a strength-sapping slog with Motherwell. We drew 1–1 with them at Tynecastle – thanks to a goal by Robbo – and won the replay 1–0, with John Colquhoun scoring late on.

We seemed to be well primed for our semi-final tie with St Mirren at Hampden, after beating Hibs 2–1 at Tynecastle in the league, courtesy of strikes by Roddy MacDonald and Sandy Clark. But injuries and suspensions took their toll of us, with Wee Robbo among those we had to play without, and a first-half goal by Ian Ferguson didn't help our cause. Could we come back? Gary Mackay answered that question when he scored with sixteen minutes remaining, but Frank McGarvey settled the issue in St Mirren's favour in the time remaining. What a disappointment.

We'd have loved to reach the final again and take our chance on beating Dundee United.

St Mirren ended up doing that, qualifying for the Cup Winners' Cup in the process. Fair play to them, but a side effect of their 1–0 win was that Dundee United took the UEFA Cup place, which otherwise would have been ours for finishing fifth in the table. In short, we didn't even have Europe to look forward to after all the effort we'd poured into the season. In the programme for our last game, a 1–1 draw with Dundee United at Tynecastle, I noted with a tinge of disappointment:

> Since Craig Levein was injured in October, we have rarely been able to field a settled team. The situation worsened around the New Year and, recently, has been a nightmare. Craig, Neil Berry, Ian and Sandy Jardine have all missed a lot of games [and] it has been difficult to find a rhythm of work to a pattern.

Injuries and suspensions tend to undermine the best of teams and, in our case, went some way to explaining why we hadn't been able to match or better the standards we'd set for ourselves the previous term. Maybe it was time to get out the Kay's catalogue. This was a standing joke between the chairman and me. Come the end of a season, or the midway point in it, I would always ask if the players' catalogue was coming out. In other words, could we stretch to buying a player for a £1 down and £1 every week thereafter? But in reality, we'd moved on a bit from when the likes of Sandy Clark was recruited on a 'never, never' basis. If we weren't in anything like the spending league of Rangers, at least we could afford to pay out some decent money for the right kind of player.

Big Davie McPherson fitted that description, and with doubts continuing about when Craig Levein might be fit again, he seemed like the kind of guy we could do with. Word had it he was surplus to Rangers' requirements, so as I prepared to go on holiday during the summer of 1987, I said to the chairman, 'If we could get him for £300,000, it would be absolutely brilliant.'

Away I went for a couple of weeks at Douglas Park's place in Marbella, if I remember correctly. The chairman duly set wheels in motion by contacting Rangers, and when he couldn't get a hold of me in the south of Spain, he phoned Sandy and got him to speak directly with Graeme Souness about Big Davie. Souness was agreeable to letting the player go for £370,000 but told Sandy, 'You'll have to take Hugh Burns as well.' I caught up with this latest development when I got back, and as it happened, I quite liked Hugh Burns. I thought he could offer us good cover for Wattie Kidd, so we ended up with the two of them. Davie went straight into our team come the new season and as everyone knows, became an absolute stalwart for us, while Hugh played his fair share of games in place of Wattie.

Our preparations for that term, 1987–88, had us in West Germany. We'd gone there in 1985 and really enjoyed the facilities and derived a benefit from the warm-up matches we'd played against local sides. This time was no different, and we came home to play Newcastle United at Tynecastle in our final warm-up, losing 1–0, before kicking off in the league with a 4–2 win over Falkirk, again at home. Wee Robbo scored twice in that game, by way of reminding his growing band of admirers that he was as sharp as ever in front of goal. A 1–0 defeat by Celtic at Parkhead followed, as did a 1–1 draw with St Mirren at Love Street. Then we were into the Skol Cup, thrashing Kilmarnock 6–1 at Tynecastle, with two goals from Sandy Clark and one goal apiece from Wayne Foster, Gary Mackay, Neil Berry and the recently signed Davie McPherson.

That result was a great fillip for us, and in its immediate wake came a 4–1 win over Dundee United in a league match at Tynecastle. Again, Sandy Clark scored twice, with the other goals being shared by Robbo and Ian Jardine. One way or another, we could be reasonably encouraged by the start we'd made, but our progress in the Skol Cup was checked soon enough, with Rangers beating us 4–1 at Ibrox in the fourth round. This was after we'd beaten Clyde 2–0 at Tynecastle in the third round with a brace from Wee Robbo. He'd also scored for us in our 1–0 derby win over Hibs at Tynecastle to maintain our momentum in the league.

Our continuing good form in the championship, underpinned by four straight wins in September, was interrupted only by a 0–0 draw with Rangers at Tynecastle. Thereafter, we beat Aberdeen 2–1, again at Tynecastle, with goals by Robbo and Davie McPherson, and Falkirk 5–1 away, with John Colquhoun (twice), Wayne Foster, Ian Jardine and Robbo all finding the net. We were sitting at the top of the Premier Division by then, and despite losing 2–1 to Hibs at Easter Road, where Robbo scored for us, we were still in that lofty position by late October when we beat Morton 3–0 at home, with two goals from Kenny Black and another by Gary Mackay.

Everton had paid us a visit by then to provide the opposition for Wattie Kidd's testimonial. I was delighted to see him honoured in such a way. What a servant he'd been to Hearts. His commitment was second to none and yes, he could play a bit as well. Those surging runs of his down the right flank earned him the nickname Zico, after the famous Brazilian. Just for the record, our scorer in a 1–1 draw with the English side was a lad just beginning to emerge, Allan Moore. Distinction of a different sort soon was conferred on Gary Mackay, as he made his international debut for Scotland in a European Championship tie against Bulgaria in Sofia. Fair to say, I was as pleased for him as he was for himself.

When a manager sees one of his players make it to that level, he knows his time hasn't been wasted. In Gary's case, he'd come a long way since he and Dave Bowman used to sort out my training kit for me when I first arrived at Tynecastle. The fact he scored Scotland's goal in a 1–0 win made the occasion all the more memorable for him. But bizarrely, the result was of greater benefit to the Republic of Ireland, who qualified for Euro '88 on the back of it. Hence the reason why, to this day, Gary could go on a pub crawl in Dublin and not have to buy a drink.

But getting back to Hearts' ongoing season, a new player was soon to join us from the lower reaches of English football and prove himself very quickly at the top level in Scotland. I'm referring to Mike Galloway, who we picked up from Halifax on the advice of my childhood pal, Jimmy Lumsden. Mike stayed with us for less than two seasons before we sold him to Celtic for £550,000. But what a job he did in that time, not least in Europe. He made his debut as a substitute against Dundee United at Tannadice, where two goals by Robbo and another by Wayne Foster gave us a 3–0 win.

We were still sitting top of the division by that point and were only removed from it by Celtic after losing 3–2 to Rangers at Ibrox, where Mike (in his first actual start) scored, along with Robbo. That match marked the half-way point in our league season, with twenty-two games played and Robbo on seventeen goals, including six penalties. How long before somebody came in for him, the country's most natural scorer? We were to get an answer before the season was out. But even he could fire blanks, as happened over the festive period when we played three goal-less draws in a row: against Dundee and Morton away and Hibs at home. He duly got his eye again by scoring twice in a 4–0 win over Dunfermline at East End Park, Mike Galloway and John Colquhoun being our other scorers there.

Then came a 1–1 draw with Rangers at Tynecastle, in which Sandy Clark got our goal. The upshot of that was Aberdeen leapfrogged us into second-top place, albeit we were only four points adrift of the leaders, Celtic, by then. Unfortunately, it was a gap we were never going to close, despite some creditable results, including a 6–0 victory over St Mirren at Love Street, where John Colquhoun claimed a hat-trick, Robbo a brace and Wayne Foster a single. Suffice to say that while eventually recovering second place in the table, we finished the season ten points behind the title winners, Celtic. It was just our luck that they put an end to our hope of winning the Scottish Cup also.

We'd set out promisingly enough in that competition by beating Falkirk 3–1 away, with two further goals by Robbo and another by Wayne Foster. Sandy Clark and Gary Mackay proceeded to give us a 2–0 win over Morton at Tynecastle in the next round. So far, so good, with the picture looking brighter still when goals from John Conquhoun, Wayne Foster and Gary Mackay resulted in our 3–0 victory over Dunfermline, again at Tynecastle. By then we were in line to meet Celtic in the semi-finals at Hampden where, I hope they won't mind my saying so, neither side's goal-keeper distinguished himself.

The game was goal-less until the sixtieth minute when Brian Whittaker rained a cross in on Pat Bonner. He must have been distracted by Davie McPherson, because the ball dropped behind him and crossed the line. Then, with just three minutes left, our own Henry Smith was caught out by a cross from which Mark McGhee equalised. Could we hold out for extra time? Sadly not. In the brief period remaining, McGhee put in a challenge on Henry, and as the ball dropped, Andy Walker slammed it into the net.

So it was a disconsolate support that followed us back to Edinburgh, with more than Celtic's 2–1 win troubling them. Gnawing away in their thoughts too was the fear they had seen the last of John Robertson in Hearts' colours.

22

SOLDIERING ON WITHOUT SANDY

Wee John Robertson's double against Dunfermline in January 1988 had seen him rack up a century of championship goals for us in little more than five years. All but the first twenty-one of these were in the Premier Division. Was there a striker anywhere in the country quite as sharp as him? Not in my estimation. Some players will score goals for you in games that don't particularly matter, but Robbo scored in even the most important ones. His record against Hibs, for example, was terrific. But there seemed to be no satisfying his demands for a new contract, with the result being that the almost inevitable happened when the chairman finally opted to sell him to Newcastle United for a fee of £750,000.

That decision was reached a couple of weeks after our Scottish Cup semi-final defeat by Celtic. By making it public immediately after we'd beaten them 2–1 in a league game at Tynecastle in mid-April, with goals by Gary Mackay and Mike Galloway, maybe Wallace Mercer softened the blow a bit as far as the fans were concerned. In saying that, I was at least as upset as them that we were losing such a valuable asset. I didn't think going to Newcastle was the right move for Robbo either.

Most of the top strikers playing in England at that time were big guys. Ok, I know Michael Owen came along some years later to buck that trend but he was a runner, while Robbo did his best work in the penalty box. If he'd got the chance to join Rangers or Celtic, feeding off the greater amount of service they could have provided him with, I think he would have been a sensation.

In my book, he was at least as effective as Ally McCoist, who didn't make a bad career for himself as a goal-scorer at Ibrox. But Robbo had a hankering to try his luck down south, and try as Hearts did to keep him, he couldn't be dissuaded.

The chairman had the last word on Robbo's way-going, writing in the programme for what was our last home match of the season, against St Mirren:

> The directors and management were disappointed to sell John Robertson to Newcastle but felt it was in the best interests of the club and the player to agree terms. We wish him well in his new career.
>
> I have written inviting John and his wife to be our guests at today's match. John has made a significant contribution to Heart of Midllothian over the last few years and he will always be welcome to return to Tynecastle.

A significant contribution, did he say? The wee fella's record for us by the time of his departure revealed that, in 297 appearances in all competitions, he'd amassed 147 goals. I could only console myself with the thought we had Scott Crabbe shaping up well as his replacement and, hopefully, a few quid to spend on new players.

Come in Eamonn Bannon and Iain Ferguson from Dundee United. Their combined experience was to serve us well in Europe as well as domestically. Eamonn had been with Hearts as a youngster before moving on to Chelsea. If I remember correctly, he'd been a skilful, right-sided midfield player in those days, but on joining Dundee United, Jim McLean converted him into something akin to a left-winger. It was in that role he went to the 1986 World Cup finals in Mexico, with Alex Ferguson in temporary charge of the Scotland team.

Could Eamonn run? His energy seemed limitless, and while Sandy Jardine and I knew his legs couldn't last forever, we recognised that his ability to put the ball into the penalty box would serve us well. Iain was altogether different in style, in that he could play up front or that bit deeper. One thing seemed guaranteed: wherever we used him, he would pitch in with his share of goals. Neither of these recruits came cheap, though. Eamonn cost us in excess of £200,000, while Iain's fee, which had to be set by a tribunal, was something of the same order. But, with Robbo having gone, we could afford to push the boat out a bit, and of course, as time was to tell, we hadn't quite seen the back of him.

Our preparations for season 1988–89 saw us return to Germany for a series of warm-up games. These were followed by a couple in the north of Scotland, then a friendly at Tynecastle against the Brazilian side, Cruzeiro. We managed to beat them 2–1, with goals by Iain Ferguson and Kenny Black, but proceeded to lose our opening league match against Celtic away by 1–0. The Skol Cup soon began to demand our attention also. But the players were at least primed for appearing in the UEFA Cup in which we'd been drawn against the Irish side, St Patrick's Athletic of Dublin. The first leg was scheduled to go ahead in Dublin, and so it did, but at the Home Farm's Tolka Park. St Pat's opted to move it there in order to maximise their income. In other words, they suspected their participation in the tournament was likely to be over almost before it had begun.

Yet, while experience told us we had to be on our guard over there, we ended up winning comfortably enough by 2–0, with a goal by Mike Galloway and a penalty by Wayne Foster. Henry Smith had an untroubled night, until sustaining a head knock in the second half. It soon became clear we would have to send young Murray McDermott on in his place, but getting Henry off the park wasn't exactly straightforward. Nobody could find a stretcher. The search went on, with Henry having to be treated where he'd fallen. Eventually he had to be led to the pavilion, where several stitches were inserted into his wound.

We proceeded to win our home leg by the same score, Mike Galloway helping himself to another goal along with Kenny Black, and were paired thereafter with Austria Vienna. In anybody's estimation, this promised to be a tougher assignment, and so it proved, as the first leg at Tynecastle ended goal-less. The Austrians played as we thought they might in that game, pulling so many men behind the ball that it was difficult for us to get in behind them. We did make a chance or two, right enough, and would have felt better about our chances over in Vienna had we taken at least one of them.

But before the return leg came around, something happened which grieves me even yet. I likened it at the time to a death in the family. On the back of a 3–0 defeat by Rangers in the league – they'd already knocked us out of the Skol Cup by the same score – Sandy Jardine and I were called individually to a meeting with the chairman and the directors. This was on a Thursday, just forty-eight hours before a championship game against St Mirren at Paisley. Neither of us had a clue what was afoot, but Sandy opted to go in first.

Out he came a few minutes later, with a shocked expression on his face. 'You'll never believe this, Dod,' he said. 'I've just been sacked.'

He was right. I couldn't believe it. My immediate thought was if Sandy goes, I go. There had always been that pact between us.

Anyway, in I went, not knowing what might happen next. Then I heard the chairman intoning, 'Mr MacDonald, we've sacked Mr Jardine. He'll get paid up for the remainder of his contract. We're not going to sack you, but if you decide to walk away, we're not going to pay you up.'

I still had a year, maybe eighteen months, left in my contract, so felt as if I was being pulled over a barrel.

Wallace Mercer didn't make the situation any easier for me when he proceeded to say, 'You're not a rich man, Mr MacDonald.'

I went, 'Aye, true.'

What he seemed to be saying, in effect, was that I couldn't afford to stand on principle.

Out I went, to find Sandy waiting for me. 'Look, they want me to stay, but if I walk, I'm getting nothing,' I told him.

'You can't walk,' he said. 'Don't do that.' Sandy couldn't have been more insistent.

'But we've got a pact,' I said.

Again, Sandy was having none of it. 'Dod,' he said, 'you stay.'

I duly went home to explain things to Christine. I couldn't think clearly. Eventually I decided on a course of action which may or not have been the correct one. It involved me going through to Tynecastle the next morning and seeking out the chairman.

'You were one hundred per cent right in what you said yesterday, Mr Mercer,' I told him. 'I'm not a rich man. Give me a new contract. You can take money off my wages every month if you like, but I want you to pay off my mortgage.'

By putting it that way, I was giving him the chance to tell me to get lost. I would have had to walk out of the door with Sandy in that case. But he agreed to what I said, and rightly or wrongly, I stayed. To this day, I don't know exactly why the chairman decided Sandy had to go. He told the press that the co-manager arrangement wasn't working, but I suspected he took the decision he did for no greater reason than Sandy was getting more publicity than him. Since we'd been made co-managers a couple of years earlier, Sandy had taken a lot of the press calls. He was good at that side of things, as well as many others. He would be answering the phone to reporters, while I was involving myself with the players, maybe at heidie tennis.

No, we didn't play just for the hell of it. I regarded heidie tennis as being an important extra in our training routine. Players had to use their feet, as well as their heads, which helped them improve their touch on the ball almost without noticing. The sessions could be very competitive, with a few quid riding on their outcomes. I've still got a couple of pound notes signed by players who'd lost out. But that's another story.

Sandy was away, having given Hearts six years of sterling service since coming from Rangers. On top of all the help he'd given me, first as assistant manager, then as co-manager, he'd made 277 first-team appearances for the club, including 184 in the championship. These statistics were noted in a brief article in a match programme a few weeks after the event of his way-going, under a wee headline which read 'Good Luck, Sandy'. The opening line said, 'No doubt the chairman will cover the departure of Sandy Jardine . . . ' But in his own notes in the same publication, Mercer made only an oblique mention of having removed Sandy from the staff. Let me just add this by way of a postscript: only the day before Sandy was sacked, Douglas Park resigned from the board for what was said to be 'business reasons'. I never did find out if that was a diplomatic way of saying he didn't want any part in Sandy's removal.

So there I was, without my best mate in football, as we approached the return match with Vienna, although I could continue to count on great support from guys like Wattie Borthwick and John Binnie. Importantly, we hadn't conceded a goal against the Austrians at Tynecastle. That meant we didn't have to go chasing the game over there. We could sit in rather and try to pick them off. Young Jimmy Sandison proved crucial to the first part of our strategy, by following their best player, Herbert Prohaska, wherever he went. It was a role I'd performed often enough in my days of playing in Europe with Rangers, marking the opposition's danger man. I had every reason to believe Jimmy could carry it out to the letter. Anyway, despite the freezing cold conditions, we managed to hang in there and put a strict hold on the Austrians' advances. Then, all of a sudden, with the second half not long underway, the game opened up for us and provided a tantalising glimpse of the next round.

Eamonn Bannon made ground on the left before switching the play to the far side with a pass to Wattie Kidd. His run took him to the by-line before he sent over a cross which big Mike Galloway, having read the situation as it was developing, knocked in at the far post with his head. The Austrians, who were unbeaten at home in domestic competition that season and had a handful of internationals as well as Prohaska in their side, could find no way back in the half hour or so remaining. We made sure of that, and as their frustration got the better of them, only their goalkeeper came between Jimmy Sandison and a second goal for us.

The press reports awaiting us on our return to Tynecastle were glowing, with Stewart Brown writing in the Edinburgh *Evening News*, 'Hearts' outstanding performance . . . was also their biggest triumph on the European front,' while Ian Wood noted in *The Scotsman*, 'This will be the first time Hearts have gone as far in European competition without the benefit of a bye for thirty years, and it was a reward tirelessly worked for and richly deserved.'

Bring on Velez Mostar, from what we'd call nowadays the 'old Yugoslavia', in the third round. No, they weren't one of Europe's bigger names, and because they'd just gone into their winter break (this was November), we didn't have an opportunity to watch them in advance of the first leg at Tynecastle.

But we didn't go blind into that game. Andy Roxburgh, the Scotland manager, gave us some useful information about the opposition, while Scottish referee David Syme, who'd handled the away leg of their previous tie in Portugal, kindly gave us a video of it. In the match programme, I urged our fans to give the players one hundred per cent support, and in the event, they didn't have to wait long to see us take the lead – seventeen minutes, to be exact. Eamonn Bannon scored then, after a move involving Iain Ferguson and Gary Mackay. We could have scored at least one more goal before half time. Then again, Velez could have equalised. They were by no means a bad side. But Mike Galloway's goal shortly into the second half put us in a more comfortable position, and John Colquhoun made it 3–0 just before the end.

Wee John, by the way, was fortunate still to be upright at that point. One of his opponents had cut the legs from him shortly beforehand and had been sent off for his troubles.

And so to the second leg in which we sensed Velez might be an entirely different proposition. Almost certainly, we would be glad of the cushion our lead from Tynecastle afforded, although nothing could have prepared us for the hostility we experienced over there. Our dugout was pelted with missiles almost throughout, so much so we had to stop players leaving it to warm up on the sidelines. It was as bad an atmosphere as I'd experienced and quite why no action was taken against the home club for the behaviour of their fans escaped me. UEFA work in funny ways. Still, we did well enough on the park. After going behind on the half-hour, we equalised midway through the second half with a header by Mike Galloway. We were as good as through to the quarter-finals by that point, and the loss of a late goal which gave Velez a 2–1 win couldn't hinder our progress.

Never before had Hearts got as far in a European tournament, and much as that fact must have cheered Wallace Mercer, he wasn't in Mostar to see us take the historic step. He'd been detained in Edinburgh to conduct an important piece of business, the re-signing from Newcastle, after less than half a season there, of John Robertson. Tosh McKinlay was recruited from Dundee at pretty much the same time, but more about these two issues later.

Everyone at Tynecastle was willing us to be paired with Napoli in the last eight. Why? Because the great Diego Maradona played for them. Had I not been passed my fortieth birthday by then, I could have been tempted out of retirement to face him. Our other possible opponents were Victoria Bucharest, Dynamo Dresden, VfB Stuttgart, Real Sociedad, Juventus . . . and the ones we finally drew, Bayern Munich. They'd actually been at Tynecastle some three years earlier for a friendly against a Hearts–Hibs select arranged as part of a twinning arrangement between the cities of Edinburgh and Munich. The game this time would be for real and players and fans couldn't wait to see it. Bayern, leading the Bundesleague, had lost several top players during the summer, including Lothar Matthaus, but brought in the likes of Stefan Reuter, Olaf Thon and Johnny Ekstroem. We couldn't promise our fans we'd get a result against the Germans. But our commitment to fight was guaranteed from the instant the tie came out of the hat, and fight we did.

I doubt if there's a Hearts fan alive who doesn't know the result of the first leg played at Tynecastle on the night of 28 February 1989. Iain Ferguson probably remembers it better than anybody, in that his superb goal gave us a famous 1–0 win. Bayern had looked every bit as menacing as we thought they might do before, with the second half not long underway, and following a free-kick by Tosh McKinlay, Fergie struck with a spectacular shot from twenty-five yards out. If only Big Davie McPherson had been as good a marksman, he could have given us a second goal shortly before the end of what was a terrific match.

'Hearts gave themselves a fighting chance of reaching the semi-finals of the UEFA Cup for the first time in their history when Iain Ferguson fired the goal which inflicted on the mighty Bayern Munich only their third defeat of the season,' Mike Aitken wrote in *The Scotsman*, while Jim Kean, just as upbeat, told *Daily Record* readers, 'Hearts' remarkable dream of European glory is very much alive and kicking.' You bet it was. We couldn't wait for the return leg at the Olympic Stadium in Munich where, unfortu-nately, we conceded a goal in only sixteen minutes to Klaus Augenthaler. Some goal it was too, struck from even further out than Iain Ferguson's at Tynecastle.

With the tie on a knife-edge, John Colquhoun proceeded to knock a chance just past the post. Then both Craig Levein and Davie McPherson headed wide. We played a lot of good football that night. There was no hint of our guys being intimidated by the quality of the opposition, or unnerved by the occasion. Far from it, indeed, as John Colquhoun proceeded to hit the post with a header before Davie McPherson sent the rebound past. That's how close we were to equalising on the night, until with sixty-nine minutes gone, Erland Johnsen scored a disputed second goal for Bayern to set them up for the semi-finals on a 2–1 aggregate.

My notes in the programme for a subsequent match at Tynecastle sounded like a lament for an honourable, if ultimately unsuc-cessful, bid to reach the semi-finals of the tournament:

The major disappointment obviously was the defeat in Munich that ended Hearts' interest in this season's UEFA Cup, a competition which brought so much excitement to Tynecastle this term. We were so desperately unlucky in the

Olympic Stadium when the players gave their all for the club. While the first German goal was a cracker, the second was most definitely offside. In between, many of our efforts came close and John Colquhoun's luck was out with a header which hit the post.

So after the champagne and caviar of Europe – well, I'm sure Wallace Mercer had indulged his appetite for fine wine and food on our trips abroad – we were left with only the bread and butter of domestic football to satisfy ours. It wasn't an especially mouth-watering prospect in that we were sitting fourth-bottom of the then ten-team B&Q Premier Division by the time of our European exit, with only six wins in twenty-seven matches. The most notable of them had been against Rangers at Tynecastle shortly before the turn of the year, ending 2–0 in our favour. It was in that game that Tosh McKinlay made what registered as a very encouraging debut for us at left-back. Various guys, including Neil Berry and Jimmy Sandison, had worn the number 3 jersey beforehand, but it fitted Tosh best. He liked to get down the flank and, of course, was capable of putting a good cross into the box.

The Rangers fixture also marked John Robertson's welcome return from Newcastle, where for one reason or another, he hadn't done as well as he might have hoped. The chairman really pushed the boat out to re-instate him, although it wasn't until the end of the month that he got himself back on the goals standard with two in a 4–2 defeat by Celtic at Parkhead. Robbo, who was carrying an injury if I recall correctly, didn't score again until early April when he and Eamonn Bannon secured a 2–1 win over Hibs at Tynecastle in our last derby of the season. We finally settled for finishing sixth-top of the table, five points adrift of Hibs but twenty-five behind the champions, Rangers. Who could have foreseen that the Ibrox side, under Graeme Souness, then Walter Smith, would retain the title for the next eight years?

We'd hoped to do so much better, having finished second to Celtic in the previous one. In saying that, it had looked as if we might go the distance in the League Cup after setting out with a 5–0 win over St Johnstone at Tynecastle. Iain Ferguson distinguished himself in that tie with a hat-trick, Gary Mackay and Ian Jardine getting our other goals. Malcolm Murray and Kenny Black duly gave us a 2–0 win over Meadowbank away, while in the round following that one, against Dunfermline away, Fergie scored twice and Gary Mackay and John Colquhoun one apiece in a 4–1 win. But Rangers awaited us in the semi-final at Hampden and won by a convincing 3–0.

The Scottish Cup could have been kinder to us also. We kicked off in that competition with a 4–1 win over Ayr United at home, Davie McPherson, Mike Galloway, John Colquhoun getting a goal each, and an Ayr player inadvertantly adding the fourth. Ah, well, they all count, don't they? Eamonn Bannon and John Colquhoun then gave us a 2–0 win over Partick Thistle, again at home. But that was as good as it got, what with Eamonn Bannon's goal not being enough to sustain us in the fifth round at Parkhead, where Celtic won 2–1. Who knows, had we not played our return match against Bayern Munich just a few days beforehand, maybe we would have done us more justice.

Still, if it had been a disappointing season on the domestic front, Davie McPherson had done well in a personal sense by winning the first of his twenty-seven caps for Scotland in a 2–1 win over Cyprus at Hampden. That result pushed Andy Roxburgh's side a bit nearer to qualifying for the Italia '90, where both Davie and Craig Levein were involved.

It's always gratifying for a manager to see his players break through at international level. Henry Smith and John Colquhoun had done so the previous season, by joining Gary Mackay in the side that drew 2–2 with Saudi Arabia in Riyadh. The recognition accorded these guys served as proof, if any was needed, about just how much Hearts had progressed as a club since the start of the 1980s. And of course, it was only a matter of time before John Robertson and Alan McLaren were similarly honoured by Scotland.

23

THEN I GET THE SACK

Here's a name that will resonate with many Hearts fans: Husref Musemić. Needless to say, it was a new one to me when Wallace Mercer recommended we sign him in time for season 1989–90. Some agent had sent us a video of the big striker in action and the chairman was quite taken by what he saw on it.

'But I could cobble together a tape of myself scoring a few goals,' I protested. Mr Mercer refused to be put off, and so Husref, who'd been with Red Star Belgrade, was on his way to Tynecastle regardless. But it wasn't long before I was wondering if Husref had a twin brother and we'd got him instead.

Ok, the big fella scored a few times for us early on, beginning in our round of pre-season games when he got a goal in a 4–0 win at Peterhead. He followed that up by giving us a 1–0 victory over Sunderland at Tynecastle and kept it going with a goal in our 3–0 win over Montrose during the Skol Cup and another in a 2–0 league win over St Mirren at Paisley. Still I had misgivings about him. He was forever running away from the ball, despite us saying he should hang back where we could pick him out. The fact the lad didn't speak English – he certainly couldn't understand my Glaswegian dialect – made it all the harder to get through to him.

Finally, at half time in a Skol Cup tie against Falkirk at Brockville in late August, my frustration boiled over. Holding out my arms like the wings on an aeroplane and making the appropriate engine noises, I indicated to Husref if he didn't cotton on quick to what we wanted of him, he would be on the first flight home to Belgrade. Gary Mackay, sitting in the background, had a job stifling his laughter. Anyway, we ended winning 4–1, with goals by Wattie Kidd, Eamonn Bannon, Scott Crabbe and Davie Kirkwood, another player we'd just signed, from Rangers for £100,000, and were suitably primed for our next match.

It was against Hibs at Tynecastle on 26 August 1989, the first league derby of the season. We won 1–0 and – guess what? – the man who scored for us was the one I'd been haranguing only the week before, Husref. With one flick of his head from a ball into the box, he secured a place for himself in the affections of all Hearts fans. But his next, and last, goal for the club was a long time arriving, in a 2–1 league defeat by Dunfermline at Tynecastle in October. Come the turn of the year, we let him return home to join Sarajevo.

I'd have to say Husref was a terrific character. He did his best to integrate with the rest of the lads, both in the dressing room and in a social sense, and had a fair degree of natural ability. It was just that he didn't suit our style of play. We needed someone who could hold the ball in and take the pressure off others, particularly in and around the penalty box. Husref simply wasn't that kind of player, and despite his insistence on us signing him, I think even the chairman agreed.

Davie McCreery, who arrived at Tynecastle a couple of months into that same season, had a lot more to offer us. I just wished we had got him several years earlier. Davie had been with Manchester United and Newcastle United before playing in the USA and, eventually, Sweden. He had sixty-three caps for Northern Ireland at the time and was to win another four with us. Experience like his wasn't readily acquired, so we considered ourselves fortunate indeed to get him after his short spell with the Swedish club, Sundsvall. Our dressing room was never the quietest of places, but it became even more animated when Davie walked in. Could he talk? I remember saying, 'We should have hired an interpreter to unscramble his machine-gun delivery.' If some of us found difficulty understanding him, Husref Musemić had no chance in the short time they were together.

Nicky Walker was another new face in our midst. We'd signed him at virtually the same time we signed Davie Kirkwood, again from Rangers, and for a similar fee. He provided reliable cover for Henry Smith, who had been a club stalwart almost throughout the decade. But like the rest of us, Henry remained desperate to get his hands on a winner's medal over and above the one we'd got for lifting the Tennents' Sixes trophy in the mid-1980s. Would this be his, and our, year? In the Skol Cup, maybe? We started off well enough in that competition by beating Montrose 3–0 at home with a couple of goals by Scott Crabbe and another by Husref. It still pained me to recall how they'd beaten us in the tournament a couple of years earlier, so any victory against them had to be regarded as a good one.

Then, having won the tie with Falkirk that I mentioned earlier, we found ourselves at home to Celtic in the quarter-finals. What a match that turned out to be! A 2–2 draw, with Scott Crabbe scoring our first goal and John Robertson our second after coming off the bench. It was the wee man's first appearance of the season, following a hernia problem. Extra time ensued, with the teams still locked, and Celtic finally won on penalties. So for the time being, with September not yet upon us, we were left to focus our attention on the championship. Celtic had beaten us 3–1 at home on opening day but a more numbing defeat by 2–1 came against Dunfermline at Tynecastle in early October.

Much more to our liking was a 3–1 win over Aberdeen, again at Tynecastle, in which Scott Crabbe underlined his potential once more with a couple of goals. Tosh McKinlay weighed in with the other. Then come November, we gave Dundee a doing at our place, beating them 6–3, with a hat-trick by John Colquhoun and additional goals by Wayne Foster, Wee Robbo and Scott. By the way, Robbo had bet Scott he would finish ahead of him in the scoring stakes that season, despite his late start. He ended up collecting, with twenty-two goals to Scott's seventeen. Yet strive as we did to achieve the consistency we craved, it continued to elude us.

Over the festive period, for example, we lost 2–0 to St Mirren at Paisley, then beat Hibs by the same score at Tynecastle. Guess who scored our goals on that occasion? Robbo, of course, one of them a penalty. What an amazing record he had in Edinburgh derbies: twenty-seven goals in all, if I remember correctly. I'm sure he could describe every one of them too, down to the last detail. Late January 1990 saw us launch into the Scottish Cup with a 2–0 win over Falkirk at Tynecastle. You got it, Robbo scored twice. Then come the fourth round, we beat Motherwell by a resounding 4–0 at home, with Robbo scoring another two and John Colquhoun and Scott Crabbe once apiece.

Could we go all the way in the tournament? We got our answer in the quarter-finals against Aberdeen at Pittodrie, and it wasn't the one we were hoping for. They thumped us 4–1. But our season didn't peter out on that disappointing note. Despite having lost at home to Dunfermline once more, this time by 2–0, there was still a good chance we could salvage a European place for the following season through our efforts in the championship. Winning 2–1 away to Hibs – yeah, Robbo scored twice – helped us to that end. In fact, we finished up trailing Aberdeen only on goal difference for second position in the Premier Division, which was won by Rangers.

But things were afoot which, in terms of headlines, would over-shadow anything we had achieved, or failed to achieve, that season. In hindsight, I got my first inkling of them when driving home one day, Wallace Mercer called me on my car-phone. 'Please don't ask me any questions,' he said. 'Just answer the ones I'm about to throw at you.' He proceeded to go through the whole Hibs squad, starting with Andy Goram, asking me what I reckoned each of them might be worth in the transfer market. I was intrigued, to say the least, but none the wiser about where he was coming from by the time we hung up.

A few weeks later, it must have been, the chairman went public with his proposed bid to buy out Hibs and make Edinburgh a one-city team. If he'd taken me into his confidence at the outset, I would have told him the very idea was nonsense and not to even think about it. Needless to say, the reaction from Hibs and their fans was exactly as he should have anticipated. They were outraged by his audacity, with the result the much-chastened Wallace had to abort the idea before heading off to Italy a short time later to watch Scotland compete in that summer's World Cup finals.

It said much about Craig Levein's dedication that, after all the problems he'd had with injuries, he found a place in Andy Roxburgh's squad along with Dave McPherson. But as I primed myself for watching the games on television, I couldn't help becoming a bit unsettled by one of the stories to come out of Rapallo where the Scots were based. It had nothing to do with the World Cup but everything to do (or so it seemed) with my future as manager of Hearts. The headline was along the lines of 'Mercer Bids for Alex Ferguson'.

My one-time Rangers colleague, having brought Manchester United to Tynecastle a few months earlier for Eamonn Bannon's testimonial match, had just won his first trophy in charge of the Old Trafford club. That was the FA Cup, after a replayed final with Crystal Palace at Wembley. It transpired quickly enough that Fergie wasn't for leaving, and if he had a sense of all the success which was in the offing for him, why should he have done? But with the story appearing to have come from Mercer himself, I couldn't help but see some unpleasant writing on the wall so far as I was concerned.

I'd been in the throes of trying to add quality and experience to our squad, with David Batty of Leeds one of the players mentioned to me as a possible recruit. My old pal Jimmy Lumsden, who had strong connections with the Elland Road club, reckoned we could get him for around £500,000. But would Batty, who'd dropped into Leeds' reserves, be interested in coming to Scotland? Somehow, I doubted it, so I went instead for Derek Ferguson of Rangers for a similar fee. He was someone I rated highly – a player who could hold the ball when he wanted or release it to good effect – and I'd no hesitation in putting him in the side when season 1990–91 got underway.

But circumstances were quick to conspire against me, for within three days of Aberdeen beating us 3–0 in the quarter-finals of the Skol Cup at Pittodrie, we lost 3–1 to Rangers at Tynecastle in the championship. The following Monday, 10 September, I was called in by the directors to be told my time as manager was up. Their perception seemed to be that things were slipping away from me. I didn't see it that way but had to allow for others viewing the situation differently. I'd often thought managers should only be in place for five years, otherwise a staleness can set it. I certainly wasn't about to break the boardroom door off its hinges, as with my P45 about to go in the post, I took my leave of the chairman and his colleagues.

I preferred to depart with a bit of dignity and made a point of going round the table, shaking each of them by the hand and saying it had been a privilege to work for as good a club as Hearts. I meant it too. I'd been with them for just over ten years and player–manager, then manager, for just under nine. I liked to think in hindsight, if not at the time, I'd left Hearts in a far better state than I'd found them when they were yo-yoing between the Premier and First Divisions. I'd enjoyed almost every minute of our asso-ciation, even though the major trophy we'd been bent on winning continued to elude us.

I also made it my duty before leaving Tynecastle for the last time to head for the dressing room and thank the players for their efforts. As I left, I bumped into Alan McLaren and remember saying to him, 'Stick in, Big Fella. You've got something which a lot of Edinburgh folk don't have.' That must have been the prej-udiced Glaswegian in me speaking. What I meant was that Alan, like Gary Mackay, John Robertson and Dave Bowman, possessed a toughness, a desire to succeed, which I didn't always detect in some others from the capital.

Wee Robbo, by the way, was absent from the stadium on that fateful day for me. He was down at Troon, preparing to play for

Scotland against Romania in his first international. But his reaction in the following morning's papers suggested he thought I'd had a raw deal.

Mercer promptly moved for Joe Jordan, then in charge of Bristol City, as my replacement. Should I have been surprised? Not really. I'd heard he took a shine to him during the World Cup finals in Italy, when Joe had acted as a conduit between the Scotland camp and the Italian media. He could speak Italian from his time of playing over there, of course. He was a big name in the game, and by that stage, I got the impression Mercer wanted a big name to bring kudos to Hearts. Hadn't he supposedly angled after Alex Ferguson during the World Cup itself? But here's a thing that can't be generally known: I actually hand a hand in Joe's installation. Let me explain.

His assistant at Bristol City was none other than Jimmy Lumsden, who, knowing that Joe would want to bring him to Tynecastle as his second in command, phoned me to ask what they should ask for in terms of contracts. I told him Joe should ask for this and that, and what Jimmy himself should be wanting. Joe got the lot, but when Jimmy outlined what he was looking for, Mercer said no, no and no again. So, good on him, Jimmy just thought, 'To hell with this', and went back down the road to take over as manager of Bristol City in his own right. Fair to say he hasn't looked back since, working with Davie Moyes at Preston and Everton and following him to Manchester United after Sir Alex Ferguson retired.

I'll add only this by way of a postscript: I was on borrowed time – five days to be precise – after that 3–0 hammering we took from Aberdeen at Pittodrie. Yet later that season, with Joe Jordan in charge, Hearts went back up there and lost by an even more numbing 5–0. How ironic.

24

INTO EUROPE WITH AIRDRIE

That winter of 1990–91 was a long time passing. For the first time in a quarter of a century, as player or manager, I didn't have to get myself up and out on a Saturday for a game. Money wasn't a problem, for Wallace Mercer was still paying me following my sacking by Hearts. Even so, I had energy to burn and was constantly on the lookout for a way back into the game. Then, in the spring that new year, with Tony Fitzpatrick standing down at Paisley, the St Mirren job came up for grabs. Davie Hay and I emerged as the frontrunners to fill it.

I spruced myself up for my interview, and while I can't remember the name of one of the directors presiding over it, I recall specifically him asking me, 'And what do you think you could do for St Mirren, Mr MacDonald?'

I answered him by saying, 'I would hope, after a bit of time – two or three seasons maybe – I can do what I did with Hearts by taking them into Europe.'

He just laughed, and Davie, an old and respected rival of mine from our playing days, ended up getting the job. I had to wait until the summer of 1991 before Airdrie took me on. And – guess what? – I took them into Europe after my first season in charge. I really liked that. The fact St Mirren ended up being relegated at the same time could have given me cause for gloating, but it didn't. It wasn't my style to take any delight from another manager's despair.

Airdrie in Europe seemed the most unlikely of scenarios. They'd never achieved such a thing before and did so this time by dint of reaching the final of the Scottish Cup and playing Rangers, who by then had won the Premier Division and qualified for the European Cup. That assured us of a place in the Cup Winners' Cup, regardless of the outcome of our showdown at Hampden. Our fateful journey to the National Stadium began with a 2–1 victory over Stranraer at Broomfield, with goals by Andy Smith and Jimmy Boyle. Then we beat the Highland League side Huntly 3–1 away, thanks to a hat-trick from Andy.

That was us into the quarter-finals in which were paired with Hibs at Easter Road. It promised to be a tough assignment, yet we got through it with a 2–0 win courtesy of goals by Owen Coyle and Sammy Conn. Could we dispose of Hearts in the semis? Here was a draw that, for obvious reasons, held great appeal for me. I was desperate for us to beat them, as were the handful of former Tynecastle players I had in my Airdrie squad. The first match between us ended goal-less, and the replay produced a 1–1 draw, with Kenny Black our scorer. So it was down to penalties, which we won 4–2. Bring on the Rangers.

The Saturday prior to the final saw us claim a 1–1 draw with St Johnstone at Perth with a goal by Andy Smith to achieve our highest-ever finish – seventh place – in the Premier Division. Needless to say, our players were feeling well pleased with themselves as we headed to our training camp at Seamill. Traditionally, that was where Celtic prepared for big games, and I took the view that if it was good enough for them, it was good enough for Airdrie. Well, just about.

Unfortunately from our point of view, two of the most important men in my squad, Jimmy Sandison and Kenny Black, had to be counted out of the final on the grounds of suspension. Jimmy was my captain, so I made an early decision to give the armband to Sandy Stewart. I should own up here to the fact that I was carrying a touchline ban at the time, which I'll tell you about later, but the SFA agreed that I should be allowed to lead the team out at Hampden.

Much of the newspaper build-up focused on our disciplinary record. We'd become known as the 'Beastie Boys' because of what might be loosely called our 'uncompromising style'. But Walter Smith, in charge of Rangers, didn't buy into any criticism of us.

He talked us up rather, saying, 'Airdrie are the team who have surprised everyone this season. They've finished seventh in the league, been unlucky to lose in the semi-finals of the Skol Cup, and now reached the Scottish Cup Final. What they've achieved is as successful as us winning the title.'

Walter and Rangers were desperate to make it a Double by winning the Cup. It had eluded them since 1981, the year after I left Ibrox for Hearts. Of course, we were the underdogs. I preferred it that way, telling the press a day or two before the game, 'I'd be worried if we were favourites. As long as we continue doing what we're good at, I'll be happy. We're under pressure but have been all season, just to survive in the Premier Division. I reckon Rangers are under greater pressure, though. They haven't won the Cup in eleven years. Having played with them, I know what it's like to be in their kind of situation. Until you get the first goal, it's all a bit edgy.'

The night before the game itself, we took our players to the cinema to see *Basic Instinct*. I was quoted as saying, 'That should take their minds off the final. If it doesn't, then nothing will.'

The following lunchtime we set off for Hampden, with me armed with a load of newspaper cuttings to pin on the wall of our dressing room. All were critical of our style of play, and I thought if the players could re-read them before kick-off, it would help fire them up for the big occasion about to begin. This, by the way, was Airdrie's first appearance in the final since 1975, when they lost 3–1 to Celtic. One of the papers valued our team at £685,000 – little more than what Rangers had paid for one of their stars, Alexei Mikhailichenko. Quite properly we were rated as underdogs.

In the event, we started well enough by making a couple of half-chances to score. But in the thirtieth minute, when Davie

Kirkwood slipped on the edge of the box, David Robertson brought the ball down on his chest before flighting it low across goal for Mark Hateley to score. Then almost on half time, with our guard having fallen again, Stuart McCall slipped a pass to Ally McCoist, who promptly beat John Martin to put his side 2–0 in front. Very few teams have ever come back against Rangers after giving them two goals of a start. But at least we pulled one back shortly before the finish, Andy Smith scoring with a volley. The game was as good as over by that point, although there was still time for Wes Reid to break through, only to shoot over.

It's not hard to imagine my disappointment at the finish, even though most folk had expected Rangers to beat us by a more convincing score than 2–1. 'We shot ourselves in the foot by giving away the two goals,' I said in the aftermath. 'That put us under the cosh. But at least we scored the best goal of the final and gave our supporters something to shout about.'

More was to come as season 1992–93 got underway, with us making our European debut in the Cup Winners' Cup against Sparta Prague. This was the very team that had beaten Rangers on the away-goals rule in the first round of the Champions Cup only twelve months earlier. I'd watched the return leg of that tie at Ibrox, so I knew how good the Czechs were. But I dare say they didn't rate us. In fact, they probably hadn't heard of Airdrie before our names came out of the hat together.

Our run-up to the first leg, which was at Broomfield, saw us lose 2–1 to Dundee United, for whom Big Duncan Ferguson scored both their goals. If Kenny Black hadn't missed a penalty in that match, we could have got a point – at least – from it. But we didn't carry any despondency into the midweek tie with Sparta. Far from it. Everybody, myself included, was buoyed up for what was to be a historic occasion for us, although we weren't going to let our hearts rule our heads once the game got going. I pointed out to the press and the players that Sparta were liable to be excellent on the break, therefore we had to keep our guard up at all times.

We honed our preparations over a couple of days at North Berwick, where my message to the lads was simple and to the point: just don't think about who we are playing, and if we stick to what we're good at, we can come through this game. In saying as much though, I suspected we might need a goal or two to spare if we were to survive the second leg in Prague. Come the night, 15 September 1992, Broomfield drew a crowd of 7,000, which, if far from startling, was big enough to unsettle Sparta. We ended up outclassing them. The papers all agreed on that point. But could we score? Their goalkeeper, Petr Kouba, kept them in the game for long periods, before in the second half Alan Lawrence missed a right good chance, better than the one that Evan Balfour had passed up. Then, with only a couple of minutes remaining, Jan Sopko scored with a header following a corner kick. Airdrie 0, Sparta 1 was the final score.

Our guys just couldn't believe their bad luck, Andy Smith feeling especially cursed. He was quoted later as saying, 'It just wouldn't happen for me. The ball kept hitting defenders' legs and bouncing away. It wouldn't go in. We made so many chances that you would have thought at least one of them would have brought us a goal. But we'll be going for a victory in the second leg. You never know, we might just spring one of the biggest European shocks ever.'

The fact we beat Hearts 1–0 at Broomfield, with an early goal by Owen Coyle, immediately before travelling to Prague helped strengthen our resolve for the game over there. Andy Smith wasn't alone in thinking we could yet land a place in the next round. My own view was that our pace, as well as determination, could see us get a result.

So it was a real setback for us that, with less than half an hour gone over there, Gus Caesar conceded a free-kick from which Petr Vrabec curled a shot past John Martin. That put the Czechs 1–0 in front on the night, and 2–0 ahead overall. But no, Airdrie weren't finished. Owen Coyle won a penalty shortly afterwards. Jimmy Boyle stepped up to take the kick, only to see goalkeeper Kouba block it. The ball broke clear, inviting somebody to knock it into the net. Sadly, no one could apply the necessary touch. The tie swung on that missed opportunity, for, still before half time, Roman Vonasek fired in a terrific second goal for Sparta.

There seemed to be no way of catching them by that point, and our sole consolation came in the fifty-fifth minute, when Jimmy Boyle slipped a free-kick to Kenny Black, whose shot from twenty-five yards went in off a post. Andy Smith ended up being stretchered off – this after having a penalty claim turned down. The final score was 2–1 to Sparta, 3–1 on aggregate. We were none too enamoured by either the outcome or the fact we'd had four players booked. George Peat, our chairman, stated later he would investigate ways in which we might protest about the Bulgarian referee's handling of the tie. But as George well knew, nothing he said or did was going to affect the result. Still, for as long as it lasted – only one round – our European adventure had left all of us with an experience worth remembering.

It might also have given a certain St Mirren director something to reflect ruefully upon. Yes, the director who had laughed at me when, at my time of being interviewed for the Paisley job, I said I could take his club into Europe. In the event, I could be pretty pleased all-round with how things had gone in those early days at Broomfield. As well as reaching the Scottish Cup Final in what was my first season in charge and qualifying for the Cup Winners' Cup on the back of that, we achieved what was Airdrie's best-ever finish in the Premier Division: seventh-top place. Then there was our feat in reaching the semi-final of the Skol Cup.

Walter Smith remarked in the build-up to the Scottish Cup Final that we'd been 'unlucky' to lose out at the stage we did in what I still called the League Cup, but I wasn't sure if I would have put it quite the same way. We were robbed, more like, of a place in the final itself. Among the teams we'd knocked out of the competition were Celtic on penalty kicks at Broomfield after a 0–0 draw. They had players like Charlie Nicholas and Tony Cascarino in their attack, so it was quite something that we kept them at bay. Dunfermline duly lined up against us in the semi-final at Tynecastle, with the records showing they beat us 3–2 on penalties after a 1–1 draw.

What they don't reveal is that the tie should have ended in our favour without going into extra time. Owen Coyle had put us in front after half an hour. Then, in the eighty-seventh minute, Dunfermline equalised with a penalty which Davie Syme awarded against Jimmy Sandison, who he reckoned had brought the ball down with his arm. It was clear to everybody else that Jimmy had used his chest to control it, and furthermore, that he'd done so outside the box. Talk about injustice. Our guys were sickened, even more so when they lost the shoot-out that need never have taken place. The fact that just about everyone present that night knew the referee had blundered was of little consolation to us.

He actually handled one of our games a short time later and indicated to our chairman, George Peat, beforehand that he wanted to speak to me. About what? To apologise? But I wanted no part in any peace talks and doubt if I've spoken to him since. Possibly the last time we saw each other was at an exhibition in Glasgow when he was selling caravans. No, I didn't buy one of them. I just gave him a nod in passing. So far as I was concerned, it was down to him that Airdrie didn't appear in two Cup finals that season. That we'd gone even close to doing so was a great credit to the players, many of whom I'd inherited from my immediate predecessor, Jimmy Bone.

Jimmy, such an important player for me when I was in charge of Hearts, had got Airdrie promoted immediately before I replaced him. Among the players he left behind was Owen Coyle, who he'd signed from Clydebank for a club record fee of £175,000. Then there was Sandy Stewart. I'd released him when we were together at Tynecastle, and as he told me later, when he heard I was coming to Airdrie, he thought, 'Aw, naw, I'm going to get punted again.' But there was never a chance of that. The reason I let Sandy leave Hearts wasn't so much a reflection of what I thought of him as a player as the simple fact I had bigger and more experienced defenders in the likes of Dave McPherson and Craig Levein.

Alan Lawrence and Davie Kirkwood were two more of the former Hearts contingent I got from Jimmy Bone, and I brought in Wattie Kidd, who'd had a great career at Tynecastle, Kenny Black and Jimmy Sandison. These were guys I could trust to do a good job for me as we battled to retain our place in the top flight and not spoil the good work done by Jimmy Bone in getting us there. I say 'battled'. According to our critics in the press, and we had many, we were nothing more than a team of fighters. I disputed that assertion at the time, just as I would dispute it now. We could play a bit, but at the same time, would stick up for ourselves.

From my latter days with Rangers, right through my time with Hearts, I'd taken the view that there was no point in a player throwing himself into tackles. It was better if he stayed on his feet and retained a chance of winning the ball. This approach used to irritate opponents. They didn't like anybody being in their faces. That is what we were about at Airdrie, harrying people, closing them down. Which brings me back to what I mentioned earlier in this chapter: our disciplinary record in that first season of mine at Broomfield. It showed us in a poorer light than actually we deserved. Our crime count throughout the term was something like eleven sendings-off and more than a hundred bookings. Referees, apparently, were no more enamoured by our style than anyone else who couldn't tell the difference between commitment and malice.

As it turned out, I myself wasn't immune to any backlash from officialdom. Around the half-way point of 1991–92, when we were sitting near the foot of the table, Hibs beat us 3–0 at Broomfield. Naturally, I was upset by the way things had gone, and as we trooped into that quaint old pavilion of ours, I became even more upset by the sight of one of the linesmen, Stuart Dougal, with a grin on his face. I laughed mockingly at him as he and his two colleagues made their way to their changing room. Then I headed disconsolately for ours, no doubt to exorcise a bit of my disappointment, only for George Peat to come in and say the referee wanted to see me.

Off I went, to hear the ref (I can't recall now who he was) accuse me of having called Dougal 'a prick'. I protested on the grounds I'd done no such thing, that the word simply wasn't one I ever used about anybody. Nor was it. I ended up losing the head a bit, if truth be told, and saying that lies were being told in order to set me up. Maybe not the most sensible way to react, whatever the real truth was. As a result, I was hauled in front of the SFA disciplinary committee and banned from the touchline for a year, as well as fined £1,000. It was for that reason I had to look on from the centre stand as we faced Rangers in the Scottish Cup Final a few months later.

As for not being allowed to sit on the bench for games at Broomfield, safe to say that was no hardship. I used to call the journey from the pavilion to our dugout 'the longest mile'. It could be something of an ordeal walking what, in fact, was only about sixty yards, with the fans giving you pelters if the team wasn't doing well. I much preferred to watch games from my office, which was stuck on the side of the pavilion. I could see everything I wanted from there. Nothing and nobody could break my concentration – and I could curse the match officials without them hearing a word.

25

ME AND MY MIDLIFE CRISIS

So there I was, sitting astride my Harley Davidson at traffic lights in the Gorbals in Glasgow, when a big Merc drew alongside me. I looked at the driver and instantly recognised him as the manager of Rangers, Wattie Smith.

'How ye doin', Big Fella?' I shouted, at the same time as giving him a wave.

He just gave me a cold stare by way of response, as if to say, 'Who the f**k are you lookin' at?' Then it dawned that because I had a helmet on he couldn't recognise me. I whipped it off when we got to the next set of lights and got a wave back. But he was bound to have been wondering what the hell Alex MacDonald was doing on a motorbike.

I'd had a thing about bikes since riding pillion on a beat-up old Royal Enfield as a fifteen-year-old. I could remember being terrified at first, then getting a real buzz of excitement that had never left me. I'd always said to myself, one day I'm going to get one of these. And that day came in what was my second season at Airdrie. Of course, it was no more than a daft notion. But I was forty-four or forty-five at the time, ready for a mid-life crisis when many of us blokes do the daftest of things. I just had to have a Harley and knew this showroom in Edinburgh where I could buy one.

Through I went, to be shown this beautiful machine. Maroon it was, the colour of Hearts. I was sorely tempted, but the salesman's spiel started to do my head in. I thought, 'I'm no' falling for all your patter, pal,' and walked away. Back I came a few days later, to be shown a different bike – a black one – by a different salesman. His sales talk wasn't quite as intense, so I could take my time about making a decision. 'This one's for me,' I finally said, and agreed the deal there and then. But what about insurance? This beast of a bike was 1500cc, an unbelievable bit of hardware, really. Nobody in Scotland would offer me cover.

I mentioned my problem to one of the Airdrie players, Justin Fashanu, who said, 'Boss, I'll phone a pal of mine in London. This guy could get you insurance if you were flying to the moon. Leave it to me.' Good on the Big Fella, he came back to me a couple of days later, saying, 'Fifteen hundred quid for a year, gaffer.' I said to myself, 'F**k it, why not?' I'd paid about £12,000 for the bike. What was another grand and a half on top of that?

Believe me, it was money well spent. I couldn't even begin to describe the adrenalin rush I got from riding my Harley.

One night I decided to show it off to Sandy Clark. We arranged to meet in this pub in Bathgate, so off I set. I was wearing this suede coat, the tails of which I had tucked in below me. When I got on to the Edinburgh Road, I thought I would give the bike full-throttle. All of a sudden, the wind caught my coat and inflated it like a balloon. No kidding, I thought I was going to take off. Steady, Doddie, steady. Anyway, I got to the pub I thought Sandy had described to me, parked the bike and threw my helmet under a bush. Well, I didn't want to walk in looking like an extra from *Easy Rider*. No sign of Sandy.

I had my half-brick-sized mobile with me, so gave him a call, only to be told I'd turned up at the wrong venue. The right one was somewhere on the other side of the town. 'Never mind,' I said. 'I'll catch you another time.' Better I headed home, I reckoned, just in case Christine thought I'd run into the back of a juggernaut somewhere along the way. No sooner had I retrieved my helmet from its hiding place and climbed back into the saddle, than this other biker roared in. 'I'll show you,' I thought to myself, giving the engine a 'vroom, vroom'. Away I went, at such a great rate of knots I mounted a grass verge and just about ran over this elderly lady who was walking past. The poor soul looked petrified, and I dare say I did too.

Another time, with my daughter Lisa on the pillion, I drove up to this eatery at Duck Bay on the banks of Loch Lomond. The young waiter recognised me as we walked in. 'How you doin'?' he asked. 'Aye, fine thanks,' I answered. Then, ordering a Coke for Lisa and a coffee for myself, I said nonchalantly, 'I just brought my daughter up on the Harley.' He looked well impressed. But when we made to leave, I realised I'd parked the bike's front wheel on a flower bed. The brute was so heavy I'd to go back in and ask the waiter to help me push it backwards. So much for my Billy Big Time impression.

I'd sat my motorcycle driving test on a wee 250cc machine and could recall the guy – a Celtic supporter – who put me through it asking beforehand how I felt. I told him I'd been less nervous playing in front of 100,000 people at Hampden. But I passed, and proceeded to have a lot of fun with the Harley. What I discovered though was that there are too many roundabouts in Scotland. No matter where I drove, every time I got up a bit of speed, I came to yet another roundabout and had to slow down. The upshot was I got rid of the thing after about a year and went back to driving a car full-time. Christine hadn't put me under any pressure. She just thought I was going through a daft phase and would come out of it soon enough. She obviously knew me better than I knew myself.

I mentioned earlier the turn Justin Fashanu did by getting me insurance for the Harley. What a turn he could have done Airdrie, if only we'd got him earlier than we did in season 1992–93. Jimmy Lumsden, my eyes and ears down south, recommended we go for him as we toiled at, or near, the foot of the table from virtually the outset. The highest position we achieved in the then twelve-team league was ninth, and that was way before the turn of the year. Justin didn't join us until the February, by which time there was almost no escaping relegation so far as we were concerned. I've got a load of stories about him, not too many of which I could print, right enough. No, just jesting. He was a smashing guy and a real gentleman. You know, the kind who would hold shop doors open for old ladies. He also had a bit of style about him, with the fancy boots he wore off the park and the designer glasses. The fact he'd come out a couple of years earlier as being gay simply wasn't an issue among the lads. Everyone liked him and I for one was shocked and saddened by the news a few years later that he had committed suicide.

What a presence he gave us in attack. One of his best performances came in a 3–1 win over Hibs at Broomfield. Justin scored twice in that game, with Sandy Stewart getting our other goal. It was only our sixth victory in the entire league campaign, and sadly, our last. But I remember Justin from an earlier game also, a 1–1 draw at home against Aberdeen. As well as scoring in it, the Big Fella fairly sorted out Alex McLeish, who was directly opposed to him. Big Eck had knocked Justin about a couple of times. Then the next thing we saw was McLeish go to ground as he let out a scream. Justin had got his revenge. Enough said. He could look after himself, of that there was no doubt. In saying that, I don't recall him being sent off. He was too cute for that.

Something else I remember about Justin was his eating habits. Once when we were having a pre-match meal, I saw him sit down to a plate of potatoes. Others were tucking into supposedly healthier stuff, while I myself was always a scrambled-eggs-and-beans man. I said to him, 'Big Fella, what's with the tatties?' He said, 'Straight energy, boss.' It so happened I was playing the next day in a charity game for Dukla Pumpherston. I had a big helping of tatties beforehand to see if it might help me. Sure enough, I had enough energy to get me through the game, with a bit left over.

Justin, of course, wasn't the only player we brought up from England around the same time. Peter Davenport, Gus Caesar and Wes Reid were among the others. I used to joke that the way to attract these guys to our place was to drive them past Ibrox on the way from Glasgow Airport, saying the Rangers stadium was our training ground. In saying that, they were guaranteed a good time once they got to Broomfield.

At Airdrie everybody pulled for one another. In many ways, I enjoyed my time there at least as much as I did at Hearts. Airdrie was fun. The expectations weighing on us weren't so great, but we did our very best to set new standards for ourselves.

One English-based player we failed to get was a guy called Phil Babb. George Peat and I went to watch this other player, a big striker called Stephen Torpey, playing for Bradford. Babb was playing in the same team, and I said to George, 'Buy him, he's a player.' We got back to Airdrie and made an enquiry about him, but Bradford said they weren't for selling. The next thing I knew, Babb had joined Coventry. We duly played them in a friendly, and there he was in opposition. He'd put on a bit of beef, which gave me cause to wonder about him, yet he went on to play with Liverpool for a time. Aye, there's always one who gets away.

Of course, just as important as the team you have on the park is the one you have off it. In that sense, I felt I did well to bring in John McVeigh as my assistant. I'd met him at a coaching school – I think he was with Clyde at the time – and thought he and I could work well together. He was an Airdrie man himself, and had played for the club. I put a lot of stock in his coaching and his ability to speak to players. He was good when it came to winding them up before games and was great company as well, a real enthusiast. But no less important in our backroom team at Broomfield was John Binnie, who had run the Hearts reserve team during most of my time in charge at Tynecastle. When it came to picking the Airdrie team, I tended to consult John. I'd a lot of respect for him. That isn't to say I had a lesser respect for John McVeigh. The two Johns were different people, with differing qualities to offer.

George Peat, the chairman, had my respect as well. He was a real fitba man, brilliant to work with, even if I didn't always agree with his methods. For example, we'd go up to Aberdeen and he'd say to me coming off the bus, 'We'll double the bonus today.' I'd say, 'George, it's Aberdeen we're playing. They're away ahead of Airdrie. Why not make the same offer when we're playing a team either just above or below us in the league?' So we started to work that way. It offered the players a more realistic incentive, in my view.

But the good times we enjoyed in my first season with Airdrie, when we finished seventh in the league and reached the final of the Scottish Cup as well as semi-final of the Skol Cup, didn't spill over into the second one. Hence we got relegated, along with Falkirk, which was a huge disappointment for all concerned. This wasn't for want of backing by the fans, who if not great in number by that time, were always vociferous and intimidating. Opposing teams didn't like playing at Broomfield, not least for the reason they got such a hard time there from the home crowd. I can remember us playing against Dundee United, who had Big Duncan Ferguson in their line-up. Our support were on his case from the start, and eventually, he lost it and got himself sent off. The power of the people, indeed.

What was the chance of us being promoted again at the first attempt? It would have been hard enough – without the additional hardship imposed by the fact the Premier Division was set on cutting back its numbers from twelve to ten. That meant only one team would go up at the end of 1993–94, and we could do no better than finish third behind winners Falkirk and Dunfermline, who we beat 1–0 at home on the second-last Saturday of the season. 7 May was the date, one that holds poignant memories for all Airdrie fans because it marked our farewell to Broomfield. The club had agreed to sell the site to the supermarket chain Safeway and planned to invest the funds in a new 10,000-seat stadium complying with the criteria set by the Premier Division. We were to decant to Broadwood, on a ground-sharing agreement with Clyde, little knowing it would be four years before we had a place to call our own again.

There weren't too many dry eyes in our dressing room as we prepared to vacate our dressing room for the last time. Broomfield, sadly, had had its day; the club's finances dictated we move. I felt at least as sorry for the fans as the players. The old stadium was situated so conveniently for the supporters that they could be supping their last pint at ten minutes to three on a Saturday afternoon and not miss the kick-off. Nothing would be quite the same for them in the future, even after the club took up residence in the Shyberry Excelsior Stadium on the outskirts of town in time for the 1998–99 season.

But the show had to go on, regardless of how many or how few supporters might follow us to Cumbernauld. We on the playing side were pledged to making the very best of a barely satisfactory situation, and if our first season of homelessness didn't deliver much success in the league (we ended up in fourth place), it confirmed our re-emergence as a force to be reckoned with in the Cups. Put it another way: having reached the quarter-finals of the League Cup, Scottish Cup and B&Q Cup in 1993–94, we were to do even better in all three tournaments in 1994–95. This fact was signalled when we beat Dundee 3–2 in the final of the B&Q Cup, courtesy of goals by Paul Harvey, Jimmy Boyle (penalty) and Andy Smith. As for the League Cup, we began quite tentatively in it with a 1–1 draw against Morton away. Fortunately, we won the resultant penalty shoot-out to face Motherwell away in the next round.

Here was a real challenge for us, against a side with whom Airdrie had contested many a thrilling Lanarkshire derby. Were we up for it? We made sure we were, winning 2–1, with Jimmy Boyle scoring the second of his goals in extra time to take us through. Hibs lay in wait for us in the quarter-finals at Easter Road, and we saw them off as well, by the same score as we beat Motherwell, with Andy Smith and Alan Lawrence scoring. And so to a semi-final tie with Raith Rovers at McDiarmid Park. It ended 1–1 after extra time, Stevie Cooper having scored for us, but we lost out 5–4 on penalties. Who could have forecast that Raith would go on to beat Celtic in the final, again on penalties?

Our guys couldn't wait to get going in the Scottish Cup, and when they did, it was with a 2–1 win away to Stirling Albion. Big Andy Smith got both our goals on that occasion, and he and Cooper were on target when we beat Dunfermline 2–0 at home in the following round.

As luck would have it, we were paired with Raith away in the quarter-finals, and for obvious reasons, didn't want for incentive to beat them. This we did, and in some style, with Harvey scoring twice and John Davies and Kenny Black once apiece in a 4–1 victory. Hampden awaited us in the semi-finals, as did my old club, Hearts. Could we put one over them again? Cooper provided the answer, scoring the only goal of the tie which saw us progress to a historic meeting with Celtic in the final.

26

HAMPDEN RE-VISITED

No sooner had the last league matches been played that season, on Saturday, 13 May, than Celtic manager Tommy Burns took his players off to Italy for a week's training in preparation for the Scottish Cup Final. As for Airdrie, well, without a ground to call our own, we had to settle for working out on the public pitches at Strathclyde Park on the fringes of Hamilton. How the other half lived, eh? But that only helped bring us closer together and strengthen the players' resolve to rise above the disadvantages weighing upon us.

As far as I was concerned, the fact of us getting to the final was at least as important as the outcome of it. My reasoning was that, with a big payday in the offing, we could look forward to the prospect of remaining full-time for another season at least. What was the chance of us actually winning the Cup, having lost to Rangers in the final those three years earlier? Even our own fans didn't hold out much hope for us, which was hardly surprising. Celtic had spent £1.3 million on their Dutch striker, Pierre van Hooijdonk, while we had paid £65,000 to York City for Stevie Cooper. In saying that, Stevie was a good player, great in the air. He'd scored sixteen goals for us that season.

If our resources and spending power were to be compared to Celtic's, it was evident the two clubs just weren't in the same league. I remember saying something to the effect that for every penny our players were paid, theirs earned a fiver. That was just one of the differences between them and us. Still, we would do our very best to give Celtic a game by putting on a performance worthy of the occasion. We could promise no more or less. In the event, the build-up to Hampden was spread over two weeks, the final being scheduled for 27 May, and proved to be fairly low-key. This was for several reasons.

Scotland were preparing to play in the Kirin Cup in Japan, while Aberdeen were involved in a play-off with Dunfermline in a bid to stay in the Premier Division. There was also the matter of the Scottish rugby team competing in the World Cup in South Africa, so there wasn't much space in the papers to publicise the Scottish Cup Final until it was almost upon us. Not that this bothered anyone concerned with Airdrie. We just kept our heads down and got on with our training. Celtic's concentration was focused on the fact that here was a chance to win their first trophy in six years. They'd suffered the ignominy of losing to Raith Rovers in the final of the League Cup that same season and were under intense pressure to avoid being beaten by us.

Celtic, furthermore, had just been ordered to pay £200,000 in compensation to Kilmarnock for poaching their management team of Tommy Burns and Billy Stark, hence the man who had taken over the Parkhead club, Fergus McCann, was looking for a quick return on that part of his investment. The other issue involving them was whether or not Peter Grant would be fit to play. He had been carried off at Tannadice in their last league game, suffering from a knee injury. We always suspected such a strong-willed character as him would make a miraculous recovery, and fair play to the fella, he did. It was just a pity from our point of view we would have to do without John Davies because of suspension.

When finally the press found the time and column inches to write about Airdrie, our goalkeeper, John Martin, found himself a focal point of their attention. It was reported he'd played 657 games for us, stretching back to his signing from Tranent in 1980. John had the name of being the photographers' best friend. Whatever props they wanted him to pose with, he was happy to oblige them. This time, as we showed off the strips we would wear at Hampden, John appeared in his underpants. I could never quite work that one out. Big John, still working down the pits in the Edinburgh area, was nothing if not a character.

I heard once he used to march with a flute band in Prestonpans, or thereabouts. He also fancied himself a singer, but with Hampden approaching, we just hoped he would continue doing what he did best, keeping the ball out of our net. He'd had no fewer than twenty-two shut-outs for us that season. If he had another, the Scottish Cup would be ours. Another Airdrie player the papers focused on a day or so before the game was Paul Harvey, who I could remember trying to sign as a kid for Hearts. He preferred to join Manchester United, only to be released after a reported disagreement with Alex Ferguson at training. Then there was Jimmy Boyle for whom playing at Hampden was hardly a unique experience. After all, as a former Queen's Park player, he apparently held the record of consecutive appearances for them there: 142.

But to the big game itself, with the papers quoting me in the final countdown as saying, 'I'm having to treat the players with kid gloves and wrap them in cotton wool. Their attitude is brilliant. They just can't wait to get out there at Hampden.' Nor could they, although nothing prepared them, or me, for what happened after only nine minutes. Tosh McKinlay, who Celtic had signed from Hearts, swung over a cross from the left, and Big Hooijdonk got above our defence to head it in. We could have lost another goal shortly afterwards, when Simon Donnelly pushed straight through on John Martin. But referee Les Mottram stopped the lad in his tracks by blowing for a foul on him just outside the box.

We never really got going, and besides those early thrusts into attack, Celtic didn't do very much either to adorn the showpiece, as they proceeded to win 1–0. It was a poor match and one which left our Graham Hay feeling even more disappointed than the rest of us. Graham, a part-timer who worked in a building society in Glasgow, felt he should have prevented van Hooijdonk from scoring. 'I lost him at the back post,' he admitted later, but considering the Dutchman was about six inches taller than him, I couldn't really be critical of any individual. Ours was a collective failure. Celtic, at that time, weren't a high-scoring team. In fact, their goals-for total of thirty-nine was the lowest in the Premier Division that season, yet a single strike was all they required to see us off.

The longer I reflected on our achievements back then, the more I realised we performed extraordinarily well in doing what we did. We didn't have a lot going for us off the field, but regardless of that, we made the very best of ourselves on it. The Beastie Boys, as our critics called us, bowed to nobody, including the Old Firm. Big John Martin typified the spirit in the team. I can remember once when we were playing a game up in the Highlands, he got badly hurt diving at somebody's feet. The skin on the top of his head was flapping about like a lid and needed stitches at half time.

'We're gonna have to put a substitute on,' I told him.

He insisted, 'No, gaffer.'

'John,' I went on at him, 'you're like the *Six-Five Special*, there's steam coming out of your heid.'

But play on he did. It was unbelievable. John was the kind of guy you would have wanted beside you in the trenches.

Jimmy Sandison was in that team also, likewise another of my old players at Hearts, Kenny Black, who came to be known by all the players as 'Son of Doddie'. The fans used to get on his back quite a lot before he left Airdrie, and when Gary Mackay eventually joined us, I can remember him asking me, 'Boss, any chance of signing Kenny again?' I said, 'How come?' and Gary replied, 'Because the fans are picking on me now.'

Jimmy Boyle was yet another craggy character. He was just a wee guy but could kick the ball further than John Greig. I used to be on his back all the time, telling him the same things over and over again. Sandy Stewart, who was his best buddy, came to me once and asked, 'Boss, why do you keep picking on Jimmy?' I said, 'I don't pick on Jimmy. I try to help him.' But then I asked

Sandy, 'Does Jimmy play every week?' Sandy acknowledged that he did, so I said, 'There you are then. Where's the problem?' When I used to sign twelve- or thirteen-year-olds, I might tell them off for something or other, but say to their parents, 'Look, it's only fitba. I'm trying to help your lad.'

Sometimes the best way to help them was by letting them go. A case in point was a youngish player who was at Airdrie when I took over. James Dick was his name. He might have been about twenty-one at the time, although I recall he was married and had a kid. The more I spoke to him, the less I seemed to get through to him. The irritating thing was that he could play a bit, but I had to make a decision, and I did. I released him. I thought that by doing so it might act as a wake-up call for the lad, help make him a better player. It was for his benefit, not mine. As things transpired, he improved one hundred per cent thereafter with, if my memory serves me well, the likes of Hamilton and St Mirren.

Years before, when I was with Rangers, I'd seen the same thing happen with a young guy on the books at Ibrox, Kenny Burns. He was a good player who used to take a delight in training in nutmegging people. But he was lazy and ended up getting a free transfer. That was the jolt he needed, and as everyone knows, he went on to win the European Cup with Nottingham Forest and play for Scotland.

But I'm digressing here. There we were at the end of that momentous season, 1994–95, still marking time on the possibility of moving to a stadium we could call our own. What a long, drawn-out process that proved to be. We were fated to continue ground sharing on match days with Clyde for another three years, which was less than ideal. The folk at Broadwood were kind to us. They did everything we could possibly have asked of them, and a bit more besides. But through the week, there was always the problem of finding places to train. Sometimes, as in the build-up to that Cup final with Celtic, we did our work at Strathclyde Park; on other occasions, we used a sports centre in Airdrie. The sands of Gullane were out of bounds for us. I'm not sure we could have afforded a bus to get us there. Yet I can recall putting the players through a similarly gruelling routine by taking them to Kilsyth and running them up the Takmedoon Road to Carron Dam. Take my word for it, their tongues were hanging out when they got there.

It was a further mark of our deprived circumstances that the players had to wash their own strips, which, of course, meant their wives becoming involved as well. Maybe, in a funny kind of way, such hardships strengthened the camaraderie there was between us, although I dare say the wives could have seen me far enough when after a defeat I would say to the players by way of punishment, 'Right, collar and tie for a month.' That, in turn, resulted in even more washing and ironing at home. Part of my thinking was that if their wives started getting on at them about the extra work they had to do, the players would react positively by doing their damned not to lose again.

Come season 1995–96, our performances in the First Division fell short of the standards we were looking for, with the result being we ended up in eighth position. This was in sharp contrast to how we did in the Cups, starting with the League Cup in which we began by winning 3–2 away to East Fife, with goals by Jimmy Boyle, Peter Duffield and Stevie Cooper. Bring on Hibs at Broadwood in the next round. They had Scotland's second most capped player, Jim Leighton, between the sticks and the likes of Darren Jackson in attack, yet we beat them 2–0, with Boyle finding the net after an own-goal by Big Steven Tweed. Once more it seemed we were a match for just about anyone in those one-off contests. For as long as I'd known Airdrie – that is to say, way before I came to manage them – they'd been a team of fighters. This lot were no different, although Partick Thistle made things difficult for us in the quarter-finals.

The tie between us, again at Broadwood, ended 1–1 after extra time, Jim McIntyre having scored our goal, but we managed to win 3–2 in a penalty shoot-out. And so to the semi-finals in which we faced Dundee, losing 2–1 to a goal by Neil McCann after Peter

Duffield had scored for us. Could we progress that bit further in the Scottish Cup? We'd give it a go, certainly, and started out promisingly by winning 3–1 at Dumbarton, with a couple of goals by Duffield and another by Andy Smith. Then came a 2–2 draw at home to Forfar, Cooper and Duffield being our scorers on that occasion, followed by a 0–0 draw in the replay. Penalties settled the issue in our favour once more, by a margin of 4–2. Aberdeen awaited us at Pittodrie in the quarter-finals and squeezed us out 2–1, with a decisive goal by Paul Bernard. At least we'd given them a run for their money.

These tournaments weren't so kind to our guys in 1996–97, Partick beating us 1–0 in the third round of the League Cup after we'd defeated Raith Rovers 3–2 at home with an extra-time goal by Ken Eadie. The Kirkcaldy side duly exacted their revenge in the Scottish Cup, thumping us 4–1 at Broadwood. But our focus that season, unlike the one that went before, was on the First Division championship in which we finished second to St Johnstone, who were promoted automatically. The format in place at the time meant that we had to beat Hibs, who'd finished second-bottom to relegated Raith in the Premier, in a play-off if we were to go up also. Talk about tension. Even yet, I can feel the hairs on the back of my neck bristling.

A crowd of more than 15,000 saw the teams meet a first time at Easter Road. We were unfortunate to lose 1–0, through an own-goal by Stevie Cooper, but fancied our chances in the return at Broadwood. The gate was 7,500, probably the biggest we'd attracted to the place. What a tussle these fans witnessed, high-lighted as it was by six goals. Unfortunately, only two of them were scored by us, Paddy Connelly and Kenny Black being our marksmen. Darren Jackson got two for Hibs, Paul Tosh and Paul Wright the others. It might give you some idea of the controversy surrounding that showdown if I tell you that both Jackson's strikes were the result of penalties, as was Black's one.

That 4–2 defeat, 5–2 on aggregate, had all of us on a real downer, and nobody more so than the player I'd signed only a month of so earlier from my old club Hearts, Gary Mackay. Given his upbringing at Tynecastle, he hated losing to Hibs. I liked to think that from the long time we'd spent together in Edinburgh, I'd helped in Gary's development as a player. Here he was, coming towards the end of a fine career, and it pleased me no end to get him for a fee of only £10,000. I distinctly recall saying to the Airdrie directors when Gary came in, 'This is your next manager.' Time proved me right, but more on that later.

The end of our time at Broadwood was within sight by then, fully three years after we'd vacated Broomfield. The sundry complications there had been about building a new stadium on the outskirts of Airdrie were ironed out at last. So season 1997–98, our last in Cumbernauld, passed quickly enough, albeit without us achieving anything out of the ordinary. Suffice to say, in terms of the league, we finished fourth. As for the League Cup, Morton knocked us out at the first go, with a 4–1 win at Cappielow. In saying that, the score was 1–1 at the end of ninety minutes. We died in the half hour added on, which wasn't like us. As for the Scottish Cup, well, we didn't last any longer in that competition either, losing 1–0 to Ross County in a third-round replay after a 2–2 draw at Broadwood. It was time we were back in our own territory after four seasons of homelessness. Mind you, they hadn't been without their happy memories.

27

ONCE A RANGER . . .

Home sweet home, indeed. Airdrie's new ground looked a treat, even if the four years of waiting for the place actually to materialise had drained the club's finances to a dangerous degree. I remember the first time being shown around, with one of the directors leading me through a door and saying, 'This is the gym you always said you wanted.' It was like a ballroom, with a polished floor on which you could have had a right good ceilidh. Not quite what I had in mind for the games of heidie tennis, which I swore by as a means of honing the players' feel for the ball. Eventually the board set up a more suitable alternative under the stand. But that's by the by.

We were at the Shyberry Excelsior to play fitba, and what a hanselling we gave it in a League Cup tie against Celtic at the start of that season, 1998–99, in front of a crowd pushing 9,000. Marvin Wilson scored early on for us, and we hung on for a famous 1–0 victory. We'd already beaten Stenhousemuir 2–0 away in the tournament, with a couple of goals from Allan Moore, so found ourselves up against Kilmarnock in the quarter-finals. Would our reputation as Cup fighters survive the trip to Rugby Park? It did, Marvin Wilson potting a goal in extra time to give us a 1–0 victory. But then came a fateful meeting with Rangers in the semis. They thumped us 5–0. That was a sore one.

Slightly less painful was the 3–1 defeat we suffered away to Celtic in the third round of the Scottish Cup. Maybe they were due their revenge for us knocking out of the other Cup, and the result left us with only the First Division to play for. We'd been second in the table for a spell early on in the campaign, this before dropping down to fourth, where, in fact, we ended up come the close of term.

But for better or worse, Alex MacDonald had taken his leave of Airdrie by then. There were still half a dozen or so games to be played when I turned up at my usual time one Saturday for a home fixture. All the scouts were in attendance, which struck me as being odd. Why weren't they away looking at players? To cut a long story short, the then chairman Campbell Craig approached me at full time, asking, 'Alex, could I see you in the boardroom?'

I must have had a sense of what was coming and said to him, 'Before you say whatever you're going to say to me, I don't want any bullshit.'

So he got to the point, which was that the club weren't going to renew my contract come the end of the season.

I said, 'That's fine, Campbell. Not a problem. I'd just like to thank you for everything you've done for me.'

He said then, 'But, Alex, there's six weeks to go.'

To which I replied, 'No, this is it, as far as I'm concerned. I'm finished.' Down the stairs I went, to shake hands with all the players and wish them all the best. When I met Gary Mackay, who was my assistant by then, in the corridor, he asked me what was going on.

I told him, 'They're not going to renew my contract, so I'm off.'

Gary said immediately, 'I'm off, too, if that's the case.'

But I insisted, 'Gary, you're not going anywhere. Go get yourself a contract to take over from me. I told the directors when you came here that you were Airdrie's next manager. You're staying, Bud, simple as that.'

He duly took over, at what was becoming an ever more stressful time for the club financially. Our support had dwindled during the time we'd been away from the town, and the novelty of turning out in greater numbers at the new stadium hadn't lasted. The effect of this was we hardly had a bean to spend on reinforcing the team.

All that said, it was still a very sad day when the Airdrie so many of us knew and loved went out of business in 2002 before being resurrected as Airdrie United. My eight years with them had been nothing if not eventful. I have to say I enjoyed that period of my managerial career at least as much as I did the time I was in charge of Hearts. We had a lot of hardships to contend with, first at Broomfield, which had almost no facilities besides a pitch to play on, then as lodgers at Cumbernauld. These had a galvanising effect on everybody involved. I worked with some very good people, among them George Peat, who had left before me. Joey Rowan, another director, was different class as well. He spent a lot of money on the club and was Airdrie through and through, while his wife, Sharelle, a wonderful person, did so much work behind the scenes. Between us all, we'd made the very best of difficult circumstances.

The highlights obviously were reaching the Scottish Cup Final on two occasions and qualifying for the Cup Winners' Cup on the first of them. I still have a wry smile to myself when I think of being interviewed by St Mirren and one of their directors laughing at me when I suggested I could take them into Europe. I never sought any credit for succeeding to that end with Airdrie. Everything was down to the players, who showed great resolve and strength of character. What a bunch they were. Among my first duties was to trim the size of the squad, which, numbering about forty, was too big for us to carry. John McDonald, who'd played with me at Rangers and was getting on a bit, happened to one of those I had to let go.

I must have given him a hint of what was in my mind when doing a television interview, and he came into Broomfield the following day, saying, 'You're in trouble, boss. That wife of mine is cracking up because you're saying I'm too old.' Tom McAdam, who'd made his name with Celtic, was in the same boat, though I kept him on as a coach. Yet another I released was Graham

Harvey, who was a great goalscorer but just lacking that wee bit of pace needed to play in the Premier Division. Joey Rowan thought a lot of him, and fully four years later, he asked me, 'Why did you let the boy Harvey go?' Obviously, my decision had bugged him for all that time. 'Joey,' I said, 'if you'd asked me four years ago, I could have taken the chip off your shoulders.'

I've mentioned earlier many of the stalwarts I either inherited or brought in, and would place Wattie Kidd up there with the best of them. Brilliant, he was. He'd been with me at Hearts, of course, and proved to be a great signing for Airdrie. Jimmy Sandison and Kenny 'Son of Doddie' Black came into the same category. This is not to forget Evan Balfour. What a player he was for us, something akin to my old Ibrox colleague, Tam Forsyth, in the sense of his wholeheartedness. Evan was a fireman, therefore only part-time with us, but his fitness level was superb. Then there was Owen Coyle, who left for England within a couple of years of my arrival. Given his achievements in management, after what was a long and successful career as a player, I'd like to think I helped him on his way. I remember dropping Owen once and him coming to see me – as you'd expect all good players to do in the same circumstances – to ask what was what. 'Look,' I told him, 'come to my office tomorrow and we'll have a chat.' I duly despatched this lad, Hughie Elliot – he organised all the playing and training kit for us, as well as did a lot of other work in and around the dressing room – to buy a box of lollipops from a shop across the street. So when Owen came to see me as arranged, I had the box sitting on my desk. 'Right,' I said to him. 'Do you want to talk this over man to man or come over all childish?' In other words, if he wanted to spit the dummy, he might want to sook a lolly instead. We talked man to man. He was a good lad, Owen, a really nice lad, who deserved to progress in the game. When he was at Airdrie, he and his brothers drove about in a van. I dare say he went on to afford a better set of wheels.

One guy I was indebted to at Airdrie, and Hearts before that, was my chief scout, Roy Tomnay. He had played as a junior, but safe to say, had allowed his fitness to dwindle in the long interim and was carrying a lot more beef than he should have been. Joey Rowan had spotted him with me and said, 'That big fat guy, is he going to be your chief scout?' I said, 'Too right, he is. Roy's a top man.' Among the players he found for me at Hearts was the young Allan Johnston, who went on to play for Rangers and Scotland. He found a few more for Airdrie, and to the best of my knowledge, never took a penny from the club. Roy had a printing business in the Springburn area of Glasgow. Between leaving Hearts and joining Airdrie, I did some work for him. Later, he gave my elder boy, Nick, a job.

Anyway, come the spring of 1999, with Airdrie having got me off the wage bill, I was looking for work again. But not necessarily in football management. I'd pretty much had my fill of it by then. I can remember Christine and I being away on holiday in Spain once when our Lisa came over to join us and said that George Peat, by then with Stenhousemuir, had been on the phone looking for me. It turned out they were searching for a manager, but when I made contact with George, I said to him, 'Thanks, but I'd rather not get involved again. It's Alex MacDonald time from now on.' In saying that, I can recall being at home this one day when I saw something on television to the effect that a club in Cyprus were going to appoint, I think, Howard Kendall in charge. I said to myself, 'Cyprus, eh? All that sunshine? I wouldn't mind being his assistant.'

It was no more than a passing fancy, so you can imagine my surprise when a few days later I got a call from an agent, the one who'd done deals for the Rangers player Andrei Kanchelskis, asking me if I would be interested in taking over this very same Cypriot club. David Murray, the Ibrox chairman, had given him my name, he said. I told him I would think about it and agreed, in the meantime, to send on my CV. But nothing ever came of the offer, and, from memory, the job went to a German. I dare say the fact I had no coaching badges as such didn't stand me in particularly good stead.

Anyway, after about two years of doing not very much, Christine and I were having a drink one night in the Kirkintilloch Rob Roy Social Club just a short walk from where we lived. We fell in with someone I'd known for years – he used to be my mother's paperboy when we lived in Easterhouse – called Tommy Stark. Tommy had this good-going business, Ticon Insulation, which was tied in to what remained of the shipyard industry in Glasgow. Christine, who must have been wearying of me hanging about the house, asked him, 'Tommy, can you not give Alex a job?' He then said to me, 'What can you do?' To which I said, 'Well, I can drive.'

Funnily enough, at pretty much the same time, my wee pal, Billy Clark, had said he would try to get me a driving job with his brother Arnold's firm. So, if you like, I had two irons in the fire. A few days later, about ten o'clock in the morning, Tommy phoned me and offered me a start. About noon, Billy called and said he had fixed something up for me.

'Billy', I said. 'You're not going to be believe this, but only a couple of hours ago I accepted this other job.' So began what became a nine-year association with Tommy's firm, which at the time had just got a contract to supply aircraft carriers. I'd go to Govan every morning and pick up material for delivery at Yarrows. Other times, if I wasn't in the office, I'd be down in Wales or the North-East of England picking things up.

I can't emphasise enough how grateful I was to Tommy for keeping me ticking over. I'm not money-orientated, but he gave me something which suited me to a T. Tommy also gave my two sons, Nick and Kris, the opportunity to work, which was great for them. Oh, and I shouldn't overlook Christine here. She did absolutely brilliantly by going out and getting a very good job selling houses. The MacDonalds were back in business, albeit with no dependence on football for putting bread on the family table.

Working in and around Yarrows was an education for me. It used to cross my mind that young footballers could do worse than spend a bit of time in the same environment, just to see how tough life can be. I never got any hassle because I'd played for Rangers. In fact, quite a few of the guys I came across at Yarrows I'd actually been to school with.

Every now and again too I'd bump into people with whom I'd been involved in football. One such occasion was when, driving my van through the middle of Glasgow, I got stuck at traffic lights. Just then, from around a corner, I saw one of my old Airdrie players, Tony Smith, pushing a wheelbarrow loaded up with stuff. I rolled down the window and shouted, 'Anthony, what the f**k happened to us, eh? Here's me behind the wheel of a truck and you pushing a barra'.' We had a laugh, then continued on our separate ways. Speaking of old Airdrie players, by the way, I'm still in occasional touch with a few of them. For example, before Sandy Stewart went away down south to Burnley as assistant to Owen Coyle, he, Allan Moore, Paul Jack and a couple of others, took me to the Rangers Club in Kirkintilloch. You can imagine the scene with them all singing Celtic songs and trying to fill me with 'slammers'. Absolutely brilliant, it was.

On a sombre note, I might add here that it was in my working togs I went and paid my last respects to one of the greatest players I ever faced, and one of the greatest characters in the Scottish game, Jimmy Johnstone, after he died in March 2006. I remember asking Sandy Jardine at Ibrox about the possibility of actually attending the funeral service, which was to take place in a chapel in Uddingston and being told it was invitation only. That left me with the thought I could join the thousands of mourners gathered around Celtic Park where the procession was due to pass. So that's what I ended up doing, having parked my van in a side street and walked along to the stadium. If any Celtic fans recognised me in their midst, they never let on.

Jinky and I had had our fall-outs on the pitch, of course, the most notable of them being in my St Johnstone days when he mistook Kenny Aird for me and got sent off for taking a swing at Kenny. But I admired him hugely for what were his breathtaking skills on the ball, and after my move to Rangers, when we became serious rivals in the Old Firm games in which both of us revelled, I came to admire him the more for his other qualities, guts and competitiveness among them. In saying as much, I retain a healthy respect for so many of Jinky's old team-mates. It still makes for an arresting thought that, had Jock Stein pushed his apparent interest in me in 1968, I could have ended up playing with them rather than against them on sundry, memorable occasions.

That, though, is another story. Joining Rangers as I did meant everything to me. If I struggled a bit in my first two years at Ibrox, the following ten were the making of me as a player and – dare I say? – as a person as well. While I never looked far enough ahead during that time to imagine myself as a manager, I was proud (if a bit daunted initially) to make that transition with as great a club as Hearts. How close we came in 1985–86 to pulling off a League and Scottish Cup Double and creating Tynecastle history in the process. Then there was my experience of managing Airdrie, which, in its different way, was at least as challenging and satisfying in a personal sense.

My involvement in the game in the interim has been pretty well confined to acting as a match-day host at Ibrox, meeting and greeting those groups of fans who enjoy the corporate hospitality on offer before, during and after games. Not the least enjoyable part of the job has been mingling with some old faces from the home dressing room – many of them older than mine, if I think of other former players like Jimmy Millar, Ralph Brand and Davie Provan. All of us who are, or have been, employed in this way behind the scenes would vouch for the truth in the enduring maxim: once a Ranger, always a Ranger. In my case, I've felt a great attachment to the club since first I kicked a ball in the streets of Kinning Park.

It shouldn't be difficult then for anyone to imagine my dismay when Rangers were plunged into administration in February 2012. Suddenly, alarmingly, the club's very future became an issue which was to embroil everyone – not least Sandy Jardine – connected with Ibrox. Sandy did a sterling job of rallying the fans behind the club's cause before being stricken with the awful news, towards the back end of 2012 that he had cancer of the throat and liver. Many anguished months of treatment lay ahead. But this I know: despite finally being liquidated and having to start afresh in the Third Division, nothing and nobody can erase what has been Rangers' marvellous history, and I remain immensely proud to have been a small part of it. Airdrie, of course, went bust way back before Rangers did and came back as Airdrie United. Now, as I sign off here, Hearts find themselves wrestling with administration. I wish them only the best for they are another club I'm honoured to have been involved with.